RURAL PLANNING: POLICY INTO ACTION?

Edited by
Paul Cloke

Harper & Row, Publishers
London

Cambridge	San Francisco
Mexico City	São Paulo
New York	Singapore
Philadelphia	Sydney

Copyright © 1987. Editorial and selection material © Paul Cloke.
Individual chapters © as credited.
All rights reserved

First published 1987

Harper & Row Ltd
28 Tavistock Street
London WC2E 7PN

No part of this book may be reproduced in any manner
whatsoever without written permission except in the
case of brief quotations embodied in critical articles
or reviews.

British Library Cataloguing in Publication Data
Rural planning: policy into action?
  1.   Regional planning——Great Britain
  I.   Cloke, Paul J.   II.   Open University
  III. Series
  711'.3'0941   HT395.G7

ISBN 0-06-318351-X

Typeset by Inforum Ltd, Portsmouth
Printed and bound by Butler & Tanner Ltd, Frome and London

CONTENTS

Section III Conclusions

CONTRIBUTORS

Philip Bell	Research Fellow, Department of Geography, St David's University College, Lampeter.
Andrew Blowers	Professor, Faculty of Social Sciences, Open University.
Paul Cloke	Senior Lecturer, Department of Geography, St David's University College, Lampeter.
Graham Cox	Lecturer in Sociology, School of Humanities and Social Sciences, University of Bath.
Gareth Edwards	Former Research Fellow, Department of Geography, St David's University College, Lampeter.
Jo Little	Research Fellow, Department of Geography, University College, London.
Philip Lowe	Lecturer in Countryside Planning, Bartlett School of Architecture and Planning, University College, London.
Liz Mills	Research Associate, Department of Social Administration, University of Bristol; and Research Fellow, Policy Studies Institute, London.
Allan Patmore	Professor, Department of Geography, University of Hull.
Paul Pettigrew	Head of Economic Development, Mid Wales Development.
Tom Rocke	Planning Officer, North Avon District Council.
Gerald Smart	Emeritus Professor, Bartlett School of Architecture and Planning, University College, London.
Mike Tricker	Lecturer, Management Centre, and Project Manager, Public Sector Management Research Unit, Aston University.
Michael Winter	Research Officer, School of Humanities and Social Sciences, University of Bath.

PREFACE

The impetus for collecting together the set of essays presented in this book stemmed directly from the small school of rural researchers interested in rural policy implementation who have been working together in Lampeter in the 1980s. Most have contributed chapters to this book and to all must be credited the stimulus of a work environment dominated by shared research interests. Only by beginning to isolate interesting and untouched research areas did we realize how little work had been done on the themes of policy and implementation in rural environments. This book is merely a start in the rectification of our ignorance.

Thanks are extended to all contributors for their cheerful cooperation in bringing the book into existence, and especially to Naomi Roth and Marianne Legrange of Harper & Row who had faith in the idea and whose technical expertise has been of enormous help. I am also grateful to Malcolm Moseley, Alan Rogers and others whose useful comments at various stages of the book have helped to refine its structure and content.

As usual the technical staff at Lampeter have performed miracles, notably Maureen Hunwicks, who typed much of the manuscript, and Trevor Harris, who did much of the artwork.

Finally, heartfelt thanks go to my family: to Elizabeth and William for keeping Daddy's study as a 'no-go area' and to Viv for sharing everything so supportively.

IMPLEMENTATION CONCEPTS
FOR RURAL AREAS

POLICY AND PLANNING
IN RURAL AREAS
Paul Cloke

INTRODUCTION

Attempts to analyse and evaluate planning processes in rural areas appear to have reached a hiatus. Certainly many of the dead concepts which have retarded a detailed understanding of planning for so long have now been cleared away. No longer are statutory planning documents viewed as a blueprint for what will actually happen in the countryside and among its people; no longer is it necessarily assumed that specific and measurable changes in rural areas should be ascribed inferentially to the planning policies adopted at that time; no longer are policy decisions characterized as neutral and apolitical acts of resource arbitration or allocation. This much at least has been put behind us as the legacy of nearly two decades of research, although with hindsight it appears that these conclusions might have been reached more quickly, in line with contemporary concepts in the urban and regional context. But where does this leave the analysis of rural planning? If the stated policies of decision-makers are not to be taken at face value, if events cannot be linked necessarily to planning action and if rational planning models do not apply, then new approaches are required to fill the void — hence the hiatus.

Two fundamental premises may be advanced as a basis for inquiry in the future:
1. Rural areas should be understood as integral elements in the outworking of contemporary capitalism. Critical social theories can usefully be employed to explore the external links of society, economy and culture which 'rural' specialists have traditionally sought to devalue as part of the legitimation of their own specialism.
2. The planning function as exercised in rural areas should be placed explicitly in the context of the state–society relationship. Plans and policies represent one mechanism (of many) used by the state to enhance conditions for capital accumulation, to deal with conflicts arising from different fractions of capital or from procedures of production, and to ensure its own survival through the justification of its activities.

These two premises are by no means innovative or unfamiliar. Nevertheless it is only recently, with the publication of key texts dealing specifically with *rural* issues (e.g. Newby, 1977; Newby *et al.*, 1978; Bradley and Lowe, 1984; Phillips and Williams, 1984), that the value of these approaches has been specifically acknowledged.

Within the wide scope offered by these issues, two initial themes appear important. First, a clear recognition of the limitations of planning in rural areas is required (Hanrahan and Cloke, 1983; Cloke and Hanrahan, 1984). Quite simply, evaluations of the impact of plans and policies have been based on too high an expectation of what planning (in its societal context) can achieve. A detailed examination of this issue is published elsewhere (Cloke and Little, forthcoming) but the introductory chapters of this book outline the background to political policy-making and the restricted impacts of planning within rural environments. Second, the issues of flexibility and discretion within this admittedly constrained planning function are also of considerable import- ance. In other words, given that planning is severely limited in scope and powers, are some 'planners' able to develop more successful forms of policy *implementation* than others? If so, what practical problems are encountered and how are they overcome? This is the central theme of this book; literally to investigate the *sharp end* of rural planning through a series of detailed case study essays which deal with a variety of planning functions in rural areas. These essays are not written from a rationalist viewpoint, even though the focus on implementation will inevitably involve a somewhat artificial divide in some cases between the issues of enactment, and the iterative and politicized events of policy-making which preceded, accompanied or followed them. It is therefore the task of these first two chapters to develop a brief conceptual foundation on which the case studies can be built.

RURAL CHANGE

Cliff Hague (1984), in his analysis of *urban* change and planning, writes:

> The physical environment is the repository of dead labour and as such, within capitalism, inhibits contemporary capital accumulation. Periodic devaluations of fixed capital are one way that capitalism responds to the falling rates of profit. Thus the crises of capitalism are written in the settlement structure and the built environment, and that structure and environment become the focus for political struggles pitched with varying degrees of consciousness at resisting the offerings and imperatives of capital. (p. 43)

This kind of political economy viewpoint has contributed substantially to the analysis of urban economic progress, societal restructuring, state roles and the links between economy, society and the state (Urry, 1981). Equally, the understanding of *rural* change benefits from the contribution of political economy concepts. Healey (1984), in a provocative discussion paper, lists three potential areas of gain:

1. The way in which the organization of the economy produces particular forms of investment in rural areas.
2. The range of social groups; their interests in land, property and the environment; and the interaction between social groups and economic processes.
3. The motives and mechanisms behind the operations of the state in response to or as initiator of economic reorganization.

It seems likely, therefore, that the implications of a political economy approach will enhance our realization of planning constraints in rural areas. For example, many

Table 1.1   Population change in rural local authorities, 1961–81, by region (Champion, 1981)

Region	No. of districts	1981 population (000s)	Percentage 1961–71	Population 1971–81	Change Difference
Scotland	24	998	−1.9	9.6	11.5
Wales	13	583	0.6	6.8	6.2
North	6	276	1.0	4.3	3.3
Yorkshire & Humberside	7	453	10.4	12.0	1.6
East Midlands	8	560	9.2	10.1	0.9
South West	20	1,368	10.3	11.0	0.7
West Midlands	8	427	7.7	8.1	0.4
East Anglia	12	1,035	14.5	12.9	−1.6
South East	4	357	21.1	12.1	−9.0
All rural districts	102	6,056	7.5	10.2	2.7
Great Britain	458	54,129	5.3	0.3	−5.0

notions of society ('the common good' or 'general interest') used in rural research could be reclassified in recognition of the irreconcilable class conflicts arising from the production and distribution of the surplus value created by labour (Healey, 1982). Furthermore, capital is currently both relocating and restructuring, with the relative mobility of contemporary monopoly-phase capitalism leading to locational footloose-ness, and technical divisions of labour resulting in branch plant developments often in marginal locations (Bradley and Lowe, 1984). Labour, on the other hand, has remained relatively static and conflict within local society therefore arises because of the recomposition effects of capital restructuring. Rees (1984) has demonstrated that contemporary capital expansion has been uneven as capital seeks out favourable locations with clear implications for valued rural environments. Meanwhile traditional capitalist elites in the agricultural sector of rural areas exert their powers gained through property and land ownership by controlling the visual rural environment. In turn agriculture itself may be seen to represent an anachronistic dominant fraction of capital which is threatened by the expansion of other fractions in rural areas. Thus it is changes in employment which have: 'resulted in radical developments in terms of rural class structures, gender divisions, the forms of political conflict occurring in rural areas, and, indeed, of the complex processes by which "rural cultures" are produced and reproduced' (Rees, 1984, p. 27).

Contemporary rural change can usefully be seen in this light. The 1981 Census exposé of dramatic population gains in the remoter rural areas and continued growth elsewhere in the countryside (except for extreme peri-urban zones where rates of growth have declined) has drawn considerable attention to the theme of counter-urbanization in rural areas. Analyses by Champion (1981), Robert and Randolph (1983) and others clearly demonstrate the enhanced status of rural localities as favoured areas for inmigration. Along with lower rates of outmigration in many of these areas, the countryside appears to be gaining from the relocation and restructuring of capital. It is all too easy to characterize these changes merely as a manifestation of urban-to-rural manufacturing shifts. Although such shifts have indeed occurred in some rural areas (see, for example, Keeble, 1980; Fothergill and Gudgin, 1982; Gould and Keeble, 1984) the use of liberal definitions for both rural localities and rurality itself in some studies has undermined the suggested overwhelming dominance of the manufacturing shift factor. In addition, the importance of the growth of service sector employment in many rural areas is often underestimated. Further, Moseley (1984) suggests that rural repopulation can be 'people led' as well as 'job led', and there is increasing evidence that the release of specific sectors of the formal labour market (through unemployment, self-employment, 'hippy culture', early retirement and so on) has resulted in population growth in some rural areas far more than have the more obvious trends of inmigration of workers to new local employment or of long-distance commuters to urban employment (Cloke, 1985).

Whether by direct relocation of labour markets or by various labour-release mechanisms, the overall changes in political economy have had a dramatic *aggregate* impact on rural areas. But it is important to recognize localized variations in the distribution of wealth and opportunity within this aggregate trend. In many cases the beneficiaries of these changes are the new middle classes (Carter, 1985) who are able to monopolize local housing markets, aided and abetted as they are by protective planning policies (Cloke, 1983). In this way, the most precious rural living environments are susceptible to a rural form of *gentrification* (see Chapter 11) and the local working-class population is displaced or disadvantaged. In a study of rural deprivation McLaughlin (1985) reports a consistent picture of the very well-off living alongside the very poor — an uneven competition in upwardly spiralling housing markets which can only be won by the more powerful and better-equipped classes. In some locations, a particular culture of this process occurs through the attraction of retirement populations—a trend for which the term 'geriatrification' has been coined. In other, perhaps more marginal areas, agricultural capital remains dominant and urban drop-outs and local school leavers are well represented among the new rural adult populations. These areas, often characterized by lower land prices because of their remoteness and climatic/ morphological characteristics, have in general only become attractive receptor areas to capital relocation through state incentives. As a consequence, gentrification trends are often less well advanced in the less attractive of these locations (as, significantly, are protective planning policies for rural settlements!).

Alongside these ramifications of transformed labour markets, rural people have also faced rationalizations in the provision of both housing and essential services. Trends of service contraction have been documented repeatedly in recent texts (see, for example, Pacione, 1983, 1984; Phillips and Williams, 1984; Gilg, 1985) demonstrating a well-honed proclivity by the private sector for profit maximization through large-scale outlets in central marketplaces. In addition there has also been a mirror-image tendency for services provided by regional and local state to react to public-sector resource constraints by rationalization in market-oriented locations. Resource concentration has thus been rife in both private and public sectors with the result that non-mobile elements of rural society bear the brunt of redistribution, being unable to purchase the necessary accessibility to cope with the new opportunity structure. Housing markets demonstrate similar distributional impacts. Local authority house-building has been heavily constrained by central state restrictions over local state expenditure. Such building as has escaped these cuts has been in centralized rural locations alongside the major estate developments financed by the private sector. In smaller settlements, where planning controls are often stricter, where Conservation

Area status is more liberally applied, and where council house sales are often highest, new housing development tends to consist either of single- or small-plot private-sector developments catering for middle-class inmigrants or, in some specific areas, single developments specifically designed and permitted for the siblings of agricultural capital. This latter occurrence reflects one particular loophole (or favour, depending on personal ideological preferences) in planning legislation in these locations.

Outside these settlements, countryside change is manifest in the balance between destruction and conservation of environment and landscape. Again, a viewpoint which gives credence to the overwhelming capacity for change associated with capital expansion and accumulation characterizes this conflict as a one-sided struggle between power and pious hope. For example, Pye-Smith and Rose (1984, p. 1) make this claim:

> Today it is more than just a few lesser-known species of insects or obscure plants that are threatened with extinction, and it is something much greater than a little-known view or infrequently trodden path that is being destroyed by the drastic changes which now sweep across Britain's countryside. Indeed we are too late to save the countryside that existed a mere ten years ago. Of the pieces of countryside recognized by the government as being nationally important for conservation more than one in ten is damaged or destroyed each year.

And who are the culprits for this damage and destruction?

> [. . .] the farming, forestry and water industries and the interest groups which support them. (p. 1)

Indeed the catalogue of activities which is seen to threaten the countryside with unacceptable change goes beyond this particular hit-list. Blunden and Curry (1985) mention the extraction of minerals, the generation of power and its transmission, communications and recreation and leisure activities in addition to farming, forestry and water gathering. Although this 'threat' may in some cases be more potential than real (given the matrix of conflict and compatibility of land uses suggested by Green in Figure 1.1) the key factor here is the ability of the planning function, and indeed wider state interests, to ameliorate the exploitative demands of capital expansion in the countryside. These bald trends greatly oversimplify the guardianship and paternalism which many fractions of agriculture capital employ towards their units of production. Nevertheless, changes to rural landscape and environment have certainly reflected the changing demands of capital accumulation in these sectors. The interesting factor here is that the benefits of production changes are not so starkly linked to class distribution as is the case with socioeconomic issues. Indeed, the old and new middle classes and some fractions of the landed gentry find it in their own interest to lend support to conservation objectives so as to sustain the environments which have proved so attractive to them (Lowe and Goyder, 1983). Conversely, the indigenous working classes have tended to concentrate their political struggles (such as they have been) in favour of exploitative non-agricultural land uses which have generated local labour requirements. Although farmers and agrobusinessmen appear isolated in this conflict of interests, their political influence on central government has been sufficiently strong to ensure the establishment of an artificially favourable economic climate in which to continue the process of capital accumulation almost unabated.

These thumb-nail sketches give an overgeneralized and conflated view of the links between power relations and rural change. Nevertheless the inexorable and changing

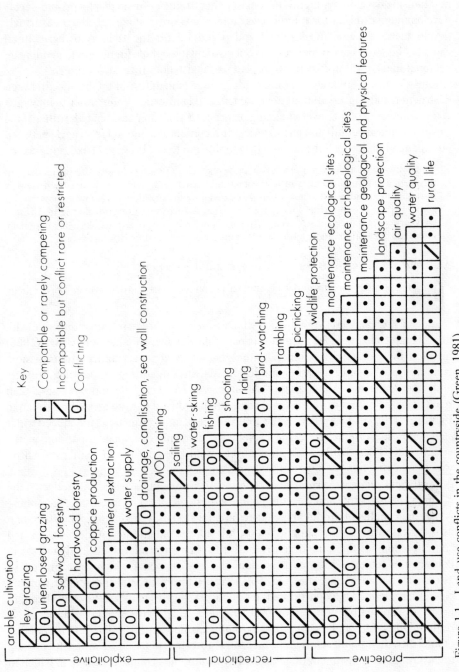

Figure 1.1 Land-use conflicts in the countryside (Green, 1981).

motion of capitalist production can be seen to be having an increasingly high-profile impact on rural society and rural land use. The distribution of negative impact is manifest in class, gender and spatial divisions, with the subsequent elites not only benefiting from the profit of production but also heavily engaged in the politics of the planning processes which are designed to regulate resource allocation conflicts. The likelihood that planning can respond with neutrality to these conflicts is, of course, thus severely compromised.

PLANNING AND DECISION-MAKING STRUCTURES
POLICY, POWER AND THE STATE

In the analysis of urban policy and power relations, the state has become the pivot of policy analysis, and this central position ascribes an overtly political nature to the evaluation of planning and decision-making. It therefore seems reasonable to recognize planning and policy-making by authorities and agencies in *rural* localities similarly as aspects of state activity which are subject to the kind of constraints recognized in the urban and regional spheres. In this way an understanding of the role of the state and its dealings in rural areas is subsumed within the overall relationship between the entire capitalist state and its host society, transcending the rather more narrow sphere of central–local government relations with which rural policy analysts have been preoccupied thus far. Detailed analyses of the concepts of the state are available elsewhere (see, for example, Saunders, 1979; Dunleavy, 1980; Johnston, 1982; Cooke, 1983; Dear and Clark, 1984; Ham and Hill, 1984). It is only possible here briefly to record the four main categories of concepts regarding the distribution of power within the state and the causes and functions therein.*

1. Pluralist/representational concepts

This group of ideas is based on the suggestion that an independent state acts in neutral arbitration of conflicts within civil society (Dahl, 1961; Polsby, 1963). Power within the state is freely available to all elements in society through democratic elections, public participation and pressure-group activities. Although the acceptance of power is not uniform there is nevertheless a supposition that even the least powerful are not powerless, and with sufficient determination any individual or group can gain access to public policy. The state does not, therefore, generate any consistent bias towards particular class groups as the causal factor behind state activity is the verdict of the majority and not any motive of the state itself.

2. Elitist/instrumentalist concepts

The supposition here is that power is held by minority elite groups and that state activities are structured so as to favour the powerful elites and their interests. Pluralism may therefore be dismissed as a series of window-dressing exercises which legitimate the processes whereby policy outcomes favour particular societal fragments. Elites may benefit from socioeconomic power (Hunter, 1953) or political power (Bottomore,

---

* A fuller analysis can be found in Cloke and Little (forthcoming).

1966). Where both power sources are transposed by individuals in key positions in the state, the state then becomes instrumental in furthering the interests of those who hold power within it. The key question here is whether different elites operate in different areas of influence or whether elitism represents a form of one-class rule with the state merely upholding capitalist interests (Miliband, 1977).

3. Managerialist concepts

In some cases it is recognized that power within the state lies in the hands of professional managers who act as 'gatekeepers' to policy-making, and by dint of technical knowledge and manipulation of decision-making are able to influence policy outcomes in favour of their own interests and those of their class peers (Pahl, 1975). The degree to which the operations of managers are a prime factor in the distribution of power within the state depends on the level of constraints imposed on their activities by the societal structures around them; that is, the level of discretion permitted by the prevailing political economy. Ray Pahl came to place more emphasis on these societal constraints in his later work on managerialism (Pahl, 1982) thus marking a significant shift in the conceptual balance between external constraint, discretion and autonomy within state activity. Managerialism might thus be viewed as a partial explanation of the distribution of power, but one which is reliant on other contextual concepts for its utility.

4. Structuralist concepts

Pluralism, elitism and managerialism highlight the power available to individuals. Structuralism suggests that class distributions represent the only real form of societal disaggregation for the analysis of power and political policy-making. Thus the state is seen to represent the current balance of class influence which in Britain at the present time favours the interests of monopoly capital. Influential theorists such as Poulantzas (1973, 1975) and Castells (1978) have therefore recognized that the major purpose of state policy is to further the requirements of capital interests. Alongside this fundamental goal, state powers are used in the short term to proffer minimal reforms for the working class in order both to diminish pressure for more far-reaching redistributions of power, and to legitimize the state as a pluralist body. Autonomy within the state arises not only from the need to promote minimal reform, but also because the ruling class may be subdivided into different fractions and therefore a particular instance of state intervention may constitute aid for one fraction of the bourgeoisie against another.

RURAL PLANNING AND THE CENTRAL STATE

Even from this simplistic and overgeneralized outline of concepts of power distribution in the state it can be recognized that policy-making and decision-taking can be interpreted in very different ways according to the theoretical position adopted. The influence of the central state on rural planning has been enormous, and yet different viewpoints on the nature of that influence abound. Gilg (1984), for example, in analysing the links between central government politics and trends in rural planning, has described the emergence of a 'consensus type of politics' between the mid-1950s and the 1970s. Consensus is seen to have produced positive benefits: 'an agriculture which provides a high proportion of Britain's dietary requirements at a reasonable price, many villages have been attractively developed or conserved, large areas of open countryside remain scenically beautiful . . .' (p. 250), but whether these are benefits for all or benefits which accrue according to a structured distribution of elites or classes should be the subject of a challenging debate. Certainly McLaughlin's (1983) analysis of the state's response to rural deprivation suggests that state elites have successfully deflected public interest away from the underlying causes of deprivation (i.e. the distribution of wealth, income and opportunity) by legitimizing 'softer' issues such as rural service provision which are not a danger to the status quo of social relations. Knox and Cullen (1981) go further in labelling the planning system as one of the state's internal survival mechanisms for capitalist interests.

It is against this background of political analysis that central state decision-making for rural areas must be viewed. Its role over recent years appears to have been:

1. To reduce the powers of local government institutions by the divide-and-rule tactics of distributing decision-making powers between several different agencies; by ever more stringent monitoring of local state activities; and by restricting the availability of finance.
2. To act in favour of particular fractions of capital interest, wherever possible preventing conflict between different fractions of its constituent classes.
3. To reinstate the priority of private-sector capital by seeking to reduce the direct involvement of public-sector agencies in some rural policies.

Several examples may be used to illustrate these trends.

The domination of the central state over its local counterpart is clearcut in urban localities where politically antagonistic metropolitan authorities have been 'Thatchered' out of existence by a Conservative government. In rural areas, however, local authorities tend to be sympathetic politically to the centre. Nevertheless, similar, if less drastic restrictions apply. The formal planning system has been constituted to ensure that local planning policies are both divided between county and district authorities, and subject to the scrutiny of the central government. From the formative 1947 Town and Country Planning Act onwards, central government advice has ensured that spatial planning in rural areas should take the form of resource concentration (Cloke, 1979) despite evidence that such policies were associated with considerable hardship for disadvantaged groups in smaller rural settlements and in some cases could be contested in terms of economic credibility (Gilder, 1979). Further reforms of the planning system following the 1968 Town and Country Planning Act established the new structure plans but weakened the power base of county councils by granting development control and local planning powers to the districts. Thus, when innovations to rural settlement policies *were* proposed by county councils such as Gloucestershire and North Yorkshire (see Cloke and Shaw, 1983) the Secretary of State was able to render them impotent and return them to the conventional pattern by claiming that the county councils concerned were invading the power territories of the districts. In fact these innovations represented a challenge to central state wisdoms and were deflected accordingly. It could be argued, therefore, that the degree of autonomy available to local-level rural planners has been significantly reduced over the past decade.

These restrictions on the statutory planning system are supplemented by more direct reductions in particular public-sector activities in rural areas, with the corollary of increased private-sector control of these opportunities. For example, the enforced reduction of local authority expenditure has entailed reductions in council housebuilding and various local authority services. Conversely, private-sector housebuilders and developers have received support in their ambitions to loosen local authority development control strictures in certain rural areas. Through the decisions of the Inspectorate at Appeals, and through guidance and advice from the Department of the Environment, the ability of local authorities to control the demands of developers for land has been eroded.

Perhaps the most striking example of policy redirection in favour of the private sector is the Transport Act 1985 (Cloke, 1984; Banister *et al.*, 1985; Knowles, 1985). Although the exact implications of the deregulation of the bus industry are as yet matters of conjecture rather than of empirical evidence, the trend behind this move to the market, and the underlying phasing-out of central government aid for local government subsidies for rural services, is clear. An area of opportunity provision in rural areas which was previously underwritten by the central state has now reverted to a global profit-making orientation with specific consequences for non profit-making locations such as most rural areas. *Either* local authorities continue to subsidize loss-making routes by diverting expenditure from other services (education, highways, etc.) within an increasingly restricted budget allocation from the central government, or services are allowed to decline.

In all these examples, there does appear to be an uneven distribution of benefit and disadvantage. The interests of private-sector entrepreneurs are being boosted by recent central government policy changes along with the interests of the middle-class consumer who has the income and wealth to purchase housing and service opportunities, and who rarely uses the rural bus! Specific provision for the working class, be it housing, transport or local services, is being withdrawn. Class polarization in rural areas is thus being exacerbated by central government policies.

So far as agriculture and rural landscape conservation are concerned, central government policies have largely faced the different objective of achieving a legitimate compromise between the demands of different fractions of the class and capital interests which elitist and structuralist concepts suggest that it upholds. Andrew Blowers (1984), in his account of the political ramifications of the London Brick Company plans to redevelop the brickworks in the Marston Vale, captures the essence of how different fractions can line up on a point of conflict:

> This caused divisions among groups normally united, and promoted alliances between strange bedfellows. It remains a matter for debate as to whether the issue was significant, whether the conflict did markedly influence the company or affect its objectives and whether the outcome was predictable. Although structuralism provides an answer to these questions it does not say anything about the significance of participation of the various groups in the conflict. Insofar as these played a significant role in altering perceptions, changing the relationship between company and community and securing greater control over environmental development, they cannot be totally ignored. (p. 249)

In some instances of high-profile planning and decision-making in the countryside, a clear advantage is held by discernible elites. Pye-Smith and Rose (1984) point out the imbalance of power and resources evident at many large-scale public inquiries. Often, government departments and surrogate agencies have an integral involvement with the development in question (the Central Electricity Generating Board at Windscale and Seiswell, the Department of Transport at Archway, the National Coal Board at the Vale of Belvoir) and thus the costs of presenting their case can be drawn from public monies. Even in instances where there is no direct state involvement the developers, as agents of capital, will invariably be able to finance their case to a far greater extent than the pluralist objectors. Furthermore, the planning mechanisms involved also favour the interests of capital:

> The developer often starts from a position of strength as he generally does not have to make his arguments clear until the P.I. (public inquiry) is convened. The developer is under no obligation to tell either the public or the local planning authority anything other than that he wishes to use a certain site for a particular purpose . . . The objecting planning authority, on the other hand, must make a statement outlining its objections twenty-eight days before the inquiry begins. (Pye-Smith and Rose, 1984, p. 60)

In the more day-to-day policy-making aspects of the countryside the interests of capital are equally well served. A global view of state resource allocations to rural areas reveals the degree to which the agricultural industry is the dominant recipient of resources (Bowers and Cheshire, 1983). The grant aid and subsidy enjoyed by agriculture offer interesting analyses of the distribution of power in this area. It is possible to recognize the success of 'pluralist' pressure groups — notably the National Farmers' Union (NFU) and the County Landowners' Association (CLA) — working on behalf of agriculture. The success of these groups, however, is not independent of the existence of parliamentary and local government elites made up of powerful decision-makers with backgrounds (and often foregrounds!) in land ownership and entrepreneurial activity in agriculture. The conjunction of socioeconomic and political elitism in this instance offers great scope for instrumentalist analysis of pro-agriculture policies. Equally, the existence of these key decision-makers permits a managerialist thesis, while in recognizing agriculturalists as a major fraction of capital in rural areas, theories of structuration also appear particularly applicable.

This range of potential interpretation should not be permitted to obscure the fundamentally privileged position of agriculture. The use of state funds to subsidize agrobusiness has espoused economic and technical objectives in the pursuit of production increases. Ensuing conflicts between farm modernization and mechaniza-tion and conservation objectives have led to a questioning of the privilege of financial aid to agriculture. Pye-Smith and North (1984), among others, argue that: 'What we urgently require is a restructuring of the entire grant-aid system to ensure that ecological and social considerations are taken into account in every development which is publicly funded' (p. 93).

The likelihood of such a re-evaluation occurring will depend on the degree to which the central state's protection of national agriculture is eroded by competition for resources by other agricultural interests within the wider sphere of the European Community. Certainly in those areas where the central state retains exclusive control, agricultural privilege has been protected against the demands of the conservation lobby. In the context of the debate over a potential introduction of planning controls over agricultural land use (see, for example, Shoard, 1980) the resultant legislation contained within the Wildlife and Countryside Act 1981 represents a victory for the status quo even though the principle of voluntary agreement by landowners over issues of landscape and wildlife conservation was successfully publicized as a compromise solution. Indeed, to some extent agricultural capital does regard the Act as less than ideal. Cox and Lowe (1983) suggest that the response of farming lobby groups to this legislation may reflect changing attitudes towards conservation:

> With a will, born of necessity the CLA and NFU have embarked on the task of creating a consensus around the Act. Concerned to ensure that the stewardship practised by farmers and landowners more than matches the rhetoric of the voluntary case, the CLA . . . are keenly aware that the crucial battle for public opinion could be lost by default. (p. 72)

By stepping back from the introduction of planning control over agricultural land use, however, the state has continued its overall policy of agricultural protection.

One outcome of the Act has been the greater politicization of the conservation lobby which, according to Cox and Lowe (1983), has adopted a more 'aggressive and confrontational style' (p. 72) than before. The very fact that countryside conservation issues have only now begun to enter the central party-political arena in Britain with any priority reinforces the necessity that analysis of countryside planning should take full account of the political context in which policy-making occurs. The fact remains, however, that the access to power enjoyed by the conservation lobby remains relatively unimportant when compared with existing power privileges of agricultural and land-owning elites.

RURAL PLANNING AND THE REGIONAL AND LOCAL STATES

Decision-making for rural areas also involves a plethora of agencies at the regional and local levels, and the activities of these bodies may also be incorporated into broader theories of the state and its societal context. Saunders (1985) has characterized the *regional state* as an undervalued dimension of central–local relationships and suggests that the proliferation of regional agencies is 'part of a long-running and fundamental attack on local democracy and on the ability of ordinary people to defend their interests as consumers in the face of demands by dominant class-based producer interests at a time of economic decline' (p. 161). Using evidence from a study of water and health agencies Saunders recognizes two forms of political power at the regional level:
1. The politics of production are characterized by class domination organized through forms of corporatism.
2. The politics of consumption are characterized by managerial aspects of bureaucracy in dealing with trends of closure of services.

As such, regional state agencies appear to display little autonomy from the constraints of central state control (see Chapter 8), and offer little hope that more radical policies to address the fundamental problems of rural areas will be introduced at the regional level.

An interesting variant on the theme of the regional state is evident in the activities of the two rural development boards in Britain — the Highlands and Islands Development Board, and Mid Wales Development. Born of a political age slightly less dominated by the central state, and constituted as part of central government's successful attempts to dictate the strength of devolutionist lobbies in the Celtic fringes, these Boards have enjoyed some financial and administrative freedom to subsidize and

otherwise encourage industrial development in their areas. A wide range o
planning tasks has also been undertaken, although these have played second fi
industrial policies in terms of finance and political will. Indeed, it could be arguec
they represent an attempt to soften and legitimize the uneven distribution of advantage
from the industrial policies. In these cases the politics of production originally favoured
the interests of large-scale industrial capital, but more recently have of necessity turned
to the smaller-scale entrepreneur as the basis of their productive activities. Abandoned
in some senses by the interests of large-scale capital, and finding themselves under
increasing scrutiny from a central state which is gradually clamping down on the
interventionist planning of lower-order agencies, the development boards have become increasingly vulnerable. Accordingly they have noticeably changed their role
from one of intervention to advice, encouragement, training and marketing — tasks
which represent less autonomy and greater reliance on the patronage of the central
state.

So far as the *local state* is concerned (see, for instance, Cockburn, 1977; Duncan and
Goodwin, 1982; Dunleavy, 1984) theorists have tended to assume a significant level of
working-class involvement both in local government and in the wider local state
activities. Hence the local state is seen as capable of withstanding central state attacks
and at the same time as a potential influence for progressive reform of central state
policy-making. In rural areas, the local state tends to be conservative in nature, and
therefore is generally supportive of the role of central government. Even so, rural
authorities have witnessed the gradual erosion of local state autonomy as centrally
derived policies become increasingly mandatory and financial support has been
reduced so as to enforce reductions in spending on social consumption at the local
level.

Despite this process, the local state still exercises some discretion. Studies of local
government (see Alexander, 1982; Byrne, 1983; Gyford, 1984) suggest that different
authorities display varying patterns of expenditure on various services and that certain
authorities have achieved some innovations in social consumption. Such discretion is
clearly borne out by Glover's (1985) study of differing attitudes towards rural transport
subsidies. However, the political allegiances and current social structure of rural areas
serve both to minimize any potential local discretion in favour of progressive policies,
and to reinforce the constraints on interventionist planning exerted by the central state.
The result is that the political conservatism of rural localities presents an ideal breeding
ground for elitist policy-making. Evidence presented by Buchanan (1982) in Suffolk
and Cloke and Little (1985) in Gloucestershire illustrates the manner in which small
elites of councillors and planning officers exert overwhelming influence over the
important aspects of plan preparation.

Effective planning action in rural localities therefore depends on the strength of local
political will and the extent of central state discretion. These two factors seem to be
self-reinforcing. As Gilg (1985) has pointed out:

> the majority of rural inhabitants are very satisfied and happy with their life-style, and have
> consciously chosen to live in the countryside. Many of these people are moreover less
> concerned with the socio-economic issues . . . but more with the changing environment of the
> countryside and the increasing pressures being placed upon it. (p. 107)

A new breed of local decision-makers espousing conservation ideals may well emerge to challenge the political dominance of farmer/landowner groups. Indeed there is evidence that some rural local authorities are already experiencing a shift away from the old-style Conservative gentry and towards the more contemporary 'town Tories' and even Alliance supporters. As Gilg (1985) suggests, a conflict could arise here between policies of agricultural support and conservation. However, as farming subsidies are controlled by the central state, and at the local level both agriculturalists and conservationists will be united in an anti-development policy stance, the potential for local-level conflict is not great. Rather, there will be a continuing pre-emption against interventionist policies in favour of socioeconomic deprivation in rural communities. As Newby (1981) has noted: 'All too often this is the political reality . . . which underlies the neglect of housing, public transport and the whole range of social, health and welfare services in rural areas' (p. 239). Local political will is thus in line with central constraints in these matters. Whereas fractions of capital, and indeed the middle class, may be divided over the physical environment, they are certainly united in opposition to further intervention in the socioeconomic environment. As a result the routine implementation of policies for rural people will be bound into a land-use planning framework from which district and county authorities would find it difficult to escape even should they wish to do so. Implementation of socioeconomic planning thus becomes a matter of constrained *opportunism*. Given little or no resources or positive powers themselves, planners have been forced (often with no little initiative on their part) to make use of any available facilities which might further their broad policies, hence the increasing endorsement by rural policy-makers of self-help and voluntary initiatives. Such factors have perennially offered intrinsically beneficial qualities but have only become important in the public sphere because self-help represents a high-profit 'resource' which can be adopted by a planning process which is often bankrupt of previously available formal resources. In Chapter 2 we turn to this theme of implementing rural planning policies.

REFERENCES

Alexander, A. (1982) *The Politics of Local Government in the United Kingdom*, Longman, London.
Banister, D.J. *et al.* (1985) Deregulating the bus industry in Britain, *Transport Reviews*, Vol. 5, 99–142.
Blowers, A. (1984) *Something in the Air: Corporate Power and the Environment*, Harper & Row, London.
Blunden, J. and Curry, N. (eds) (1985) *The Changing Countryside*, Croom Helm, London.
Bottomore, T.B. (1966) *Elites and Society*, Penguin, Harmondsworth.
Bowers, J.K. and Cheshire, P. (1983) *Agriculture, The Countryside and Land Use*, Methuen, London.
Bradley, T. and Lowe, P. (eds) (1984) *Locality and Rurality*, Geo Books, Norwich.
Buchanan, S. (1982) Power and planning in rural areas: preparation of the Suffolk county structure plan. In Moseley, M.J. (ed.) *Power Planning and People in Rural East Anglia*, Centre of East Anglian Studies, Norwich.
Byrne, T. (1983) *Local Government in Britain* (2nd ed.), Penguin, Harmondsworth.
Carter, R. (1985) *Capitalism, Class Conflict and the New Middle Class*, Routledge & Kegan Paul, London.
Castells, M. (1978) *City, Class and Power*, Macmillan, London.
Champion, A.G. (1981) Population trends in rural Britain, *Population Trends*, Vol. 26, 20–23.
Cloke, P.J. (1979) *Key Settlements in Rural Areas*, Methuen, London.
Cloke, P.J. (1983) *An Introduction to Rural Settlement Planning*, Methuen, London.

Cloke, P.J. (ed.) (1984) *Wheels Within Wales*, Centre for Rural Transport, Lampeter.

Cloke, P.J. (1985) Counterurbanisation: a rural perspective, *Geography*, Vol. 70, 1–9.

Cloke, P.J. and Hanrahan, P. (1984) Policy and implementation in rural planning, *Geoforum*, Vol. 15, 261–269.

Cloke, P.J. and Little, J.K. (1985) *Rural Policy-Making in the Gloucestershire Structure Plan: A Study of Motives and Mechanisms*, Rural Policy Implementation Project Working Paper 6, Department of Geography, St David's University College, Lampeter.

Cloke, P.J. and Little, J.K. (forthcoming) *The Limits to Planning in Rural Society*.

Cloke, P.J. and Shaw, D.P. (1983) Rural settlement policies in structure plans, *Town Planning Review*, Vol. 54, 338–354.

Cockburn, C. (1977) *The Local State: Management of Cities and People*, Pluto Press, London.

Cooke, P. (1983) *Theories of Planning and Spatial Development*, Hutchinson, London.

Cox, G. and Lowe, P. (1983) A battle not the war: the politics of the Wildlife and Countryside Act, *Countryside Planning Yearbook*, Vol. 4, 48–76.

Dahl, R.A. (1961) *Who Governs?* Yale University Press, New Haven.

Dear, M. and Clark, G. (1984) *State Apparatus: Structures and Language of Legitimacy*, Allen & Unwin, Boston.

Duncan, S. and Goodwin, M. (1982) The local state and restructuring social relations, *International Journal of Urban and Regional Research*, Vol. 6, 157–186.

Dunleavy, P. (1980) *Urban Political Analysis: The Politics of Collective Consumption*, Macmillan, London.

Dunleavy, P. (1984) The limits to local government. In Boddy, M. and Fudge, C. (eds) *Local Socialism?* Macmillan, London.

Fothergill, S. and Gudgin, G. (1982) *Unequal Growth: Urban and Regional Employment Change in the U.K.*, Heinemann, London.

Gilder, I.M. (1979) Rural planning policies: an economic appraisal, *Progress in Planning*, Vol. 11, 213–217.

Gilg, A. (1984) Politics and the countryside: the British example. In Clark, G., Groenendijk, J. and Thissen, J. (eds) *The Changing Countryside*, Geo Books, Norwich.

Gilg, A. (1985) *An Introduction to Rural Geography*, Edward Arnold, London.

Glover, R. (1985) Local decision-making and rural public transport. In Cloke, P.J. (ed.) *Rural Accessibility and Mobility*, Centre for Rural Transport, Lampeter.

Gould, A. and Keeble, D. (1984) New firms and rural industrialisation in East Anglia, *Regional Studies*, Vol. 18, 189–201.

Green, B. (1981) *Countryside Conservation*, Allen & Unwin, London.

Gyford, J. (1984) *Local Politics in Britain* (2nd ed.), Croom Helm, London.

Hague, C. (1984) *The Development of Planning Thought*, Hutchinson, London.

Ham, C. and Hill, M. (1984) *The Policy Process in the Modern Capitalist State*, Wheatsheaf Press, Brighton.

Hanrahan, P. and Cloke, P.J. (1983) Towards a critical appraisal of rural settlement planning in England and Wales, *Sociologia Ruralis*, Vol. 23, 109–129.

Healey, P. (1982) Understanding land use planning: the contribution of recent developments in political economy and policy studies. In Healey, P., McDougall, G. and Thomas, M.J. (eds) *Planning Theory: Prospects for the 1980s*, Pergamon, Oxford.

Healey, P. (1984) Emerging directions for research on local land use planning. Paper presented to the Research in Local Land Use Planning Seminar, Oxford Polytechnic, May/June 1985.

Hunter, F. (1953) *Community Power Structure*, University of North Carolina Press, Chapel Hill.

Johnston, R.J. (1982) *Geography and the State: An Essay in Political Geography*, Macmillan, London.

Keeble, D.E. (1980) Industrial decline, regional policy and the urban-rural manufacturing shift in the United Kingdom, *Environment and Planning A*, Vol. 12, 945–962.

Knowles, R. (ed.) (1985) *Implications of the 1985 Transport Bill*, Transport Geography Study Group, Salford.

Knox, P. and Cullen, J. (1981) Town planning and the internal survival mechanisms of urbanised capitalism, *Area*, Vol. 13, 183–188.

Lowe, P. and Goyder, J. (1983) *Environmental Groups in British Politics*, Allen & Unwin, London.

McLaughlin, B. (1983) The rural deprivation debate — retrospect and prospect. Paper presented to the Rural Economy and Society Study Group Conference, Keele University.

McLaughlin, B. (1985) What causes rural deprivation? Paper presented to the Welsh Rural Forum, St David's University College, Lampeter.

Miliband, R. (1977) *Marxism and Politics*, Oxford University Press.

Moseley, M.J. (1984) The revival of rural areas in advanced economies: a review of some causes and consequences, *Geoforum*, Vol. 15, 447–456.

Newby, H. (1977) *The Deferential Worker*, Allen Lane, London.

Newby, H. (1981) Urbanism and the rural class structure. In Harloe, M. (ed.) *New Perspectives in Urban Change and Conflict*, Heinemann, London.

Newby, H., Bell, C., Rose, D. and Saunders, P. (1978) *Property, Paternalism and Power*, Hutchinson, London.

Pacione, M. (ed.) (1983) *Progress in Rural Geography*, Croom Helm, London.

Pacione, M. (1984) *Rural Geography*, Harper & Row, London.

Pahl, R.E. (1975) *Whose City?* (2nd ed.), Penguin, Harmondsworth.

Pahl, R.E. (1982) Urban managerialism reconsidered. In Paris, C. (ed.) *Critical Readings in Planning Theory*, Pergamon, Oxford. (Originally published as Chapter 13 of *Whose City?*)

Phillips, D. and Williams, A. (1984) *Rural Britain: A Social Geography*, Blackwell, Oxford.

Polsby, N.W. (1963) *Community Power and Political Theory*, Yale University Press, New Haven.

Poulantzas, N. (1973) The problems of the capitalist state. In Urry, J. and Wakefield, J. (eds) *Power in Britain*, Heinemann, London.

Poulantzas, N. (1975) *Classes in Contemporary Capitalism*, New Left Books, London.

Pye-Smith, C. and North, R. (1984) *Working the Land*, Temple Smith, London.

Pye-Smith, C. and Rose, C. (1984) *Crisis and Conservation: Conflict in the British Countryside*, Penguin, Harmondsworth.

Rees, G. (1984) Rural regions in national and international economies. In Bradley, T. and Lowe, P. (eds) *Locality and Rurality*, Geo Books, Norwich.

Robert, S. and Randolph, W.G. (1983) Beyond decentralisation: the evolution of population distribution in England and Wales, 1961–1981, *Geoforum*, Vol. 14, No. 1, 75–102.

Saunders, P. (1979) *Urban Politics: A Sociological Interpretation*, Hutchinson, London.

Saunders, P. (1984) Rethinking local politics. In Boddy, M. and Fudge, C. (eds) *Local Socialism?* Macmillan, London.

Saunders, P. (1985) The forgotten dimension of central–local relations: theorising the 'regional state', *Government and Policy*, Vol. 3, 149–162.

Shoard, M. (1980) *The Theft of the Countryside*, Temple Smith, London.

Urry, J. (1981) Localities, regions and social class, *International Journal of Urban and Regional Research*, Vol. 5, 455–473.

2

POLICY AND IMPLEMENTATION DECISIONS

Paul Cloke

CONCEPTS OF IMPLEMENTATION

The implementation problem is assumed to be a series of mundane decisions and interactions unworthy of the attention of scholars seeking the heady stuff of politics. Implementation is deceptively simple: it does not appear to involve any great issues. (Van Meter and Van Horn, 1975, p. 450)

One of the two major issues facing a contemporary analysis of rural planning (as identified in Chapter 1) is the degree to which autonomy and discretion are available to planners in the implementation of their policies. Interest in the topic of implementation has been spawned by an increasingly widespread realization that rural policies and promises are not matched by planning action. Indeed, a substantial conclusion illustrated in the previous chapter is that planning has largely failed to regulate the market-based trends which would, planning or no planning, have exacerbated both social problems of polarization and disadvantage in rural areas and rural land-use problems connected with landscape and wildlife conservation.

The yawning divide between planning intentions and practices can initially be viewed from two basic perspectives (Cloke and Hanrahan, 1984). A traditional approach would be to recognize an *implementation problem* as the major cause of inadequate planning responses to perceived needs. A logical outcome of this perspective is that if only the techniques of implementation could be improved then planning would have a realistic opportunity of ameliorating rural ills. Alternatively, a *policy problem* can be adopted, suggesting that 'suitable' policies for rural areas are being precluded within the complex manoeuvres of the planning process in rural areas. In other words, we have expected far too much from planning in rural areas (Hanrahan and Cloke, 1983) which is unable to deliver its objectives because there is no rational and sequential dichotomy between policy and implementation. Moreover, any such perspective not only ignores the complexities of how things get done within planning but also falsely represents the strength of the internal survival mechanisms in planning which repel the adoption of socially progressive policies. Further exploration of

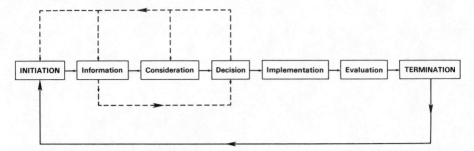

Figure 2.1   A rational decision-making view of the policy process (Jenkins, 1978).

implementation concepts is usefully carried out using this framework of rational and political approaches and indeed of the various hybrids which have sought to combine them.

RATIONAL MODELS — THE TOP–DOWN APPROACH

Alterman (1982) has compared the study of implementation to an analysis of a black box. The input and the output have become reasonably clear to researchers over the years but the throughput of decision-making has until fairly recently remained a dark and mysterious secret. Traditional attempts to enlighten this black box have described implementation as a discrete stage in a rational process of decision-making. Such attempts stem from strong but rather simplistic theoretical roots which assume that policy represents the decision as to what to do, and implementation represents getting it done (Baker, 1972). Thus planning is viewed as a sequence of distinct steps and implementation constitutes a rational stage of decision-making following 'policy-making' and preceding policy evaluation. Figure 2.1 demonstrates a fairly typical illustration of such a rational decision-making chain. In stressing stepwise progression from 'policy' to 'implementation' this framework for analysis constitutes a *top–down* approach. Implementation is thus characterized and constrained by decisions from above, rather than by the ground-level environment in which any action takes place. Within this rational context, implementation has been variously defined as:

1.   'Those outputs (actions) of an agency which derive from a particular decision sequence, the outputs being supposed to achieve, or implement, the policy' (Healey, 1979, p. 5).
2.   'The ability to forge subsequent links in the causal chain so as to obtain desired results' (Pressman and Wildavsky, 1973, p. 15).
3.   'Those actions by public and private individuals (or groups) that are directed at the achievement of objectives set forth in prior policy decisions' (Van Meter and Van Horn, 1975, p. 447).

   In many ways this rational top–down model has been tacitly and implicitly accepted by analysts and decision-makers alike. Smith (1973) highlights the widespread assumption that once a policy has been made it will be implemented and the outcome of implementation will be close to that anticipated by policy-makers. Planning in this mode is thus an inexorable and logical process whereby actions follow decisions. It follows, therefore, that reasonable expectations are generated among both planners and the community that recognizable aims and objectives can be fulfilled during the implementation stage of the process. Any breakdown of the process at the implementation stage would thus be an illogicality in a logical system, and so problems of policy enactment are seen as confined to the technicalities of implementation, rather than stemming from any previous stages of the chain. Dunsire (1978) confirms the blinkered nature of this diagnosis of implementation problems within the rational decision-making model. He recognizes three forms of implementation failure:

1. When the outcome of implementation differs from expectation, even though the actions taken were predicted to achieve the desired outcomes.
2. When the prescribed actions were not carried out.
3. When the prescribed actions were carried out but the desired outcomes were not achieved because there were errors in predicting the results of the prescribed actions.

All these variations of implementation problem are confined to the implementation stage of the model. The changing environment in which actions are taken means that good implementation techniques are overtaken by events; the breakdown in actually carrying out implementation procedures; and the erroneous selection of implementation procedures in order to procure agreed objectives; are all representative of situations whereby the top–down policy is not seen to be at fault. The assumption is that an improvement in the technical procedures of implementation will restore the rational planning process and therefore achieve the desired outcomes.

The power of rational decision-making models depends on the degree to which the scale and frequency of implementation failures can continue to be explained away in technical and procedural terms. Certainly, in Chapter 1 a summary was made of the range of circumstances in rural areas where planning has been unable to respond to pressing problems of society, economy and environment. The notion that somehow planners still have not got their implementation procedures up to the required technical standards is a rather facile one. Moreover, by allowing the blame for rural problems consistently to be laid at the door of the planning system there is a danger that the state, in combination with those capital interests responsible for provoking change in rural areas, is effectively diverting interest away from its own liabilities in these matters. Analysis of policy and implementation has therefore moved beyond the rational model in search of a more realistic view of the political and organizational context of planning action.

BOTTOM–UP AND HYBRID MODELS

Healey (1979, 1982) has been prominent in the analysis of alternative models of planning and policy-making processes. In eschewing the idea of 'decisions–means–ends' sequences she focuses rather on the mechanisms and contexts which explain how policies are made and pursued. Specifically she recounts the influence of political and economic institutions on the activities of planning and policy-making agencies. From this perspective, gaps between policy and implementation merely reflect the changing balance of influence among these institutions, and decision-making processes represent bargaining and negotiation between different interests. Any such framework for investigation will lead to the rejection of the notion of an implementation problem (as

Figure 2.2   A behavioural model of policy-making (Lewis and Flynn, 1978, p. 11).

outlined above) in favour of a more complex view of policy problems arising from the distribution of power within society and within relevant organizations.

This reorientation of the focus for planning analysis encapsulates a range of different viewpoints on implementation. Lewis and Flynn (1978, 1979), for example, favour a behavioural model of policy-making in which implementation is viewed simply as 'action'. Using evidence from interviews with individuals working in a range of planning agencies, they analyse the dual concerns of such individuals: the exterior world and the interior institutional context within which they work (Figure 2.2). Far from exposing a rational decision-making process in this context, Lewis and Flynn (1978) uncover a haphazard and complex combination of circumstances:

> In reality there are disagreements about policy goals and objectives; vagueness and ambiguity about policies and uncertainty about their operationalisation in practice; procedural complexity; inconsistency between powers available and existing problems; and conflict arising from public participation, pressure group activity and political dissensus. (p. 5)

Given this complexity, they adopt a view of implementation in which the baseline is 'getting things done' and the predominant line of inquiry is how things get done. In some circumstances they found that such action did follow previously defined policy objectives. More frequently, however, they discovered that:

> [. . .] actions result from the resolution of conflicts between two sets of priorities and policy areas; may precede the formulation of a procedure for dealing with similar cases in future and therefore the policy; or may result from what is feasible in the circumstances rather than the fulfilment of the original objectives. (p. 5)

As Rocke (1985) has pointed out, Lewis and Flynn's framework constitutes a concerted attempt to prise apart the psychologically conditioned link between policy and implementation. Top–down approaches have usefully directed attention towards the implementation concept, but a series of 'bottom–up' approaches is required to understand how and why individuals and groups of decision-makers act the way they do (Hambleton, 1981).

A pure bottom–up approach is equally capable of offering a blinkered view of implementation. To get bogged down in the day-to-day minutiae of decisions, thereby losing sight of the less tangible but crucially important higher-level political constraints on those decisions, will lead to distortion and oversimplification in our understanding of the sharp end of planning in rural areas. It would be useful, therefore, to superimpose the best elements of top–down and bottom–up approaches in any synthesis of the policy–implementation phenomenon. For example, Barrett and Fudge (1981), bringing together a most useful collection of essays on policy and action in the urban sphere, outline four factors which underlie the enactment of policy (a top–down perspective):

1. Knowing what you want to do.
2. Gaining access to the required resources.
3. Marshalling and controlling these resources.
4. Communicating with and controlling the performance of other agencies involved
    in the process.

At the same time, however, they acknowledge that the relationship between policy and action (from a bottom–up viewpoint) is not a straightforward one because implementation also constitutes a series of responses — to ideological leanings, to environmental pressures, to pressures from other agencies and so on. As a result, implementation is inextricably bound up with power relations and the various mechanisms for gaining influence and control over the allocation of resources. It follows from these views of policy enactment and the policy–action relationship that elements of both top–down and bottom–up perspectives are required to fully explain the complexities of implementation.

The value of hybrid approaches to the understanding of how things get done within political and institutional contexts has been recognized by many recent researchers. Hambleton (1981), for example, recognizes that the existence of policies can create expectations and influence behaviour but that implementation should not be viewed as the inexorable outcome of these policies. He points out that, in practice, it is difficult if not impossible to delineate where policy ends and implementation starts. This analysis concurs with that of Barrett (1980) who prefers to describe implementation as a policy–action continuum which represents an iterative negotiation between actors and agencies whose task it is to put policy into effect, and those who control the means to such action.

Hybrid approaches, although offering deeper insights into the complicated realities of decision-making, offer less scope for straightforward analyses of 'success' or 'failure' in implementation. Different actors in the policy–action continuum will have different perceptions of success or failure (Hill *et al.*, 1979). What actually happens is that delays occur, objectives are altered, some parts of policies are prioritized over others, implementation difficulties lead to new policy goals and so on. Moreover, implementation is not static either in time or in relation to other policies being pursued contemporaneously. Alterman (1982) thus regards implementation as a *relative* concept:

> To talk about an implementation process usefully, one must state what is the 'policy of reference' and what are the 'persons, groups or agencies of reference' from whose point of view implementation is described and assessed. One policy's implementation is another policy's deviation: and one group's success in implementation is another group's failure. (p. 229)

Despite their inability to give clear indications of success or failure of implementation, the hybrid models do present clear and important conclusions for the understanding of rural planning at the sharp end. Policy and implementation are not sequential; rather they are dynamic and interactive processes, each creating an impact on the other. Hence Anderson's (1975) now classic statement: 'Policy is being made as it is being administered and administered as it is being made' (p. 98).

Moreover, these interactive negotiations are being carried out within broad political

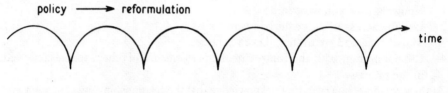

Figure 2.3   The policy-action continuum (Barrett and Fudge, 1981, p. 25).

constraints — what Barrett and Fudge (1981) have termed 'bargaining within negotiated order'. Policy, therefore, is not a fixed entity. Instead it has the status of *intentions*
which are bargained over and modified through negotiations with other agencies and
interests seeking to exert control and maximize their own priorities. Implementation is
the continuum of these policy–action interactions, representing the bargaining and
negotiation procedures between those wishing to influence the course of events and
those who control the access to power required for any such change. Barrett and
Fudge's (1981) diagrammatic illustration of these concepts is shown in Figure 2.3.

   The key to our understanding of these processes, therefore, lies in analyses both of
the *constraints* on the operation of the policy–action continuum, and of attempts to
structure this operation in order to limit the autonomy and discretion available to
competing actors and agencies. Clearly the ability to impose structuring and constraints
reflects the distribution of power as discussed in Chapter 1. The key question once
again appears to be whether the central state permits significant discretion to its
regional and local counterparts in the structuring of planning and policy-making
processes, or whether the imperative of central state provision for expansion by the
interests of capital deters any real autonomy within localized planning in rural areas. It
is to these matters of structuration and constraint that we now turn our attention.

THE CONTEXT OF IMPLEMENTATION

Thus far, it has been established that explanations of the erstwhile failure of policy-
makers to achieve any lasting impact on rural problems should transcend a mere search
for technical and operational weaknesses of a rational implementation process of
'putting policies into action'. In so doing explanations should not be hindered or
restricted by the need to resort to conventional lines of analysis in the rigid separation of
policy and implementation. Minay (1979), for example, argues that the policy–action
continuum encounters varying levels of constraint according to the nature of the
planning being attempted. He outlines four differing views of planning:
1.   Planning as a response to private action
2.   Planning as the positive promotion of environmental change
3.   Planning as coordination
4.   Planning as resource management
and suggests that the degree of difficulty in achieving a negotiated outcome varies
considerably. There is an evident strength in this assertion. Planning as development
control, for example, encompasses the kinds of bargaining procedures outlined above
but does not involve the pervasive issues of resource availability and allocation which

are vital to positive and interventionist planning. Similarly the task of coordinating the activities of different resource–allocating agencies, difficult though that might be, is less dependent on the national political will than a form of planning which seeks to enact, say, a major redistribution of wealth within society. This analysis of 'degree of difficulty' in implementation has some merit.

A more fruitful line of analysis, however, is to mimic the progress made in the urban and regional contexts by firmly placing rural policy and action in position as one activity within the broader spectrum of government. Planning is part of the state, and is therefore subject to and subsumed by the macro-scale relationship between the state and civil society. Thereby if an analysis of the state and its institutions permits the view that planning is a neutral arbitration service for competing resource-bidders, then the degree of centralized constraint exerted on decision-makers within planning might be construed as unimportant. If, however, the state is viewed as performing the more conservative function of preserving societal status quo so as to permit the expansion of capital (Poulantzas, 1973), then extreme doubt must be cast on the assumption that planning through the state can be either independent or apolitical in its dealings with different social or class groupings. Evidence for the latter view is becoming increasingly compelling (Cloke and Little, 1985, 1986a). It can certainly be argued that rural policy-makers, before they even start their negotiations within the policy–action continuum, are constrained by an artificially delimited range of options, and accept an externally imposed definition of the 'art of the possible' which is dictated by a recognition of the need to retain societal status quo.

The primary constraints on rural policy options are therefore the restrictions imposed by the state/society relationship. Underneath this primary constraint, how-ever, occurs a series of more recognizable secondary restrictions, further constraining the already delimited range of options open to policy-makers. Briefly, these secondary constraints occur in three areas of the political environment in which planning functions (Hanrahan and Cloke, 1983; Cloke and Hanrahan, 1984).

1. CENTRAL–LOCAL GOVERNMENT RELATIONS

The issues of planning as part of the central, local and regional states have been discussed in Chapter 1. Recent years have witnessed the development of a complex range of state agencies, representing or mediating between the central and local levels of state (Boddy, 1983). The increasing complexity of state agencies creates constraints on the implementation of rural policies, as overlap and conflict arise between different agencies. At the centre, for example, the activities of the Ministry of Agriculture, Fisheries and Food (MAFF) in supporting the modernization of agriculture and the improvement of agricultural land conflict with the role of the Department of the Environment (DoE) in promoting rural landscape conservation. Local agencies thus receive confused signals from the centre, clarified only by the relatively powerful nature of the interests of agricultural capital at the centre compared with their environ-mentalist rivals. The complexity of agencies also creates problems of accountability, particularly where inter-tier mediation agencies are granted decision-making powers without reference to the rules of representation expected by some segments of a democratic society and embodied in more traditional aspects of the central and local state.

The allocation of resources to rural areas is thus channelled through a fragmented system of public administration. A key concern, therefore, is not only the coordination of agencies between the centre and the locality but, more importantly, the degree of discretion afforded to local elites, managers or society more generally, in arriving at policy decisions. An accompanying factor relates to the degree of willingness demonstrated by often conservative rural representatives to accept and make use of such discretion which is made available. Wright (1982) makes the point that local state programmes of investment are devised: 'with at least one eye on the central department's policies and priorities, and are implemented with the knowledge that the central department monitors the implementation of programmes closely' (pp 6–7). In addition, evidence concerning the take-up of available discretion (see, for example, Newby *et al.*, 1978; Glover, 1985) suggests that local authority members are often ideologically reluctant to agree to feasible levels of intervention in local housing and service markets.

With high-profile incursions by central government into the local state domain over recent years, it can be strongly suggested that local government is becoming increasingly subordinated to externally defined priorities rather than being unfettered in its policy and implementation decisions (Harloe, 1981). Through restrictive financial and legislative controls, the central state appears to be tightening its grip over the local arena, and these restrictions have significant impacts on policy decisions by officers and members at the local level.

2. INTER-AGENCY RELATIONS

Although central state restrictions on local agencies are becoming more severe, further implementation restraints occur when such agencies have to interact with each other. A traditional panacea for the ills associated with putting into practice rural policies has been the recommendation for greater coordination and integration of decision-making agencies (Working Party on Rural Settlement Policies, 1979; Smart and Wright, 1983). Behind this recommendation lies a chequered history of poor coordination and isolationist stances by many rural agencies, including individual departments within local authorities.

The notion of corporate planning has been officially adopted by many agencies, particularly local authorities following the reorganization of local government in 1974. Any great expectation that agency coordination will radically improve the ability of rural planning to respond to problems is likely, however, to be misplaced. Aside from the very important consideration that the removal of this one secondary constraint does not alter the overbearing primary constraints of the state/society relationship (see above), it is clear that agencies continue to preserve their spheres of influence and power wherever possible. The compromises inherent in corporate decision-making have tended to founder on this rock of agency egocentricity. Many examples of this process in rural areas support these contentions. Packman and Wallace (1982), for instance, in their survey of the management of rural services in East Anglia, demonstrate that each agency involved operates within a clearly defined and jealously guarded delimitation of responsibility, and services a distinct group of clients. Any cooperation in service provision is greatly inhibited by these factors.

Discord between agencies should not merely be put down to inept coordination.

There are several circumstances in rural areas when deliberate non-cooperation takes place between agencies. Healey (1979) has demonstrated that the uneasy division of planning responsibilities between county-level strategic policies and district-level development control is often marked by opposition between the two agencies. District authorities will sometimes stretch to the limits the discretion available to them so that local preferences can override strategic policies. They are aided and abetted in this task by central government, which has supported districts both by amending structure plans to their advantage and by ruling against counties in key appeals procedures.

Interagency relations are thus pervaded by conflicts of interest, and policy and action in rural areas are distorted as a consequence. The situation is thus ripe for any divide-and-rule tactics which the central state might wish to employ to maintain its own dominance.

3. PUBLIC–PRIVATE-SECTOR RELATIONS

Private-sector agencies and the capital at their disposal are usually a vital factor in the enactment of public-sector policy. In many instances, pressure for development from the private sector represents the motive force for change in an area and planning *per se* is merely a passive or reactive mechanism to this pressure. In terms of service provision, market-led trends have sought the concentrated clientele and economies of scale to be found in growth centre locations. Such objectives have led to a contraction of private-sector services from many locations. Similarly in the public sector, limited finance for direct provision of rural opportunities has prompted the pursuit of rationalization policies, effectively mirroring the private sector's locational decisions. The dependence on private capital to finance development ensures that investment patterns in rural areas are dominated by the logic of the marketplace and the motive of profit.

The role of planners in this relationship is reduced to one of advocacy and informal persuasion, seeking to encourage private-sector interests to provide opportunities in locations recognized by planners as zones of need but not necessarily by developers as zones of demand. Patently, however, the distribution of this investment occurs well beyond the direct control of planning and as a consequence further significant restrictions are placed on the 'art of the possible' for rural policies and planning options.

The private sector is also instrumental in exerting indirect influence on public policy through activities aimed at reducing such overhead costs as tax payments. Austin (1983) suggests that corporate pressure is brought to bear on policy-makers to encourage them to minimize collective expenditure on public services. Such less obvious factors in the public–private-sector relationship are particularly important in those rural areas whose conservative political representatives often rely on these very same corporate interests for the continuation of their political and economic status.

Planning and policy-making for rural areas can be rendered relatively impotent if the will and motivation of private-sector interests do not happen to comply with public-sector aspirations. Indeed, public policy usually takes full account of known private interests prior to the finalization of rural planning strategies.

The primary constraint of the state/society relationship, and the secondary constraints arising from central–local, interagency and public–private-sector relationships offer an interesting framework for understanding the structuration of the policy–action continuum in rural planning. These issues are neither innovative nor necessarily contemporary, as they have been adopted widely in the analysis of planning at the urban and regional scales. They have, however, been less readily accepted as the basis for understanding rural policies and planning, perhaps because analyses of rural planning have been more devoted to the rational and apolitical notions of public policy and less willing to countenance the centrality of political and organizational factors in constraining the art of the possible for rural policies. It is one thing to reach these conclusions via abstract academic analysis, however, and quite another to relate them to the everyday experience of planning practice. The remainder of this chapter offers some corroborative evidence for these findings from the local political ferment.

THE PRACTICAL CIRCUMSTANCES OF IMPLEMENTATION

As part of the Rural Policy Implementation Project at Lampeter, a questionnaire survey of a sample of 36 county planning authorities was carried out on themes of practical policy-making and implementation. A full account of the methodological and technical limitations of this survey is published elsewhere, along with detailed results (Cloke and Little, 1985, 1986b) but a summary of four groups of salient findings serves to reinforce the preceding discussion on the nature of policy and implementation in rural planning.

THE NATURE OF IMPLEMENTATION

All respondents were involved with the structure plans of their respective counties and therefore their answers, when questioned on the nature of implementation, are coloured by the practicalities of the implementation task. The majority of respondents defined implementation in terms of the most tangible of their tasks — that is, those activities of land-use control. Here there are established legislative controls to be performed, and implementation is perhaps at its most rational. Definitions of implementation were founded on this incontrovertible base. Some respondents viewed implementation as the pursuit of agreed policies by county council departments; others included the work undertaken by external agencies in pursuit of agreed policies. A small minority defined implementation as the pursuance of a wide agenda of activities, unrestrained by 'official' policies. Obviously the perceived successes and problems of implementation will depend on the initially defined ambit of implementation activities. Given a narrow definition, implementation can be seen as unproblematic, whereas more ambitious objectives are frustratingly difficult to enact. A clear schism emerged from the survey between perceivedly straightforward development control tasks, and the wider ambitions of policy. The latter area of policy and action gives a relatively unconstrained scope for action. According to one respondent: 'it [implementation] is also any involvement with what is happening in the area. It is a wide-ranging definition that encompasses virtually anything which helps to achieve the objectives of the local authority'.

Although the scope is unrestrained, the means of enactment were seen by many planners to be dominated by the external restrictions within which planning operates.

The following comment is typical: 'Implementation, without power . . . is merely an acceptance of the market mechanisms and their resulting actions, whether in line with policy or not'. The nature of implementation, then, differs with the scope of the aims and objectives of policy and this survey therefore seems to support the idea of a policy–action continuum. Narrowly defined tasks such as development control provide the tangible, straightforward element, while the wider socioeconomic and environmental concerns are very definitely seen as subject to many of the external constraints discussed above.

IMPLEMENTATION PROBLEMS

Although the activities perceived to be associated with implementation varied from county to county, the difficulties experienced in enacting agreed policies or broader objectives were uniform. Five problems predominated:

1. *Interorganizational conflicts* — wherein local planning authorities have no direct control or influence over other resource-allocating agencies.
2. *Lack of finance* — a reflex response, of 'obvious' relevance and importance but rarely detailed as to finance from what source and for what purpose.
3. *Lack of control over private-sector interests* — what happens in rural areas is often dictated by a relatively undirected wealth of private resources whose investment may not concur with policy goals, and indeed may conflict with them.
4. *Government policies* — deficiencies were highlighted here due to the fragmentary nature of enabling legislation and lack of statutory support for local authority initiatives in rural areas.
5. *Local political and public commitment* — the survey consistently exposed a lack of political resolve to go beyond the status quo and to opt for rural development policies rather than conservation. This backwashes to the vocal opposition from many sectors of rural communities (frequently non-indigenous fractions) to rate-based spending on rural services and development proposals.

These five groups of difficulties experienced by those involved with practical policy and action closely reflect the theoretical constraints on implementation analysed in the earlier part of this chapter. Central–local (2, 4, 5), interagency (1) and public–private-sector (3) relationships all figure prominently in this one illustration of implementation in practice. The primary constraint of the state/society relationship remains as the unspoken foundation for secondary constraints rather than as a recognizable element in its own right.

OVERCOMING IMPLEMENTATION PROBLEMS

A third element of the survey begged the question to planners of *how* these recognized problems might be overcome. The structural nature of perceived implementation problems means that few simple or immediate methods are available to planners with which to improve their implementation procedures. Three types of answer were suggested in this context:

1. Alterations to the implementation process.
2. Alterations to policy.
3. Changes in the central government framework for planning.

In their discussion of these three options, two consistent reflections on the interrelations of (1) to (3) were in evidence. *First*, planners who by the very sampling frame of the survey had necessarily been deeply involved in structure plan policy-making were inclined to look upwards to the central state and downwards to the 'implementers' for improvements rather than to potential policy alterations. Clearly, it is both convenient and organizationally responsible for planning officers to identify potential changes in the actions of other decision-making agencies and in the administrative and financial groundrules laid down by central government, rather than in the agreed policies of their own authority, which in any case had been subjected to the 'feasibility test' before they were agreed. *Second*, the range of options for overcoming implementation problems was viewed as being an interdependent vested hierarchy of proposals. Alterations to implementation processes were viewed as dependent on policy changes, which in turn relied on changes in central government attitudes towards planning so as to provide scope for wider policy options. Apart, then, from some very small-scale fine tuning, the notion of being able to overcome perceived implementation problems is viewed as involving far-reaching structural changes to the discretion granted to local-level policy-making and planning.

RECENT IMPLEMENTATION IMPROVEMENTS

In a final section of the survey, respondents were requested to provide detailed examples of circumstances in which previous difficulties in policy implementation had in fact been overcome in their areas. More than half of the sample reported no significant improvements although some of this negative response may have hinged on varying definitions of 'significant'. The nature of the positive responses, however, suggests that no important improvements were missed by this semantic difficulty, in that the reported improvements tended to be low level and pragmatic in nature. The funds of initiative and technical competence within county planning departments are clearly being outworked not in the conventional implementation role but rather in an environment of *opportunism* for the practical enactment of policies and objectives. Any resource either directly available to the authority, such as Manpower Services Commission labour, or indirectly available through localized coordination schemes (often liaising with the voluntary sector), will be fully utilized to pursue the planning task. It was stressed by respondents, however, that planning-by-opportunism has arisen because of the severe restrictions on straightforward rational planning imposed by the central state's view of the role of planning and public-sector intervention in rural affairs. These external restrictions are reiterated throughout the survey responses.

This survey, due to its technical limitations and restricted scope, dealing with only a sample of practitioners engaged in structure planning, provides only a small part of the evidence required to give practical credence to the theoretical issues discussed earlier. As a limited example, however, it does tend to confirm many of the conceptual submissions which arise from the perspective of rural planning as a constraint-ridden part of state activity. To some extent, therefore, analysis of rural planning and policy-making seems to be aided by the beginnings of a conjunction of theory and practice.

CONCLUSIONS

Analysis of rural planning at the sharp end has consistently expected far too much of the planners' ability to achieve their objectives. The reality of planning is that it is heftily constrained both by the state/society relations and by central–local government, interagency and public–private-sector conflicts. These constraints explain the apparent lack of impact achieved by policy-makers on recent and contemporary changes in rural Britain, and point us in various directions towards a greater understanding of the complex interactions of coordinative planning. It certainly seems that a dichotomous view of 'policy' and 'implementation' as two rational and sequential stages of the planning process will not greatly aid such an understanding. Respondents to the survey of county planning authorities confirm this. One states:

> Whilst a sequential view may appear rational and have value in justifying or explaining what is happening it does not adequately represent the actual processes of change. Policies of the authority are intentions, desirable courses of action, a base line for negotiation, and implementation can be putting these policies into effect. The distinction between policy and implementation is in practice blurred and artificial when the main emphasis is how can the local authority best respond to the problems that exist in its area.

Placed in a broader context, conclusions such as these suggest that rural planning and policy-making do not suffer from an 'implementation problem' *per se*. Attention should rather be focused on how to develop a response to rural problems within a climate of insufficient corporate responsibility for planners and inadequate financial resources for their projects. This response can be *pragmatic* within current restraints, or *progressive* in removing some current constraints.

There is something of a dilemma between these pragmatic and progressive options. Policy-making is essentially a public-sector activity, while enactment of policies is essentially a private-sector activity in combination with crucial contributions from fragmented and uncoordinated public agencies. These arrangements would only be altered by a considerable change in political will, yet rural areas show no signs of such political initiative, and in any case represent too few votes to influence the central state in this direction. Given these circumstances, rural policy and action continue to represent something of a political gesture rather than any real attempt to resolve actual problems.

REFERENCES

Alterman, R. (1982) Implementation analysis in urban and regional planning. In Healey, P., McDougall, G. and Thomas, M. (eds) *Planning Theory: Prospects for the 1980s*, Pergamon, Oxford.

Anderson, J.E. (1975) *Public Policy Making*, Nelson, London.

Austin, D.M. (1983) The political economy of human services, *Policy and Politics*, Vol. 11, 343–359.

Baker, R.J.S. (1972) *Administrative Theory and Public Administration*, Hutchinson, London.

Barrett, S. (1980) Perspectives on implementation. Paper presented to the SSRC Central-Local Government Relationships Conference, INLOGOV.

Barrett, S. and Fudge, C. (1981) Examining the policy-action relationship. In Barrett, S. and Fudge, C. (eds) *Policy and Action*, Methuen, London.

Boddy, M. (1983) Central–local government relations: theory and practice, *Political Geography Quarterly*, Vol. 2, 119–138.

Cloke, P.J. and Hanrahan, P.J. (1984) Policy and implementation in rural planning, *Geoforum*, Vol. 15, 261–269.

Cloke, P.J. and Little, J.K. (1985) *Implementation and County Level Planning*, Rural Policy Implementation Project WP1, SDUC, Lampeter.

Cloke, P.J. and Little, J.K. (1986a) Implementation and county structure plan policies for rural areas, *Planning Perspectives* (in press).

Cloke, P.J. and Little, J.K. (1986b) The implementation of rural policies: a survey of county planning authorities, *Town Planning Review*, Vol. 1, 257–277.

Dunsire, A. (1978) *The Execution Process, Vol. II: Control in a Bureaucracy*, Martin Robertson, Oxford.

Glover, R. (1985) Local decision-making and rural public transport. In Cloke, P.J. (ed.) *Rural Accessibility and Mobility*, Centre for Rural Transport, Lampeter.

Hambleton, R. (1981) Policy planning systems and implementation: some implications for planning theory. Paper presented to the Planning Theory in the 1980s Conference, Department of Town Planning, Oxford Polytechnic.

Hanrahan, P.J. and Cloke, P.J. (1983) Towards a critical appraisal of rural settlement planning in England and Wales, *Sociologia Ruralis*, Vol. 23, 109–129.

Harloe, M. (ed.) (1981) *New Perspectives in Urban Change and Conflict*, Heinemann, London.

Healey, P. (1979) On implementation: some thoughts on the issues raised by planners' current interest in implementation. In Minay, C. (ed.) *Implementation: Views from an Ivory Tower*, Department of Town Planning, Oxford Polytechnic.

Healey, P. (1982) Understanding land use planning. In Healey, P., McDougall, G. and Thomas, M. (eds) *Planning Theory: Prospects for the 1980s*, Pergamon, Oxford.

Hill, M.J. *et al.* (1979) Implementation and the central-local relationship. In Social Science Research Council (1979) *Central–Local Government Relationships*, Report of an SSRC Panel to the Research Initiatives Board, SSRC, London.

Jenkins, W.I. (1978) *Policy Analysis: A Political and Organisational Perspective*, Martin Robertson, Oxford.

Lewis, J. and Flynn, R. (1978) *The Implementation of Urban and Regional Planning Policies*, Final report of a feasibility study for the Department of the Environment.

Lewis, J. and Flynn, R. (1979) The implementation of urban and regional planning policies, *Policy and Politics*, Vol. 7, 123–142.

Minay, C. (1979) Four types of planning implementation. In Minay, C. (ed.) *Implementation: Views from an Ivory Tower*, Department of Town Planning, Oxford Polytechnic.

Newby, H., Bell, C., Rose, D. and Saunders, P. (1978) *Property Paternalism and Power*, Hutchinson, London.

Packman, J. and Wallace, D. (1982) Rural services in Norfolk and Suffolk: the management of change. In Moseley, M.J. (ed.) *Power, Planning and People in Rural East Anglia*, Centre for East Anglian Studies, Norwich.

Poulantzas, N. (1973) The problems of the capitalist state. In Urry, J. and Wakeford, J. (eds) *Power in Britain*, Heinemann, London.

Pressman, J. and Wildavsky, A. (1973) *Implementation*, University of California Press, Berkeley.

Rocke, T. (1985) *Implementation of Rural Housing Policy*. Unpublished Ph.D. Thesis, Department of Geography, SDUC, Lampeter.

Smart, G. and Wright, S. (1983) *Decision Making for Rural Areas*, Bartlett School of Architecture and Planning, University College, London.

Smith, T.B. (1973) The policy implementation process, *Policy Sciences*, Vol. 4, 197–209.

Van Meter, D.S. and Van Horn, C.E. (1975) The policy implementation process: a conceptual framework, *Administration and Society*, Vol. 6, 445–488.

Working Party on Rural Settlement Policies (1979) *A Future for the Village*, HMSO, Bristol.

Wright, S. (1982) Parish to Whitehall: administrative structure and perceptions of community in rural areas, *Gloucestershire Papers in Local and Rural Planning*, No. 16.

SECTION II

CASE STUDIES

INTRODUCTION

The case studies which follow are ordered in terms of the scale of planning for rural areas which is being examined. As a collection they present material which covers a wide spread of the functions performed by planning in rural areas, although particular aspects are particularly suited to investigation at a particular scale.

Mike Tricker and Liz Mills concentrate their analysis of education services in rural planning on national level policies and directives from central government, and analyse the central–local relations involved in the implementation of these directives by local authorities. Similarly, Graham Cox, Philip Lowe and Michael Winter begin by introducing an analysis of the circumstances which spawned the 1981 Wildlife and Countryside Act and then trace the progress of the enactment of this legislation in four regional case study areas. Inevitably in a book of this nature the legislative, regulatory and financial activities of the central government are crucial factors in understanding the implementation of policies at ground level.

A further group of studies is set at the regional level, dealing principally with the activities of particular agencies in managing development. Andrew Blowers illustrates a conceptual analysis of power and consensus with a study of the planning considerations of mineral extraction in Bedfordshire; Allan Patmore provides a case study of national park planning in the North York Moors National Park; and Paul Pettigrew provides an insider's account of industrial development planning in Mid Wales. At this regional level, the relationships between and within agencies are highlighted and the fundamental role of private-sector actors and institutions is examined. In all three cases, however, continuous reference has to be made to the importance of central government as the overriding context for lower-order decision-making.

The work of individuals associated with the school of rural policy implementation research at Lampeter has tended to seek out particular localities in which to uncover the mechanisms and outcomes of policy and action. Such studies may lack the wider applicability of others at the larger scale but they do permit a detailed understanding both of the degree to which central government policies are channelled in a top–down manner into particular communities and of any bottom–up initiatives which might permeate into planning processes. These studies also allow the local distributions of *power* to be accounted for in decision-making. Thus, Philip Bell investigates the planning-related workings of a regional state agency — Southern Water Authority — in the local context of Lewes District in Sussex. Similarly, Gareth Edwards presents a study of national policies for highways and public transport as they are translated through local authority management into a number of different localities in Mid Wales. Even more localized are Tom Rocke's findings on the implementation of housing policy in Wansdyke District in Avon, and Jo Little's examination of how local planning has influenced gentrification in two Wiltshire villages. Once again, however, these local-scale studies inevitably involve consideration of the state and power relations which form the constraining context within which local planning operates.

With this broad spread of both scale and planning function, the conceptual discussions of rural change, planning and the state, and the policy/implementation relations in Chapters 1 and 2, find repeated practical expression in the case study essays. The final essay represents something of a summary by Gerald Smart of decision-making procedures for rural areas. His research constitutes a government-funded review of many of the preceding issues, and provides an essential counterpoint for the drawing together of conceptual and practical issues in the final chapter of the book.

3

EDUCATION SERVICES

Mike Tricker and Liz Mills

POLICY COORDINATION

The retention of services in rural areas has been a major objective for rural planning practice since the 1940s. During the postwar period, in response to a combination of organizational changes and demographic trends, educational provision in rural areas has been progressively withdrawn from the smallest settlements and concentrated in larger centres further up the urban hierarchy. This rationalization raises a series of issues which extend beyond the quality of educational provision in its narrowest sense. It has been widely argued, for example, that the closure of a rural school has a profound effect on community life and on the future size and type of population in the local community. In his classic study of rural depopulation in England and Wales, Saville (1957) observed that

> The centralisation of educational facilities is almost certainly affecting the rural population adversely, for the acquisition of urban values by the children and the loss to each village of the important social figure of the school master or mistress are widely recognised as significant items on the side of the debit balance. (p. 170)

Even the Plowden Report, which arguably accelerated this process of centralization, noted that 'To close a primary school may in fact diminish a village in more senses than one and provide a further reason why young married couples will want to leave it' (Central Advisory Council, 1967).

The presence or absence of a school may also weigh heavily in a local planning authority's assessment of the suitability of a particular settlement for future housing development. At the same time, settlement policies have themselves had an important impact on the demographic characteristics of individual settlements and thus on the demand for educational facilities. In this situation the achievement of close coordination between the policies implemented by local education authorities (LEAs) and those pursued by local planning authorities is clearly crucial.

The rural settlement policies of the 1950s and early 1960s had as their major emphasis the selective expansion of 'key' or 'main' settlements — identified as 'holding points' or 'growth points'. Implicit in policies of this kind was the expectation that the benefits of development would spread outwards from these centres to their rural hinterlands (Cloke, 1979). The close links which might exist between settlement policies and the organization of education services were illustrated as early as 1949 in a plan for the Sudbury district in Suffolk. This proposed the development of a series of village 'clusters', the size of which was determined by the number of children required to feed a one-stream primary school, generally situated in the central village of the group. Here, educational buildings were to be grouped with a health centre and with a community centre performing a wider social function. It was also envisaged that a transport service, using small vehicles, would serve the educational, social, health and other demands of the associated smaller settlements (Jeremiah, 1949).

In preparing the county development plans required by the 1947 Town and Country Planning Act, the school was one of an array of local services used by local planning authorities to rank settlements according to their importance as service centres. In most cases, however, analysis of this type was largely static, being simply an inventory of services existing at the time the plan was prepared, and little account was taken of the likely future of individual schools, let alone the possible impacts of changes in the future pattern of educational facilities on the operation of key settlement policies (Woodruffe, 1976; Mills, 1986). Particularly surprising is the fact that the separate development plans drawn up by LEAs in response to the 1944 Education Act seem to have been prepared without serious reference to the settlement policies which were central to the county development plans. Later guidance issued by the Ministry of Housing and Local Government stressed the need for an overall county policy framework and for a coordinated programme for public investment in villages and elsewhere (Ministry of Housing and Local Government, 1970). Achieving this coordination in practice has, however, proved to be less than straightforward. More seriously, public money has been channelled into marginal rural areas by central government agencies in partnership with local planning authorities in an attempt to stem depopulation and offset imbalances in population structure when, at the same time, support for services such as schools in these areas is being withdrawn (Development Commission, 1984).

Local education authorities have in general been slow to accept the shift towards corporate management within local authorities and this has been recognized as a particular problem in rural areas. In 1982, following representations from the Development Commission and Rural Voice, the Department of Education and Science (DES) asked the Association of County Councils to draw their members' attention to the need to consider educational provision as an integral part of rural settlement planning and to improve consultation procedures to take account of the activities of other agencies in their areas (Development Commission, 1984). There is, however, little indication that this request has had any real impact. To understand why, it is necessary to appreciate both the way in which the education services for rural areas have evolved and the tensions and conflicts which are built into the decision-making processes of LEAs.

CHANGING CENTRAL–LOCAL RELATIONS

The education service in Britain is a national system which is locally administered and as such it has traditionally been viewed as one of the most decentralized models of public service provision (Kogan, 1983). Since 1944, however, views on the rationale for and the means of providing the service have undergone a series of radical changes and, as a result, LEAs have come under increasing pressure to respond to national needs and externally expressed norms. In consequence, efficiency has increasingly displaced philanthropy as the dominant motive in education provision. One result has been a succession of schemes to rationalize and centralize educational provision for rural areas.

THE EMERGENCE OF THE DUAL SYSTEM

The wide geographical distribution of schools within rural areas is attributable to the efforts of voluntary bodies and in particular the churches. Large numbers of village schools were established in the early eighteenth century by the Society for Promoting Christian Knowledge (SPCK). In 1811 this work was taken over by the National Society which aimed to establish a church school in every parish. From 1833 these efforts were aided by the provision of government grants towards construction costs (Bamford, 1973). Ironically, the success of the pioneering work undertaken by these voluntary agencies has left LEAs with a heavy legacy of problems which they are still struggling to solve.

In the mid-nineteenth century opinion began to harden in favour of state supervision of education. The first move to loosen the tie to religious influence came with the 1870 Elementary Education Act which introduced compulsory education for 5–13-year-olds and made religion an adjunct to education rather than an integrating factor (Thomas, 1973). This Act, which empowered the government to provide elementary schools directly, marked the beginning of the dual system — a partnership between church and state. As a result, a new network of *ad hoc* authorities — school boards — concerned solely with education, was set up to organize the building programme and to manage schools in areas where no voluntary provision existed. The Act also introduced the concept of minimum effective standards for school buildings. Initially, this produced a frenzy of rebuilding activity by the Church of England in an effort to combat state intervention. Nevertheless, the period after 1875 saw a major change in the pattern of rural schools — with fewer and fewer church schools and a rapidly growing number provided by school boards (Bamford, 1973).

The 1902 Education Act carried this reorganization one stage further by abolishing school boards and establishing a network of LEAs based on the county councils and county boroughs and financed by local rates. A provision of the Act meant that 'non-provided' schools, which previously had no state assistance, were now eligible for grant aid and, apart from religious education, all their activities became the responsibility of the LEAs. The Act also gave LEAs the power to provide higher (secondary) as well as elementary education. In practice, however, in the period up to 1939, secondary education was developed in towns and cities and lagged behind in rural areas (Bamford, 1973). The problems of providing such facilities for rural areas were seen as partly economic and partly social. The official viewpoint was that children should not be enticed away from the countryside by educational opportunity (Board of Education, 1907).

THE 1944 EDUCATION ACT

The situation was radically changed by the 1944 Education Act, marking the beginning of a vast expansion of the education system. Administratively it was a centralizing Act: it removed much of the power previously given to LEAs and placed the initiative for educational policy firmly in the hands of national government. The most visible sign of this centralization was the creation of a Ministry of Education, under whose direction LEAs were placed.

The Act required LEAs to replace the two-tier system of elementary and higher education by a three-tier system of primary, secondary and further education and gave them the duty '. . . to contribute towards the spiritual, oral, mental and physical development of the community by ensuring that efficient education throughout these stages shall be available to meet the needs of the population of their area' (Ministry of Education, 1944). The legislation also extended the ancillary services (including the supply of school meals, transport and milk) that LEAs were required to provide and gave backing to the Burnham Committee's scheme for standardizing teachers' pay, which had previously been subject to wide regional variations.

Under the terms of the Act church schools could choose either 'aided' or 'controlled' status. Aided schools received grants of 50 per cent (later increased to 75 per cent) towards the cost of essential improvements. Controlled schools, in contrast, became the financial responsibility of the LEA. The original choice between aided and controlled status appears to have been heavily influenced by the 'high' or 'low' nature of the diocese. However, many voluntary-aided schools subsequently opted for controlled status because of the heavy demands of the new building regulations. They were thus caught up in subsequent reorganizations initiated by the LEAs.

Section 2 of the 1944 Act required each LEA to prepare a development plan for converting existing elementary and secondary schools into primary and secondary schools. Inevitably, many 'all-age' village schools, which often had only a few children in the first instance, had their numbers further reduced by the withdrawal of their 11–14 age groups to purpose-built secondary schools in the larger population centres. The major changes proposed on the ground were therefore closures and amalgamations of small schools and their consolidation into larger units serving wider catchment areas. A crucial factor in deciding which schools would close and which ones should be retained was the condition of the buildings. In rural areas the vast majority of buildings dated from the nineteenth century and lacked modern amenities. Whether the building could be extended and remodelled depended on the state of the fabric and on whether the site was large enough to satisfy current building regulations. The ground had been prepared for the development of such 'area' schools more than 10 years earlier in an experimental reorganization scheme implemented in East Suffolk (Board of Education, 1933).

THE PLOWDEN AND GITTINS REPORTS

The Plowden Report (Central Advisory Council, 1967) provided a further impetus to this rationalization process. The report, which was clearly dominated by urban considerations, concluded that the optimum size for a primary school was in the range 280–320 pupils and that:

> Despite the achievements of one and two teacher schools, their difficulties and their cost, particularly in teachers, lead us to recommend that schools with an age range of 5 to 11 should usually have at least three classes, each covering two age groups. (Central Advisory Council, 1967, para. 480)

Against this criterion a school with less than 60 pupils and 3 teachers might not be considered viable. The report did stress, however, that local circumstances would make exceptions inevitable and emphasized that the decision whether or not to close schools must depend on factors such as the siting of villages, whether they were growing or declining and the possible effects of closure on them (ibid., para. 483).

The need to balance these considerations in preparing reorganization proposals was also emphasized in the separate inquiry into primary education in Wales. The report, prepared under the chairmanship of Gittins, concluded that:

> It is preferable to reorganise schools so as to make them as large as possible consistent with the conditions imposed by the geographical area and the natural community from which the school will draw its pupils . . . and the time taken to travel to schools. (Central Advisory Council (Wales), 1967, para. 7.6.1)

The strong link between reorganization proposals and conventional wisdom on rural settlement policies was also emphasized:

> These area schools should be situated in key villages as far as possible on good lines of communication serving an area covered by two to four existing schools. The guiding principles are that the area school should serve an area which covers existing communities and remain a rural school. (ibid., para. 7.6.3)

PLANNING IN A CLIMATE OF UNCERTAINTY

Like most public services, education is responsive to demand, expressed in terms of the number of actual or potential clients, the standards expected of the service and the costs of providing and maintaining the service. The recent history of education within rural areas illustrates the difficulty that LEAs have experienced in anticipating and balancing these often conflicting requirements.

THE POLITICAL DIMENSION

The sharp division of education policy along party political lines has meant that proposals enacted while one government is in power have been withdrawn or repealed by the next. At the same time, individual LEAs have resisted directives issued by the DES. The major example of this is the issue of comprehensive education.

These changes in education policy, coupled with marked changes in the population structure of rural areas, the disappearance of many rural public transport services and the increasing reluctance of teachers to accept posts in more remote rural schools, have caused severe problems for LEAs, particularly for those in relatively remote areas which have experienced selective depopulation. In Northumberland, for example, no less than three development plans were drawn up between 1944 and 1966.

During the 1950s and early 1960s progress in improving buildings to facilitate reorganization was held up by the priority given to secondary school reorganization and the provision of schools to serve new housing estates. In other instances, lack of finance and the revised building regulations issued by the Ministry after the approval of the original development plans helped to make the original proposals unrealistic. These constraints also prevented the building of dual-use facilities which were envisaged for some villages. During the postwar period, proposals to remodel or replace voluntary schools have been further complicated by the need to reach agreement with the dioceses. In many instances this has involved attempts to maintain a 'balance' between voluntary and county schools. This combination of long-term and unreasonably optimistic planning has meant that many schools which were designated for closure have suffered a form of planning 'blight' for more than 30 years (Shropshire County Council, 1978). Others have been lulled into a false sense of security which has been shattered by recent demographic trends.

DEMOGRAPHIC FACTORS

In the past three decades LEAs have been riding a demographic roller-coaster as the child population first soared and then fell. During the 1950s and early 1960s there was a steady increase in the number of children being born and as late as 1963 the Ministry of Education's annual report expressed confidence that '. . . although the birth rate has still not returned to the 1947 peak it has risen in every year since 1955 and is expected to set a new sixty year record in the 1970s'. Instead, live births fell steadily every year from a peak of 876 000 in 1964 to a low of 569 000 in 1977 — a fall of 35 per cent. As a result, the number of pupils in primary schools fell by 30 per cent between 1973 and 1985 (Figure 3.1). A decline of this scale has, naturally enough, posed severe managerial problems for every level of the education system.

The problem is compounded by the fact that planning more than five years ahead clearly involves predicting the number of children likely to be born. The number of births depends on two things: the number of women of child-bearing age, and the number of live births per woman — the fertility rate. Nationally it is known that the number of women of child-bearing age will increase up until the early 1990s when it will start to decline. The fertility rate, however, is far less predictable — being influenced by a range of external factors such as living costs, wage rates, security of employment and so on (Bainbridge, 1980; Rogers, 1985). Expressed as the average completed family size the fertility rate fell from 3.0 in 1964, to 1.7 by 1977 only to rise to 1.9 by 1980. The latest projections are for an average completed family size of 2.1 children by the early 1990s. The uncertainties surrounding this important variable mean that educational planners are having to formulate strategies on projections possessing wide margins of error, as Figure 3.1 shows.

FORECASTING AT THE LOCAL LEVEL

Against this uncertain background LEAs have been requested by the DES 'to make the

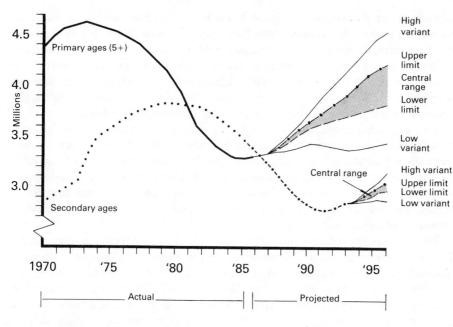

Sources: DES, 1982; DES, 1985

Figure 3.1   Pupils in maintained primary and secondary schools in England (DES, 1982, 1985).

most realistic possible assessments of future school population trends in their own areas with a view to closing under-utilised schools' (Department of Education and Science, 1977, 1981). As a general rule, the uncertainty of such forecasts increases as the size of the area under consideration decreases and the further ahead the period for which projections are being made. Indeed, the practical difficulties of producing longer-term forecasts are so great that many LEAs produce detailed forecasts on a five-year horizon only (Aston University, 1980).

Methods of forecasting in current use range from simple manual techniques employing one or two data sources, to highly sophisticated statistical forecasting models. Virtually all methods, however, rely on the same basic technique of *cohort progression*. This involves projecting forward the numbers within particular age groups while making a variety of adjustments for a range of additional variables such as migration, household formation and the rate of new housebuilding. Clearly, the structure of age groups already in schools can be readily assessed; indeed, LEAs are required to provide the DES with such information as part of the annual 'Form 7' returns. Information on the number of pre-school children already living in an area is usually derived from the health authority's records of births and vaccinations; these provide the basis for projections at the bottom end of the age ranges. Such information generally has a high, but not absolute, degree of accuracy and it has become more difficult to interpret as a result of the recent fall in the take-up of vaccinations.

Information on current and future housing developments and occupancy rates, which may be regarded as of peripheral importance to projections for a whole county, becomes increasingly significant as the size of the area under consideration decreases. At worst, such estimates can amount to little more than informed guesswork, dependent on the accuracy of information regarding the residential development programmes of private developers, the type and price range of units proposed, and the local economic conditions prevailing at the time development is completed.

The increasing importance of producing accurate forecasts provides planning authorities with an opportunity to improve their often tenuous links with their LEAs. In the more sophisticated forecasting systems, such as those developed by Oxfordshire and Berkshire, information on planning permissions and housing completions is integrated through a computer system used by county and district planning departments, and the catchment areas of individual schools are monitored by the LEA through a computerized register.

The problem of predicting individual school rolls has been further compounded by the provisions of the 1980 Education Act, which introduced a greater degree of parental choice. Prior to this it could be expected that children would go to the nearest appropriate school. However, as falling rolls have resulted in spare capacity appearing in many schools, parents have frequently opted to send their children to more distant schools — with the result that catchment areas have increasingly overlapped. For a small village school the transfer of even one family can effect a change of plus or minus 10 per cent in projections.

TRENDS AND EXPECTATIONS

Census data for England and Wales indicate that the number of children aged 5–15 living within rural areas increased by 4.2 per cent between 1971 and 1981 (Table 3.1). This growth was, however, concentrated within settlements with populations of between 2000 and 5000 — which experienced an average increase of 8.3 per cent (Tricker *et al.*, 1986). Those settlements with populations of less than 2000 experienced a far lower increase and in more than one-third of districts there was an overall

Table 3.1   Change in the number of children aged 5–15 years 1971–81 (Tricker *et al.*, 1986).

Region	Percentage change in settlements with a normally resident population of		
	<5000	*2000–5000*	*<2000*
Southeast	+ 1.1	+ 6.4	−2.1
West Midlands	+ 6.0	+ 9.4	+4.7
Northwest	+ 6.1	+11.1	+3.7
Yorkshire and Humberside	+ 8.2	+13.3	+4.0
Northern	− 6.3	− 7.0	−5.8
East Midlands	+ 5.2	+ 8.4	+2.8
Southwest	+ 2.8	+ 8.1	+0.4
East Anglia	+13.2	+22.3	+9.0
Wales	+ 5.8	+ 6.0	+5.7
England and Wales	+ 4.2	+ 8.3	+2.0

decline (Figure 3.2). This pattern reflects, in part, the effectiveness of the 'key' settlement policies in channelling new housing development into the larger settlements. The same policies have certainly helped to reduce the viability of schools within the smaller 'non-key' settlements. This decline has been particularly marked in areas

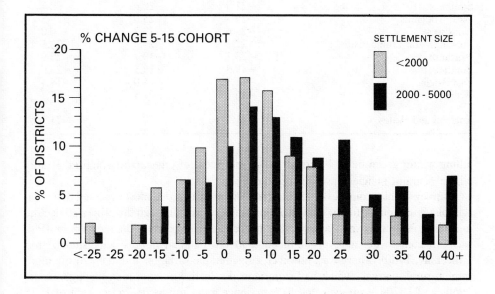

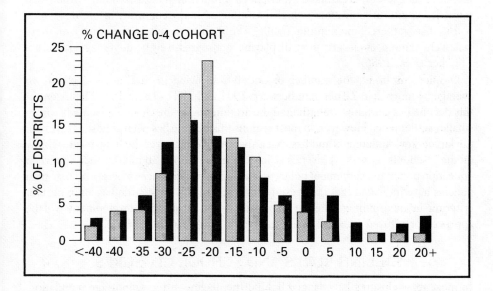

Figure 3.2   Change in school-age groups within rural areas of districts in England and Wales 1971–81.

Table 3.2   Change in the number of children aged less than five years 1971–81 (Tricker *et al.*, 1986)

Region	*Percentage change in settlements with a normally resident population of*		
	<5000	*2000–5000*	*<2000*
Southeast	−21.9	−20.6	−22.7
West Midlands	−28.3	−25.0	−29.5
Northwest	−26.6	−27.7	−26.0
Yorkshire and Humberside	−22.2	−20.6	−23.5
Northern	−23.1	−19.7	−25.9
Southwest	−19.8	−19.5	−20.0
East Anglia	−11.5	− 6.0	−14.4
Wales	−16.5	−21.5	−13.7
England and Wales	−21.1	−20.1	−21.7

falling within green belts, National Parks and Areas of Outstanding Natural Beauty where restraint policies have been pursued.

A survey of shire counties carried out in 1980 indicated that most expected their own school populations to follow the DES's central forecast, although the projected decline in rolls by 1986 was expected to be less marked and the extent of the recovery by 1990 was expected to be more pronounced than the national figures suggested (Aston University, 1980). There was, however, considerable variation and many of the more remote rural districts, which had experienced selective outmigration throughout the 1960s and 1970s, were expected to experience a decline to 70–75 per cent of 1975 levels. In fact several areas have experienced a fundamental turnaround as the trend towards 'counterurbanization', which has affected many countries in the developed world, has gathered momentum (Mills, 1985). The result is that many of these relatively remote areas are now displaying a progressively younger age structure (Tricker *et al.*, 1986).

Despite this trend, the number of under-fives living in rural areas declined on average by more than 21 per cent between 1971 and 1981 (Table 3.2). The extent of this decline has certainly strengthened the arguments for the closure of schools within smaller settlements. However, in most regions this decline has been almost as severe in the larger 'key' settlements and has cast a shadow of doubt over the long-term viability of their schools as well. This raises important questions about the links between education policy and settlement policy — particularly in instances where structure plan policies have indicated that the presence of a school will be regarded as an important criterion in determining whether applications for residential development will be approved or refused (see, for example, Avon County Council, 1981).

FALLING ROLLS AND SCHOOL CLOSURES

In most areas closures have lagged behind the decline in the school-age population. Thus, while the national primary school population declined by 22 per cent between 1978 and 1985, over the same period 1137 primary schools were closed — representing just under 5 per cent of the total. Just under half of these (556) were within rural

Table 3.3 School closures approved by the Department of Education and Science (DES, unpublished statistics)

	1978	1979	1980	1981	1982	1983	1984	1985
Rural areas								
Primary	49	26	43	88	75	127	100	48
Secondary	4	–	2	1	1	4	3	5
Urban areas								
Primary	28	25	40	101	100	98	103	186
Secondary	9	16	25	35	71	66	53	50

areas (Table 3.3). The pressure to close small rural schools has, however, been given fresh impetus by a series of DES circulars and advice notes (Department of Education and Science, 1981, 1985).

The quickening pace of closures has led to increasing concern over possible effects on the children themselves, on parental and community involvement and on the viability of rural communities (Tricker, 1984). Central government guidance to LEAs stresses the need to weigh such potential social consequences against the possible educational and economic costs and benefits (Department of Education and Science, 1977). This implies that a full appraisal of alternative patterns of reorganization should be undertaken before decisions are taken. The techniques for carrying out such comprehensive social impact assessments are well developed and have been available for many years. Many of them involve the use of priority rating techniques, traditionally associated with market research (Carley and Derow, 1983). However, while a few planning authorities have experimented with such techniques as a means of measuring community preferences for alternative structure plan policies (Hedges, 1975), the majority of public agencies have been slow to adopt them, and in practice comprehensive appraisals of the social costs and benefits of alternative patterns of reorganization have very rarely been attempted (Aston University, 1981).

THE CLOSURE EQUATION

The major factors which influence the DES when considering whether to maintain a small school are the educational advantages and disadvantages of alternative arrangements and the financial implications (Table 3.4). The key questions for planners are therefore:
Does reorganization make economic sense?
Will reorganization affect the quality of educational provision?
What will be the impacts of closure on the local community?

Economic factors
The extra expenditure incurred by LEAs as a result of the need to maintain some schools in sparsely populated areas is taken account of through the so-called 'sparsity factor' in calculating the rate support grant. This does not, however, cover all the costs. LEAs have therefore come under increasing pressure to examine the financial

Table 3.4   Factors taken into account by the Department of Education and Science when considering proposals to cease to maintain a school under Section 13 of the Education Act 1944 (DES, 1977)

A.   *Educational factors*
1.   The number of children in each age group and future trends.
2.   The number of teachers, pupils and classes and the possibility of better deployment of the available teaching staff to improve the educational opportunities offered to the pupils.
3.   The size of the catchment area and the travelling distances to the school.
4.   The state of the schools involved (including those which are to receive the remaining pupils) as regards educational standards, suitability, site, proportion of temporary accommodation and structural condition.
5.   Pupil–teacher ratio compared with the overall pupil–teacher ratio in the authority's area.
6.   The ratio of the number on roll to the capacity of the permanent accommodation.

B.   *Economic trends*
1.   Unit teaching costs per child.
2.   Unit non-teaching costs, other than premises, per child (compared with those of other schools within the authority).
3.   Unit premises costs per child (compared with those of other schools within the authority).
4.   The effect on transport costs.
5.   The potential of the premises for educational or other purposes.

---

implications of maintaining small schools and to consider what economies might be achieved by closure and reorganization.

Because of the large 'fixed' element, unit costs increase rapidly when the number of pupils in a school falls below about 50 (Figure 3.3). At the other extreme the variable costs curve tends to flatten out and economies of scale become appreciably less at school sizes of around 150 pupils (Curry and West, 1981). The form of this relationship is determined almost wholly by teachers' salaries which account for around 60–70 per cent of total running costs. Clearly, staff costs are not just a function of staff numbers, but also of salary scales, staffing structure and length of service. This substantially complicates attempts to bring about economies of scale in particular cases. In practice, however, impending retirement or movement to an alternative post on the part of the headteacher is likely to prompt a review of the future of a small school and may act as a trigger to closure procedures.

Estimates produced by various LEAs suggest that where a small school with 25–40 pupils can be closed and the pupils sent to a nearby school where spare capacity exists, virtually the whole cost of the smaller school can be saved (Aston University, 1980). In most cases there will be some additional expenditure on transport, but unless the distances are unusually great these are unlikely to offset the salaries of one or two teachers and the maintenance of a building. Nevertheless, a number of authorities have shown that in some instances any savings from amalgamation would be more than offset by the cost of providing transport. In the case of voluntary schools, reversion clauses will usually mean that the LEA gains no capital receipts from the sale of the buildings. The variations in the financial benefits to be derived from alternative reorganization schemes emphasize that each situation needs to be examined on its merits and all feasible alternatives thoroughly appraised, taking account of possible educational and social factors before deciding on a course of action.

COST PER PUPIL

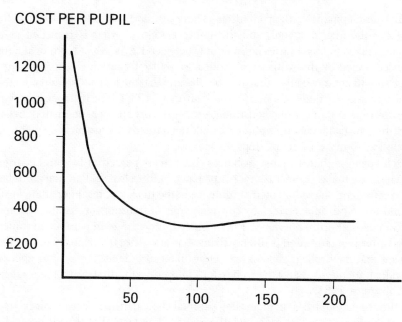

SIZE OF PRIMARY SCHOOL

Source: Association of County Councils, 1979

Figure 3.3   Relationship between unit costs and size of primary schools (Association of County Councils, 1979).

Educational factors

The educational arguments for closing small rural schools are based on the belief that a small school, with few pupils and only one or two teachers, gives too narrow a base for the wider education that follows and also makes too great a demand on the teachers to cope with a wide range of age groups within a single class. Limited evidence exists to suggest that the supposed disadvantages of mixed age groups characteristic of small schools are reflected in the results of standardized tests (Department of Education and Science, 1978). However, the validity of these findings has been seriously questioned and recent studies have provided no convincing evidence to suggest that pupils attending small rural primary schools are educationally or socially disadvantaged (Aston University, 1981; Community Council of Northumberland, 1983; Forsythe *et al.*, 1983).

Parental attitudes towards reorganization proposals typically reveal widespread concern over the possible effects of longer travel time and distances on the social and educational development of their children. There are no fixed rules governing the length of the journey to school, and the interpretation of what is regarded as a reasonable distance to travel varies considerably between LEAs. Most seem to adhere to the advice issued by the Ministry of Education in 1950 that children of primary school age should not travel more than 5 or 6 miles and that the journey should not take longer than 45 minutes door-to-door (Aston University, 1980). The distance criterion is unlikely to represent a serious constraint, except in very sparsely populated areas. However, the time factor can be important if children have to walk to a pick-up point, or if a vehicle has to make frequent stops or detours.

Research suggests that, in most instances, the effects perceived by parents after reorganization are not as serious as those anticipated before closure. Parental attitudes are, to a great extent, shaped by their confidence in the quality of teaching at the local schools and this tends to override any considerations of transport or distance (Community Council of Northumberland, 1983). Indeed, the change in parental attitudes before and after reorganization is often striking. Nevertheless, the majority of parents retain a view that small village schools are better (in terms of their 'family' atmosphere and individual attention) than larger ones for children in the first-school age range (Aston University, 1981).

Given the recent emphasis on increasing parental choice, the perceived 'image' of a school is likely to have a crucial effect on its future roll. This factor has also introduced a new uncertainty into reorganization schemes. In particular, attempts to bolster numbers at a small school by closing one nearby may well fail if parents respond to perceived differences in the quality of education and opt to send their children elsewhere (Aston University, 1981; Brook, 1981).

Impacts on the community

Proposals to close almost any school are likely to be met with strident opposition, particularly from parents. In recent years this opposition, with the assistance of bodies such as the Advisory Centre for Education (ACE) and the National Association for the Support of Small Schools (NASSS), has become increasingly well organized and sophisticated (Rogers, 1979; Avon Community Council, 1985). In addition to challenging the economic and educational arguments already discussed, these pressure groups have stressed a wide range of social consequences which might result from closure and reorganization. As a result, LEAs and the DES have been forced to place these factors on the agenda.

Because of its central place in the popular concept of the rural community — and particularly its role in maintaining continuity and tradition — the school is seen not merely as an educational institution but as an integral part of village life, whose presence touches all parts of the community (Blyth, 1965). Consequently, the closure of village schools is generally believed to have social effects which extend well beyond the lives of pupils, parents and teachers. This historical concept of the school as a natural and necessary ingredient of the village is basic to an understanding of reactions to a closure proposal (Bell, 1982). Potential impacts include a reduction in community participation in school-related activities, a reduction in the amount of social interaction within the community, and consequent adverse effects on the viability of settlements (Garvey, 1976; Jones, 1980).

Research indicates that formal community involvement with schools is mainly confined to parents. Nevertheless, a marked reduction in community participation in school-related activities is likely to occur after closure and reorganization. Whereas a gradual process of adjustment may occur as parents are drawn into the 'community of interest' focusing on their children's new school, involvement by non-parents is likely to remain well below that of similar groups living closer to schools (Aston University, 1981). The pattern of free transport provision may also constrain the choice of schools for those families without day-time access to private transport and may expose income and class divisions which remain latent while the majority of children attend the same school. The opportunity for informal social contact with their children's school is also likely to be substantially diminished for such parents. Clearly, therefore, unless special efforts are made, the integrative function of school-related activities is not likely to be as effective over the catchment of a new 'area' school (Hereford & Worcester County Council, 1980).

Arguments advanced in favour of retention also reflect widespread concern that closure of the local school will make a village less attractive for households which have, or intend to have, young children. Furthermore, there is a strong belief that taking young people out of their home environment at the age of five (or even earlier) will prevent them from developing strong ties with their home community and learning its values. Closure, therefore, is felt to decrease the chances of young people born locally wanting to stay. Research indicates that parishes which have lost schools have generally experienced a decrease in population, while those which have retained schools have experienced an increase. However, there is very little evidence that school closures have triggered extensive movements of existing households, and in many instances this differential growth may be attributed to a general trend towards smaller household sizes coupled with restraints on the building of new houses in the smaller 'non-key' settlements (Aston University, 1981). This tends to support the argument that school closures are a response to, rather than a prime cause of, population changes in rural areas. In several instances the number of children of primary school age in settlements which have lost their schools now exceeds the number present at the time of closure. It is therefore difficult to detect any clear link between school closure and subsequent changes in age structure. There is, however, some indication that changes are occurring in the population structure of settlements which have lost facilities like schools and that, as a result, their residents are increasingly those who have a relatively high degree of mobility and are therefore less sensitive to the availability of local services (Aston University, 1981).

The social effects of closure must, therefore, be seen in the wider context of social and economic changes which are taking place in the rural areas, within which the reorganization and rationalization of educational facilities are merely elements. Change in any of these elements is, however, likely to alter the structure of social interactions which contribute to a sense of identity or 'community'. Moreover, a major impact of school closure may be a greatly increased sense of powerlessness and alienation from decision-makers which creates generalized dissatisfaction and doubts about the future viability of the community as a whole (Forsythe et al., 1983). These are likely to be greatest where a strong local protest preceded closure. The way in which the closure process is managed is therefore an important factor in achieving acceptance of a new pattern of educational provision. In particular, it is important that consultation procedures should be seen as genuine rather than a mere formality, and that the LEA acknowledges that the 'client' group extends beyond current parents and their children. Those groups which stand to lose most directly from school closure — the less affluent and the less mobile — are also likely to experience varying degrees of deprivation as a result of the progressive withdrawal of other services and facilities. It is important, therefore, that local authorities should consider educational provision as an integral part of rural settlement planning and that reorganization takes account of wider community development issues, in which the schools themselves have a role to play. Seen in this wider perspective, an appropriate reorganization scheme for a rural area is one which creates effective and efficient teaching groups while retaining, as far as possible, a local educational presence; minimizing the burden of travel for young children; and maximizing the possibilities of parental involvement.

ALTERNATIVE PATTERNS OF REORGANIZATION

The DES has recently suggested that in order to provide a full range of educational experiences a first school should ideally have at least 4 teachers and 120 pupils (Department of Education and Science, 1980). Alternative ways of reorganizing provision to achieve this in a rural context include the creation of 'area' schools, where one school serves an area containing several villages; 'nuclear' schools, where two or more existing schools are combined with one as a centre or nucleus and others as satellites; and variations on the 'nuclear' solution such as 'clustering' or 'federation' schemes. The appraisal of alternative schemes against these criteria requires application of a wide-ranging form of cost-benefit analysis in order to assess their value for money rather than the narrower, cost-effectiveness analysis traditionally used by LEAs.

THE 'NUCLEAR' OPTION

In the past most LEAs have decided that the educational advantages of having larger peer groups and a wider range of teaching skills within one building outweigh the disadvantages of the greater burden of travel for young children and the possible inhibition of parental involvement arising from a larger catchment area. The traditional approach has therefore been to plan for the replacement of small rural schools by a network of area schools. However, a small number of authorities, including Norfolk, Cambridgeshire and Oxfordshire, have experimented with 'clustering' or 'federation' schemes. These attempt to satisfy the criteria of educational effectiveness while avoiding the less acceptable consequences of a straightforward area school solution. Legally and administratively the 'cluster' becomes one school under the direction of a single headteacher. As originally envisaged, the main communal facilities of the school, such as the hall and playing field, would generally be at the central school while the 'satellites' would provide teaching accommodation for the children in whose villages they were situated. Each nuclear school would have its own minibus which would bring pupils from home to school, ferry teachers and pupils between satellites and the nucleus and also transport school meals (Department of Education and Science, 1980). A satellite might be smaller than a self-standing school because it shares resources with the centre, but it should still be large enough to support teaching groups of an economic size and a manageable age span — ideally not less than 30–35 pupils — and 2 teachers. It might still be necessary, therefore, to close some of the smaller schools within a cluster.

The capital costs of establishing such a grouping in practice are likely to be considerably less than the area school option, in the short term at least, and implementation can obviously be spread over a number of years. The revenue costs, and in particular the teaching costs, are, however, likely to be appreciably greater. Nevertheless, the opportunity for staff to work together as a team offers significant benefits and thus will almost certainly represent better value for money than a system of separate small schools. The future transport costs of operating either option are a significant unknown factor.

This highly flexible pattern of organization is also in tune with the increasing emphasis that planning authorities are placing on 'clustering' approaches as alternatives to key settlement policies. The successful implementation of such policies, however, requires particularly detailed knowledge of rural communities and their interactions (Mills, 1986). Where the schools in question are a mixture of voluntary and county schools, achieving such a merger can present considerable technical difficulties. Moreover, the fact that the satellites can be closed without reinvoking formal closure procedures is likely to be met with some suspicion on the part of the communities in question.

THE DEVELOPMENT OF COMMUNITY SCHOOLS

The process of 'consolidation' and reorganization can also provide opportunities to develop new social focuses. There are now several examples of reorganization and remodelling of school buildings which have provided opportunities to incorporate dual-use facilities — used mainly for school purposes during the day-time and for community activities in the evenings and at weekends. These efforts have in some instances been aided by the Sports Council and rural development agencies (Sports Council, 1979). Where such 'community schools' have been created there is evidence that they may emerge as significant focuses for the newly enlarged catchment areas, particularly those with relatively dispersed settlement patterns (Aston University, 1981).

INTEGRATED RURAL DEVELOPMENT

This wider view of the role of education services and the use of educational facilities and the exploration of alternatives to traditional patterns of reorganization is consistent with the concepts of 'integrated rural development' which are currently being promoted by rural development agencies and the European Community (McNab, 1983; Development Commission, 1984). However, the implementation of such projects depends on political will, since they may imply the diversion of resources from other areas of education to the needs of rural schools, which are generally catering for smaller numbers of children. Rational analysis can help in identifying the wider benefits of such options and their relative costs, but when it comes to making decisions the most important consideration is mobilizing political support or finding a course of action which carries enough support to be feasible.

REFERENCES

Association of County Councils (1979) *Rural Deprivation*, ACC, London.

Aston University (1980) *The Social Effects of Rural Primary School Reorganisation.* A study on behalf of the Department of Environment and Department of Education and Science, Second Interim Report, Aston University, Birmingham.

Aston University (1981) *The Social Effects of Rural Primary School Reorganisation.* A study on behalf of the Department of Environment and Department of Education and Science, Final Report, Aston University, Birmingham.

Avon Community Council (1985) *Small Schools Information Pack*, Avon Community Council, Bristol.

Avon County Council (1981) *Avon County Structure Plan Written Statement*, Avon County Council, Bristol.

Bainbridge, W. (1980) Falling rolls: predictions and prospects, *Durham and Newcastle Research Review*, Vol. 9, 17–36.

Bamford, M. (1973) Trends in village life and education since 1850. In Warner, P.W. (ed.) *Rural Education*, University of Hull.

Bell, D.M. (1982) *The Social Effects of the Closure of Village Schools in Northumberland*, Community Council of Northumberland, Morpeth.

Blyth, W.A.L. (1965) *English Primary Education: A Sociological Description*, Routledge & Kegan Paul, London.

Board of Education (1907) *Supplementary Regulations for Secondary Schools in England*, Board of Education, London.

Board of Education(1933) An experiment in rural reorganisation, *Educational Pamphlets*, No. 93, HMSO, London.

Brook, J.S. (1981) Village school closures: rural planning and primary education in Gloucestershire, Unpublished dissertation, Oxford Polytechnic Department of Town Planning.

Carley, M.J. and Derow, E.O. (1983) *Social Impact Assessment: A Cross-Disciplinary Guide to the Literature*, Policy Studies Institute, London.

Central Advisory Council (1967) *Children and Their Primary Schools* (The Plowden Report), HMSO, London.

Central Advisory Council (Wales) (1967) *Primary Education in Wales* (The Gittins Report), HMSO, London.

Cloke, P.J. (1979) *Key Settlements in Rural Areas*, Methuen, London.

Community Council of Northumberland (1983) *The Social Effects of the Closure of Village Schools in Northumberland*, Community Council of Northumberland, Morpeth.

Curry, N. and West, C. (1981) Internal economies of scale in rural primary education, *Gloucestershire Papers in Local and Rural Planning*, No. 12, pp. 18–33.

Department of Education and Science (1965) Circular 10/65, DES, London.

Department of Education and Science (1977) *Falling Rolls and School Closures*, Circular 5/77, DES, London.

Department of Education and Science (1978) *Primary Education in England: A Survey by Her Majesty's Inspectors of Schools*, HMSO, London.

Department of Education and Science (1980) The renewal of primary schools: planning for the Eighties, *Building Bulletin*, No. 57.

Department of Education and Science (1981) *Falling Rolls and Surplus Places*, Circular 2/81, DES, London.

Department of Education and Science (1982) Pupils and school leavers: future numbers, *DES Report on Education*, No. 97.

Department of Education and Science (1985) Statistics of schools in England, *DES Statistical Bulletin*, 4/85.

Development Commission (1984) *Forty-first Report on the Work of the Development Commission*, HMSO, London.

Forsythe, D. *et al.* (1983) *The Rural Community and the Small School*, Aberdeen University Press.

Garvey, R. (1976) Closing down the village schools, *Where?*, 119.

Hedges, B.M. (1975) *Community Preferences in Structure Planning*, SCPR, London.

Hereford & Worcester County Council (1980) *Rural Community Development Project: Schools Study*, Hereford & Worcester County Council, Worcester.

Horsnell, M. (1978) How the village rot can start, *The Times*, 7 November 1978.

Jeremiah, K. (1949) *A Full Life in the Country*, Batsford, London.

Jones, P. (1980) Primary school provision in rural areas, *The Planner*, Vol. 66, 4–6.

Kogan, M. (1983) The case of education. In Young, K. (ed.) *National Interests and Local Government*, Heinemann, London.

McNab, A. (1983) Integrated rural development in Britain: concepts and practice, *Gloucestershire Papers in Local and Rural Planning*, No. 22.

Mills, L. (1985) Recent changes in the urban systems of advanced industrial nations: trends, causes and problems. Paper prepared for World Resources '86 (International Institute for Environment and Development/World Resources Institute), Washington.

Mills, L. (1986) Changes in the rural spatial economy of an English county (Somerset 1947–1980). Unpublished Ph.D. Thesis, University of Bristol, Department of Geography.

Ministry of Education (1944) *Education Act 1944*, HMSO, London.

Ministry of Education (1963) *Annual Report*, HMSO, London.

Ministry of Housing and Local Government (1970) *Development Plans: A Manual of Form and Content*, HMSO, London.

Rogers, A. (1985) *Regional Population Projection Models*, Sage, London.

Rogers, R. (1979) *Schools Under Threat: A Handbook on Closures*, Advisory Centre for Education, London.

Saville, J. (1957) *Rural Depopulation in England and Wales*, Routledge & Kegan Paul, London.

Shropshire County Council (1978) Primary education: implications of declining numbers, *Report to Education Committee*, October 1978.

Sports Council (1979) Opportunities and constraints in community use of education facilities, *Research Working Papers*, No. 15, Sports Council, London.

Thomas, C.J.A. (1973) Planning and the rationalisation of primary school provision in rural areas. Unpublished dissertation, Oxford Polytechnic, Department of Town Planning.

Tricker, M.J. (1984) Rural education services: the social effects of reorganisation. In Clark, G., Groenedijk, J. and Thissen, F. (eds), *The Changing Countryside*, Geo Books, Norwich.

Tricker, M.J., Hems, L.C. and Martin, S.J. (1986) A rural analysis of the 1971 and 1981 censuses: population change, *PSMRU Working Paper*, No. 12, Aston University, Birmingham.

Woodruffe, B.J. (1976) *Rural Settlement Policies and Plans*, Oxford University Press, Oxford.

4

LANDSCAPE PROTECTION AND NATURE CONSERVATION

Graham Cox, Philip Lowe and Michael Winter

Doubtless there will be further evolution of policy in the future. That this should be so does not invalidate the Act; rather on the contrary, it is the basic foundation for the future. (Government reply to the First Report from the Environment Committee on the Operation and Effectiveness of the Wildlife and Countryside Act 1981, para. 1.5, 1985)

INTRODUCTION

A shrewd observer wishing to characterize the legislation to protect landscape and conserve nature in Britain might be tempted by a Great War analogy. The heavier kinds of artillery in that conflict had serious disadvantages. By the time something like Big Bertha had been trundled into position, aimed, primed and fired, the enemy was quite likely to have gone away. Even if the enemy was still there the accuracy of such guns was as disappointing as their range was huge. In many respects the National Parks and Access to the Countryside Act 1949, the Countryside Act 1968 and the Wildlife and Countryside Act 1981 have been the Big Berthas of rural conservation planning. Grandiose aims have often been accompanied by a long period of cumbersome limbering-up and the preparation of elaborate machinery only to be followed by a spectacular anticlimax — an explosion way off target or a dud shell.

But if such pieces of legislation have dominated the scene and provided the context within which policy has been elaborated, it is at least as obvious that the character of that policy has been forged by a parallel series of essentially pragmatic responses to problems which have been forced into prominence. To understand why this should be so involves seeing the policy process as a continuous one anchored in the social construction of power. From this perspective, the moments in the policy formation–policy implementation dialectic are separable only with considerable conceptual ingenuity. Any piece of legislation will have, embedded within it, sets of more or less developed potentialities, and implementation analysis must concern itself with the political processes through which such potentialities are realized and thwarted — or, in terms of our opening metaphor, with that never-ending attrition of trench warfare. The alignments of interest and deployment of resources which prompt compromise in policy-making continue to shape and influence implementation and with most legislation the period after the Parliamentary phase, like that before, is more important in determining the extent and nature of what is reformed. This is partly because much legislation is enabling and allows considerable discretion to Ministers, civil servants and statutory bodies, but also because its implementation requires new administrative procedures to be worked out and, in the process, those closely involved may seek to enlarge or diminish the spirit of the legislation. Implementation, in short, is the continuation of politics by other means (Majone and Wildavsky, 1978).

In this chapter we consider the recent history of rural conservation, which has been dominated by preparations for and struggles over the passage and implementation of the Wildlife and Countryside Act 1981. The episode illustrates many of the general points painstakingly generated by policy analysts (Barrett and Hill, 1984) and we suggest that their importance is made self-evident by any approach which appropriately emphasizes power relations within policy-making. Like its postwar predecessors the 1981 Act is an ambitious and complex piece of legislation with diverse aims whose effectiveness has been substantially undermined by the chronic underfunding and understaffing of those agencies most concerned with its implementation. Moreover, like the 1949 Act, it has already done much to focus and complicate conflict in the countryside.

THE 1981 ACT

The Wildlife and Countryside Act 1981 received the Royal Assent on 30 October 1981, after several hundred hours of Parliamentary debate stretching over 11 months, having attracted a greater number of amendments than any previous piece of legislation in Parliamentary history. Conservationists had pressed for general powers to regulate the environmental impact of agricultural development but the Act represented a success for the astute and carefully sustained lobbying of farming and landowning interests which resisted such suggestions (Cox and Lowe, 1983a). Working to bolster the government's commitment to an essentially voluntary philosophy, the National Farmers' Union (NFU) and the Country Landowners' Association (CLA) stressed the need to retain the goodwill and cooperation of the farming community. They would not countenance any significant erosion of the peculiarly privileged freedom from controls which had characterized the agricultural industry since the 1947 Town and Country Planning Act effectively excluded agricultural and forestry operations from its definition of 'development' (Cox and Lowe, 1983b).

Although Parts I and III of the Act are concerned with species protection and questions of access, it has been Part II, dealing with nature conservation, the countryside and National Parks, whose passage and implementation have been steeped in controversy: indeed when the House of Commons Environment Committee was prompted to review the operation and effectiveness of the Act it specifically restricted its inquiry to that part (HMSO, 1985a). The policies in it are environmental rather than agricultural and their thrust is directed principally towards environmentally designated areas. The principal form of protection both for Sites of Special Scientific Interest

(SSSI) and the countryside in National Parks is the management agreement whereby an owner or occupier is offered a contract by the appropriate conservation authority (the Nature Conservancy Council (NCC) in SSSIs and county planning authorities in National Parks), perhaps in return for monetary compensation, to manage the land so as to retain its conservation interest. Where conflict arises between farming and conservation objectives, Part II of the 1981 Act requies farmers to give three months' notice to the NCC of their intention to carry out potentially damaging operations (PDO) in SSSIs. It also exhorts the Minister of Agriculture, when considering grant applications from farmers in environmentally designated areas, to further the aims of conservation, but only so far as these may be consistent with the agricultural purposes of a scheme. In cases where the Minister upholds the objection of a conservation authority to the award of an agricultural grant, the authority is required to compensate the farmer. Conservationists were alarmed that this seemed to give farmers a legal right to agricultural grant aid since if aid is denied on conservation grounds they must be compensated for the resulting hypothetical 'losses' from the meagre budgets of the conservation agencies.

The passing of the Act, by raising expectations and heightening awareness of the issues, shifted the terms and context of debate. The 'countryside' is now a thoroughly politicized issue (Cox and Lowe, 1983b) and chastened by its experiences during 1981 the conservation lobby has come of age politically. Whereas previously the onus was on conservationists to demonstrate the damaging effects of changing farming and forestry practices, the agricultural community and the government are now obliged to show that the Act is being effective in halting the destruction of wildlife habitats and landscapes. The politics of landscape protection and nature conservation are thus currently dominated by the careful monitoring, consensus building (Cox *et al.*, 1985c) and precedent setting associated with a piece of legislation which, for many conservation activists, was a profound disappointment.

The requirements for owners of SSSIs to give notice of potentially damaging operations and for National Park authorities to monitor the loss of open moorland ensure continued prominence for disputes between agriculture and conservation. The provision for consultation before new SSSI designations has also meant more publicity for the process of designation itself. Accordingly the focus of attention shifted during 1982 and beyond to a series of 'local' issues which involved the new machinery of the Act. The most prominent of these issues — Exmoor, the Berwyns, West Sedgemoor and Halvergate Marshes — are reviewed below. They were controversial before the advent of the Act but, as they unfolded, they assumed a perversely symbiotic relationship with it. Indeed, they successively presented bigger challenges to the Act's procedures for rural conservation, and moves towards their resolution both bypassed and extended its provisions (Lowe *et al.*, 1986).

To understand the significance of these issues demands an appreciation of the ways in which much of the Act's implementation threatened to confirm the worst fears of its critics. Since its main mechanism was a market one, apprehension centred on the amount of money needed or available for its implementation and the related concern about the way in which the conservation agencies would discharge their new powers and duties, given that financial pressure might deter them from objecting to schemes of agricultural intensification supported by the Ministry of Agriculture, Fisheries and

Food (MAFF). For although the concept of the management agreement had its origins and initial success in the struggle to preserve moorland, in Exmoor certain features of that instance of conflict made it a misleading examplar.

EXMOOR

Controversy over the reclamation of moorland in Exmoor has raged with varying degrees of intensity for more than 20 years (Lowe *et al.*, 1986). Although conditions for reclamation were relatively favourable technological developments in the 1960s gave it a new impetus. The Ministry of Agriculture, Fisheries and Food, for its part, encouraged change and offered capital grants of 50 per cent or more for improvements and headage payments on the additional stock that could be carried. Studies documenting substantial loss of moorland to agriculture were questioned by the NFU and CLA who were successful in encouraging the government to ignore requests that powers and resources to regulate moorland loss be made available under the 1968 Countryside Act. Instead the NFU and CLA proposed a 'gentleman's agreement' under which they would advise their members to notify the park committees of their intention to reclaim moorland within a critical amenity area which was to be revised. This voluntary notification system, however, failed to slow the pace of reclamation, and MAFF gave little form or substance here or elsewhere to its obligation under the 1968 Act to 'have regard to the desirability of conserving the natural beauty and amenity of the countryside'. After some widely publicized controversies in the 1970s, in 1977 Lord Porchester was appointed, jointly by the Secretary of State for the Environment and the Minister of Agriculture, to study 'land use in Exmoor'.

Porchester's findings confirmed that one-fifth of the open land in Exmoor had been enclosed and improved since it was designated a National Park in 1954. He therefore recommended giving statutory force to the notification system and enabling the National Park Committee to make moorland conservation orders binding in perpetuity. In addition he proposed that farmers should receive once and for all compensation for the permanent loss of their rights to reclaim, equal to the loss in land value.

These recommendations were broadly accepted by the then Labour government but, following the election of a Conservative government in May 1979, requests from a number of quarters for the power to make moorland conservation orders were thwarted. The NFU and CLA sought to demonstrate that Lord Porchester had been premature in his judgement that a voluntary approach had failed and pointed instead to Exmoor as the place where, more recently and with their encouragement, the principles and practice of a voluntary agreement between an owner and responsible bodies had been pioneered. Mr Ben Halliday's agreement with the Exmoor National Park Authority to achieve optimum uses of the land for public recreation, conservation and amenity consistent with good husbandry and efficient farming on his Glenthorne estate by means of a management plan presaged, for them, the elements of an effective yet voluntary approach to conservation.

The negotiations which began in November 1979 between the NFU, the CLA and the Park Authority to determine the financial guidelines for such agreements understandably attracted the close attention of MAFF, the Department of the Environment (DoE) and the Countryside Commission. Against Porchester's recommendation, the

NFU and CLA insisted that those who voluntarily set aside the option to reclaim should have the right to choose to be compensated by annual payments related to loss of profit including potential grant aid. The guidelines which were finally signed on 7 April 1981 (at the time of the Wildlife and Countryside Bill's second reading in the House of Commons) treated the two schemes as alternatives and allowed farmers to choose between them.

When the government's determination to reject any form of compulsion came under severe pressure during the passage of the Bill, it had to devise some national machinery for making its 'voluntary approach' feasible so it turned to the Exmoor voluntary system and transformed it into a statutory system. As a guide to future policy, however, the Exmoor system was in many ways a misleading and extravagant template. First, the previous government had accorded Exmoor a special status by introducing in 1978–79 the principle of 90 per cent grants, and the Conservative government confirmed this decision to underwrite a special Exmoor moorland conservation fund. This compares with 75 per cent grants in other National Parks and with 50 per cent grants for local authorities entering into management agreements. The relatively uniform conditions on Exmoor made possible the calculation of an annually fluctuating 'standard sum' (reflecting the difference in profitability between intensive and extensive livestock activities) as the basis for compensation in potentially all cases. This avoided the costly farm-by-farm negotiations which are necessary where a wider range of options is open to farmers.

A further factor making Exmoor atypical was a recognition, borne of 20 years' sustained controversy, that management agreements represented the last chance to avert some form of compulsion. In the North York Moors National Park for instance, where there have been no comparable pressures (although the scale of the problem is the same), five of the first seven farmers who were offered management agreements after the passage of the Act, rejected them and went ahead with reclamation without grant. Finally, so far as the prospective cost of such agreements generally is concerned, the Exmoor situation was deceptive in that the difference between the restricted and unrestricted values of affected land in Exmoor is small compared to other areas where drainage and other operations can yield substantial financial gains to farmers. Despite these differences the compensation terms negotiated by the NFU and CLA with the Exmoor National Park Committee in 1981 proved to be the blueprint for the national guidelines on management agreements issued by the DoE two years later. Exmoor, the place where previous countryside policies had come to grief, had effectively furnished the context for forging new principles and procedures and, by extending them to the national scene, the government contrived — however unwittingly — dramatically to raise the cost of conservation.

Understandably, despite Ministerial assurances that adequate funds would be made available, there was considerable caution on the part of the conservation agencies, the NFU and the CLA regarding the financing of management agreements. As the NCC commented in its annual report after the passage of the Act, 'in future the cost of nature conservation will be more closely related to normal market prices determined by current agricultural grants and price support systems . . . we can no longer rely on securing land for conservation at minimal cost to the exchequer, (Nature Conservancy Council, 1981).

Fears that the costs of management agreements would rapidly render the Act unworkable have so far proved premature, however. To date all agreements have been within budget and that budget has been increasing. The money spent on site acquisition and safeguard by the NCC rose from £756 000 in 1980–81 to £1.2 million in 1982–83. For 1984–85, £1.9 million was budgeted, but in July 1984 the government announced that it was providing an additional £2.5 million making a total of £4.4 million for the year. It is always open for the NCC, if an important site cannot be safeguarded within its prevailing budget, to ask the government for additional money and since 1977 no such request has been refused. This may be more an indication of the NCC's care in selecting cases than confirmation of government generosity in this area of expenditure.

Although the NFU declared in June 1984 that the cost of agreements was modest, representing good value for the nation, figures for existing agreements give a misleading impression of the eventual recurrent costs of implementing the Act's compensation requirements. This is partly because the 'going rate' for management agreements rose rapidly in this period, but more importantly because there are many more agreements in the pipeline than have been finalized. In a detailed study for the British Association of Nature Conservationists and the World Wildlife Fund, Adams (1984) estimated that the full potential cost of management agreements for the SSSI system alone could be up to £40 million a year — more than two and a half times the NCC's total grant in aid for 1984–85. Even if such a calculation is considered unduly alarmist, the NCC itself now expects that eventually one-third of SSSIs will need management agreements and that compensation will be running at £15 million a year (*The Times*, 13 November 1984). Its estimates have previously proved to be very conservative. Such figures contrast with the £600 000 envisaged by the government in 1981 as the annual cost of the Bill's habitat protection measures. The NCC, though, has expressed qualified optimism: 'since the new Act our impression is that damage to SSSIs has diminished' (Press Release, 2 February 1984).

If the overall picture in relation to SSSIs remains hazy, that in relation to National Park landscapes is positively opaque, though a study by Ian Brotherton (1984) for the Countryside Commission gives some indication of the developing situation. He examined proposals for grant-aided agricultural operations notified to National Park authorities in accordance with grant regulations which came into force in October 1980. These notifications can trigger the provision of Section 41 of the Act, which requires the Park authority to offer a compensatory management agreement if the Minister of Agriculture upholds its objection to the operation. Of 2757 notifications processed between April and September 1983 Park authorities sought modifications in 151 cases but there were only 6 cases over which agreement could not be reached. This may seem reassuring but there are no grounds for complacency. In 20 per cent of the cases work had started or even been completed before notification and since MAFF did not regard failure to notify as grounds for refusing a grant, farmers were effectively encouraged to embark on new operations and notify afterwards.

There are several reasons why Park authorities may be taking a lenient line. Many of their members have a background in farming or forestry and are likely to be favourably disposed to agricultural developments, and with each National Park having to handle on average 500 notifications a year, time and staff constraints must mean that many are passed on the nod. Most Park authorities have difficulty in finding time for appropriately trained and competent personnel to implement the scheme. Limited funding also creates extreme reluctance to finance compensatory payments. Indeed, by September 1984 not a single management agreement had been negotiated by a National Park authority under Section 41 of the Act. Those authorities willing to enter into management agreements have used the Section 39 provisions for voluntary agreements which are not formally tied to the complex financial guidelines governing Section 41 agreements. But many Park authorities are reluctant to enter into any agreement with a sizeable or long-term financial commitment. By September 1984, only 13 management agreements involving financial consideration had been entered into by National Park authorities; 7 of these were for Exmoor, and only two other National Parks were represented — Dartmoor and the Lake District. The Park authorities, unlike the NCC, have no powers to stop or delay proposed developments so farmers may choose to refuse the offer of compensation under a management agreement. Finally, since the Park authorities merely act as advisers to MAFF or the Welsh Office Agriculture Department (WOAD), they invariably temper their objections and limit them to cases which they guess the departments will concede. Where compromise ultimately proves impossible a Park authority may formally object to the Minister of Agriculture. But in four of the eight cases that went to Ministers in 1982 and 1983 the strong objections of National Park authorities or the NCC were overruled, and in the fifth the Minister granted part payment. A record showing that objections were upheld in only three cases does not inspire confidence in the resolve with which Ministers of Agriculture are discharging their statutory duty under Sections 32 and 41 to promote conservation by awarding grants in designated areas.

THE BERWYN MOUNTAINS

Because the financial implications of the Act seem so disturbing increased attention has been focused on the process of SSSI designation lest the NCC, in attempting to husband its limited resources, wavers in its statutory obligation to designate when appropriate scientific criteria are met. Conservationists also became concerned that the NCC's wariness of antagonizing local farmers was leading to considerable delay and reluctance in the designation of new SSSIs, particularly where forestry or agricultural development was in prospect. Certainly the process of designation has often been the occasion for acrimonious wrangling with farmers and forestry groups fiercely resisting the moderate constraints on their autonomy which designation might entail.

But the imminence of the 1981 Act gave the particular case of the Berwyn Mountains a wider relevance that it might not otherwise have had, as farming organizations effectively used it to challenge the NCC's independence in designating SSSIs (Lowe *et al.*, 1986). Most of the land is above 1475 ft, rising to over 2625 ft and its wildlife importance has long been recognized. Moel Sych, an SSSI of 9637 acres, was designated for its botanical interest as long ago as 1957 but it was not until the 1970s that moves were made to extend the SSSI to include the area's ornithological interest as well. Following a large-scale survey of bird populations throughout upland Wales, the Royal Society for the Protection of Birds (RSPB) in September 1977 presented details of nine upland sites — three of them in the Berwyns — and the NCC agreed that, on the evidence presented, they appeared to be of sufficient importance for scheduling.

Although there is no requirement for the NCC to enter into consultations, discussions were started with the Forestry Commission, WOAD and the Agricultural Development and Advisory Service (ADAS), which soon revealed radically different assessments of the area's potential. An appraisal was subsequently sought from an independent consultant, Reginald Lofthouse. His conciliatory report of November 1979 presented a broad zoning of the area indicating where particular uses should be given priority and suggesting guidelines for harmonizing the concerns of the interested bodies.

As the Lofthouse Report was being prepared proposals by the Economic Forestry Group (EFG) for a major afforestation scheme in the Llanbrynmair Moors catapulted the case to political prominence in the run-up to the Wildlife and Countryside Bill. The public release in September 1980 of the Lofthouse Report simply fuelled the controversy. The farming unions and the Timber Growers' Organization complained, without justification, about being excluded from the study and their protestations highlighted the dilemmas associated with the attempt to safeguard extensive areas. SSSI designation, under the 1949 Act and even under the 1981 Act, is only contestable on the basis of contrary scientific evidence and before 1981 there was no requirement for the NCC to consult on the matter. Yet implicit in the Lofthouse Report was the question of whether SSSI designation is negotiable.

The NCC had objected to the EFG scheme in August 1979 only to withdraw three months later, unable to contemplate purchasing or even renting the area and effectively committed itself to the Lofthouse Report, which had zoned a large area elsewhere for nature conservation. To the considerable dismay of the RSPB the NCC decided to cut its losses in relation to Llanbrynmair Moors. With their fate decided, attention turned to the NCC's intentions regarding a new Berwyn SSSI to be created by expanding the Moel Sych site. The Llanbrynmair concession did nothing to forestall further impassioned objections, however, and in June 1980 the NCC agreed to a further three-month postponement of designation. Another six-month deferment was announced in September so that further talks could be held with farmers, and following a thaw in attitudes the NFU, FUW (Farmers' Union of Wales) and CLA organized a meeting in Bala which proposed a deal whereby the farmers would promise good conservation practices in return for the NCC not designating such a large area. A Berwyn Society was formed and after many meetings with officers of the NCC, designation was again postponed. This left the NCC in the impossible position of having to either jeopardize the goodwill of local farmers or compromise its legal duty by accepting the Berwyn Society's offer of active cooperation, which was conditional on designation being dropped or greatly diminished.

In February 1982 a unique compromise was announced whereby the designation of a smaller SSSI was to be accompanied by the establishment, around the edge of the 37 805-acre site, of a further 12 010 acres which came to be known as a 'consultation zone' (a shadowy concept of indeterminate status) and which occupies the lower, potentially improvable land. Farmers have undertaken to approach the NCC if contemplating any changes and to seek management agreements in much the same way as within an SSSI. The government, for its part, has given assurance that money for such agreements will be made available. However effective it may prove to be, the scheme lacks statutory back-up and the record of voluntary arrangements, notably on

Exmoor between 1968 and 1977, is not encouraging. Farmers' willingness to contemplate an arrangement with conditions broadly equivalent to those within an SSSI, while objecting so vehemently to designation itself and its accompanying legal guarantee of compensation, invites scepticism. Part of the answer can be found in the Berwyn farmers' suspicion of any government order or imposition: the designation procedure itself and the lack of established means of consultation or facility for involving the local farmers were also at the heart of much of the opposition. And this led to the insertion into the 1981 Act of a statutory requirement on the NCC to consult owners before the designation of new SSSIs, although the NFU and the CLA failed to secure a right of appeal against SSSI designation.

WEST SEDGEMOOR

Similar considerations loomed large on the Somerset Levels where West Sedgemoor acquired even greater notoriety in the politics of designation immediately after the passage of the 1981 Act (Lowe *et al.*, 1986). Following what they regarded as the débâcle over the Berwyns, first Friends of the Earth (FoE), and then the RSPB threatened the NCC with legal action if it failed to designate land which met its scientific criteria. In reaction to such criticisms and 'to remove any misunderstandings about how it intends to implement the SSSI provisions', the NCC issued a formal statement on 10 August 1982 detailing its commitment to using fully the powers of the Act to safeguard SSSIs. The decision, finally announced on 17 November 1982, to designate 2470 acres in West Sedgemoor was widely seen by interests opposed to such an extensive designation as a political sop to 'buy off' conservationist discontent.

Drainage operations had always been central to life on the Levels but it was in the mid-1970s that the particular implications of the advent of the pump drain and its dramatic lowering of the water table, were brought to the attention of the NCC. A working party, the Somerset Wetlands Project Group, was set up and their 1977 report confirmed the high conservation and potentially high agricultural value of the area and drew attention, among other things, to the unreconciled terms of reference of various government departments and statutory bodies with an interest in the area. Because the report's conclusions had major policy implications it was referred to the Department of the Environment who, in turn, requested the County Council to undertake a Somerset Levels and Moors study preparatory to a local subject plan. But its deliberations were overtaken by the transformed legislative context. A very general consultative letter indicating intent had been sent to owners and occupiers on West Sedgemoor in 1978 but it was not until March 1982 that the NCC sent a formal standard letter under Section 28 of the Wildlife and Countryside Act announcing that it proposed to designate the whole 2470 acres of the moor.

The designation, which would have the effect of drastically restricting land drainage and other farming methods in the interests of conserving wetland flora and fauna in the only important inland breeding area for wading birds left in southwest England, was vigorously opposed by the NFU and CLA and some naturalists. They pointed to a report prepared for the CLA by the distinguished ecologist Sir Kenneth Mellanby which suggested that an area somewhat less than half that proposed would be sufficient to retain the moor's scientific interest. During the passage of the Wildlife and

Countryside Act both the NFU and the CLA had taken great exception to the absence of any provision for a right of appeal against designation (Cox and Lowe, 1983a) and predictably they embarked on a campaign to reduce substantially the area subject to designation. Visits by the NCC Chairman in July 1982 and later in the year by the whole council of the NCC failed to placate local opinion. Farmers and landowners were incensed by the manner in which the intention to designate had been announced without — as they saw it — full consultation and before the publication of the government's compensation guidelines. In a series of extraordinary developments the NCC was put under quite improper pressure by Ministers and local politicians to moderate its proposal and early in February 1983 Environment Minister Tom King told Sir Ralph Verney that he would not be reappointed as its chairman. Worried by effects on land values and potential difficulties with landlord–tenant relationships, local farmers charged that they were victims of 'conservation blight'. Their protests culminated with a meeting (frowned on by the NFU) at Stathe, on the northern edge of the moor, on 22 February 1983 when effigies of the outgoing NCC Chairman, its Regional Officer and the RSPB Regional Officer were burned along with the letters from the NCC advising farmers of their new obligations. The row, which threatened to undermine the Wildlife and Countryside Act, was only calmed by the personal intervention of the Minister who, in a private meeting on March 5 at Burrow Bridge, on the edge of his own constituency, assured landowners that their livelihoods would not be damaged by the designation. In particular he offered a pledge regarding compensation for possible loss of capital value which went beyond any provisions of the 1981 Act.

The West Sedgemoor episode, like its precursor in the Berwyns, had shown the determination of farming and landowning interests, irrespective of the legal situation, to regard SSSI designation as essentially contestable and had offered the spectacle of *ad hoc* arrangements and assurances being called forth to assuage carefully orchestrated local opposition. Having risked compromising its authority in the Berwyns, the NCC had confronted the challenges over West Sedgemoor with a will borne of necessity, thwarting — for the time being — the attempt to modify power relations in the nature conservation legislative space. Implementation, like the preceding legislative process, was shown to be no less a political process anchored in the social construction of power.

Management agreements to protect the wildlife interest of West Sedgemoor are likely to cost £150 000 a year and the RSPB has ruefully contrasted this annual commitment for conserving two-thirds of the moor with its own expenditure of £1 million in acquiring the other third, to which the NCC contributed just £67 000 in grant aid. There are 10 areas in the Levels considered exceptional by the NCC and if all were designated in keeping with its statutory obligations annual management agreement costs could exceed £1 million. Other important wetlands such as Whittlesey Marshes, Amberley Wildbrooks, the Idle Washlands, the Cambridgeshire Fens and the Derwent Ings are under threat and wetlands are only one of several types of habitat under great pressure from agricultural intensification, so the NCC's annual expenditure on servicing management agreements can only rise dramatically.

The main reason why current costs are only a fraction of what they may be in future is that, even after four years, the Act has still not been fully implemented. While National Park authorities have seemed reluctant to use the Act's provisions for fear of its financial implications the NCC has, despite its initial equivocation over costs, shown every commitment to the legislation. But the task of implementing its new responsibilities is enormous and beyond anything anticipated by Ministers, or indeed the NCC itself. Under Section 28 of the Act the NCC has to renotify some 30 000 owners and occupiers of the 4000 or so SSSIs. To win their understanding and sympathy — a requirement whose dimensions are amply demonstrated by the Berwyn and West Sedgemoor designations — NCC regional staff try to make personal contact before formal notification is sent. Reappraisal, the making of detailed site descriptions and maps and site-specific lists of potentially damaging operations (PDO) are equally time-consuming elements of a necessarily protracted process. New designations inevitably involve an even more complex sequence of procedures and the consultation period before a new designation can be confirmed has encouraged unscrupulous owners to take pre-emptive destructive action during what quickly came to be known as the 'three-month loophole'. Not surprisingly a large part of NCC regional staff time is being taken up with an exercise which the NCC initially expected to complete by the end of 1983, but which it now recognizes will not be finished before 1990. To date just over one-quarter of sites have been renotified.

Until a site is notified or renotified it is without even the modest safeguards the Act affords, and only then does the real work of site protection begin. In the event of a farmer wishing to carry out a PDO, under the Act the NCC has three months in which to respond, though it undertook to make an initial response within one month. If the response is unfavourable, the ensuing negotiations may be complex and protracted, whether the NCC seeks a management agreement or acquisition of the site or merely to secure the status quo, while negotiations continue, through the cumbrous device of a nature conservation order (under Section 29 of the Act). The Act is, in short, a bureaucratic as well as a financial nightmare. The NCC's all too limited powers are rendered even more inadequate by the Act's cumbersome procedures. The Rayner review, instigated by the Secretary of State for the Environment in the hope of finding scope for economies, concluded in March 1983 that many of the staff were overworked and, exceptionally, even proposed a small increase in numbers. As a result, 43 extra posts were created bringing the staff complement to 590 in 1984. The NCC estimated that a further 400 posts would be needed to fulfil all its statutory responsibilities, and a further increase in its grant for 1985–86 allowed for 100 more posts to be created to nearly double the field staff involved in implementing the Act. But the NCC remains understaffed and inevitably its general advisory role and responsibility for the wider countryside have been neglected in the wake of the 1981 Act's workload.

It is hard not to conclude that, consequently, the monitoring of the Act's effectiveness in safeguarding landscapes and habitats has been inadequate. NCC statistics revealed that in the year April 1983–March 1984 damage occurred on 156 existing and proposed SSSIs, and that figure is bound to be an underestimate because information is patchy about sites awaiting renotification. Damage varied from the very minor to the total loss of three sites with agricultural activities such as ploughing, drainage, reseeding and the use of fertilizers and chemical sprays responsible in over half the cases. As evidence accumulated of the costs, difficulties and complexities of the Act, pressure increased to remedy its most obvious defects. Early in 1984 the new NCC Chairman, William Wilkinson, wrote to William Waldegrave (Under-Secretary of State at the DoE) requesting that steps be taken to close the three-month loophole; that the notification period for PDOs be extended to six months to allow for adequate negotiation; and finally that the processing of nature conservation orders be speeded up, because a number of sites had been damaged because of delay in obtaining an order. The NCC proposed that it should have an emergency 28-day 'stop' power to cover the period in which the Secretary of State reached his decision on an order. The Treasury was also beginning to express unease at the increasing cost of management agreements and in March 1984, in the context of the Halvergate controversy, William Waldegrave announced that he was asking MAFF to find ways of protecting valuable sites without invoking the Sections of the Act which obliged conservation agencies to make substantial compensation payments to landowners.

HALVERGATE

Conflict between conservation and agricultural interests on the Halvergate Marshes in Norfolk has proved both tortuous and intractable (Lowe *et al.*, 1986). A 1980 proposal by the Lower Bure Internal Drainage Board (IDB) to improve arterial drainage and pumping capacity on three drainage levels resulted in a Ministerial decision in November 1982 to grant aid one new pump but withhold it for two others. The decision took Section 48 of the 1981 Act further than originally intended since it effectively restrained the IDB from promoting agricultural business but MAFF, supported by the DoE, hoped thereby to deflect conservationist outrage without frustrating agricultural interests. But such were the pressures impelling farmers towards arable conversion that what had been claimed as an imaginative decision did not even provide a temporary resolution. In May 1983 two landowners approached the Broads Authority with a view either to getting the Authority to buy their land, or to obtaining compensation for potential profit lost, highlighting once again the spectacular gains to be made from conversion to highly subsidized cereal crops.

The Broads Authority had seen 3705 acres of grassland disappear since 1981 and the three management agreements it had entered into, each on poor-quality marsh, were already costing £10 000 annually. With the prospective notification of a further 4940 acres, payments of over £1 million annually could be expected in an area entitled to only 50 per cent support from the Countryside Commission. At a meeting in March 1984 between the Broads Authority, the Countryside Commission and MAFF and DoE Ministers, the Ministers turned down a request that the Broads be placed on a par with Exmoor and be given 90 per cent grant aid. They did, however, respond positively — although cautiously — to the proposal that MAFF act to increase the effective revenue from livestock. A working party was set up to make proposals and in the meantime the Broads Authority sought to stop four landowners from ploughing for a year by offering a token payment. But David and Michael Wright, joint owners of 370 acres, refused, giving the Authority until 10 June to reach an agreement.

The working party could not agree but the deadlock was broken by an ingenious Countryside Commission proposal whereby it undertook to finance an alternative system of livestock support payments for three years in an attempt to sustain the traditional grazing regime on the marshes. The Commission stipulated that MAFF should subsequently take over the support payments should they prove effective but when the working party reported in mid-May there was still no Ministerial agreement on future financing. The Authority sought a one-year agreement with Michael Wright whose land was critical to the landscape value of the core marshes but decided not to negotiate with his brother who, on 10 June, duly began to prepare his ground for ploughing only to be thwarted by direct action from the local FoE. He subsequently sought to negotiate but agreement could not be reached and ploughing recommenced.

Another landowner, some distance from Halvergate, who seemed wholly uninterested in any form of management agreement, also indicated his intent to plough. The publicity attracted by this case caused Ministers acute political embarrassment. The Broads Authority and the Council for the Protection of Rural England (CPRE) successfully encouraged the Secretary of State for the Environment to prevent the drainage by using an Article 4 Direction, which effectively placed the designated works under the development control system. Its imposition simultaneously exposed the voluntary philosophy underlying the 1981 Act and delivered a body blow to the argument that planning controls are wholly inappropriate in regulating agricultural development. The DoE action had its effect and the landowner settled for a one-year holding payment pending the outcome of discussions on the Countryside Commission's experimental scheme. But the DoE would not consider the 'blanket' Article 4 Direction over all the grade 1 and grade 2 landscape areas which FoE and the CPRE lobbied for, and the Minister faced a barrage of hostile Parliamentary questions throughout July as the activities of David Wright caused continued outrage.

Though the government could point to the refusal of the Broads Authority to seek a management agreement it had to recognize that the Authority's inability to finance many management agreements indicated that other ways of protecting this highly valued landscape must be found. But with MAFF committed to a narrow interpretation of the scope for making payments under the European Community's (EC) Common Agricultural Policy (CAP), further progress awaited agreement on new EC Farm Structures Regulations specifically authorizing payments towards farming practices sympathetic to conservation in environmentally sensitive areas. Finally on 15 March 1985 MAFF announced that the Broads Authority Area would be designated under Section 41 of the 1981 Act, thus requiring farmers there to notify the Authority of their intention to undertake grant-aidable improvements. In addition, the Authority was required to compensate them if, consequently, they were denied a grant and it was to contribute 50 per cent of the cost of the experimental Broads Grazing Marshes Conservation Scheme. The arrangement was hailed as proof that by working together agriculture and conservation interests can give practical support for the livelihood of farmers and the protection of the landscape, and MAFF indicated its intention to seek the necessary powers from Parliament to enable the introduction of such schemes on a longer-term basis.

The spectacle of an *ad hoc* arrangement — however worthy in itself — being formulated to resolve a conflict which could not be contained within the bounds of the Wildlife and Countryside Act not only exposed the Act's limitations but re-enacted the pragmatic and incrementalist policy sequence which had earlier, on Exmoor, given rise to its philosophy and mechanisms. While it is always possible to present such developments in a positive light the process by which successive crises prompt new policy departures, or decisions with potentially major policy implications, suggests an inadequate strategy and a need to examine the social construction of power within a broader context to explain that inadequacy. The embarrassment of Halvergate was especially acute because it coincided with a number of developments which were leading to just such examinations.

The passage of the Wildlife and Countryside Act and the publicity which accompanied the difficulties of its implementation played an important role in opening up a wide-ranging debate on agricultural policy in its broadest sense. Other factors were also important in partially prising apart a 'policy community' which had hitherto been notoriously closed (Cox *et al.*, 1985b). By early 1984, the European Council of Ministers, faced with the bankruptcy of the EC, accepted financial ceilings in principle in most areas of CAP expenditure. The quotas on milk production imposed in April signalled to the farming and landowning lobby the probable end of the era, ushered in by the 1947 Agriculture Act, during which a sustained commitment to increased agricultural production gave them a potential for power which their own organization and competence did much to maximize (Cox and Lowe, 1984). Both the NFU and the CLA embarked on major reappraisals of agricultural and environmental policy (Cox *et al.*, 1985a).

Two influential books had done much to fuse the economic and environmental critiques of agricultural policy (Body, 1982; Bowers and Cheshire, 1983) and even within the Conservative Party there emerged a preparedness to question agricultural priorities (Carlisle, 1984; Patterson, 1984). In January 1984 the CPRE launched a campaign which developed strong links with a parallel one launched in April by *The Observer* to reform the agricultural support system. With the environmental absurdities of agricultural policy being demonstrated daily by developments on Halvergate the conservation agencies adopted a more public and sceptical stance towards government policies. The NCC, in particular, detailed 'the overwhelmingly adverse impact of modern agriculture on wildlife and its habitat in Britain' in its report *Nature Conservation in Great Britain.* There was agreement across the whole conservation movement, from the Countryside Commission to FoE, that at least part of the agricultural budget should be redirected to support conservation-oriented husbandry. A House of Lords Select Committee inquiry into agriculture and the environment conducted throughout the winter and spring of 1983–84 had given the whole range of conservation organizations the opportunity to argue, with unprecedented unanimity, for such changes. In its report, the Committee called for 'the revision of existing priorities and greater co-ordination and co-operation' between MAFF and the DoE (HMSO, 1984a). Similar points were made by the House of Lords Select Committee on Science and Technology report on agriculture and environmental research (HMSO, 1984b). In January 1985 the report from the House of Commons Environment Committee on the operation and effectiveness of Part II of the Wildlife and Countryside Act (HMSO, 1985a) expressed concern that even if its recommendations were acted on, the wider agricultural structure might still fuel the 'engine of destruction'. Despite this extraordinary pressure the Government's reply to the Environment Committee (HMSO, 1985b) contented itself with asserting the sufficiency of what was already being done.

Coincidentally Dr David Clark's very limited private member's Wildlife and Countryside Amendment Bill was being emasculated in the committee stage. Despite the blandness of government responses to this sustained criticism it is apparent that, for a number of reasons, policies relating to landscape protection and nature conservation are being appraised as never before. Prompted by the need to respond to an EC Directive relating to the conservation of wild birds the debate occasioned by the introduction of the Wildlife and Countryside Bill had presented an opportunity for conservation interests to capture the policy-making terrain and secure fundamental change. But the Act which emerged from the Parliamentary process represented a rearguard attempt at incremental adjustment which could not easily be sustained given the inadequate resources available for its implementation. By a familiar process which has yet to resolve itself the problems of implementation have focused attention on the contradictions of agricultural and environmental policies and have thereby stimulated a much broader debate accompanied by policy changes which go beyond the procedures envisaged by the Act. The agricultural policy community, whose unity and power were so important in determining the character of the legislation, meanwhile finds itself on the defensive as never before in the postwar period, not least because of the changed context which that legislation has helped to form.

Policy, as the framework for action, is only really created during the implementation process. The politics of environmental policy thus exemplify the processes by which rationalist policy initiatives are propped up and extended by the real policy world of *ad hoc* responses to crisis management: for just as the 1949 Act had its back broken on Exmoor, the 1981 Act which emerged from that crisis has come to grief on the Halvergate Marshes. That the developments can plausibly be presented as a smooth process of policy evolution should delude no one disposed to see policy-making and policy implementation as political processes anchored in the social construction of power.

REFERENCES

Adams, W.M. (1984) *Implementing the Act*, British Association of Nature Conservationists, World Wildlife Fund.

Barrett, S. and Hill, M. (1984) Policy, bargaining and structure in implementation theory: towards an integrated perspective, *Policy and Politics*, Vol. 12, No. 3, 219–240.

Body, R. (1982) *Agriculture, the Triumph and the Shame*, Maurice Temple-Smith, London.

Bowers, J. and Cheshire, P. (1983) *Agriculture: the Countryside and Land Use*, Methuen, London.

Brotherton, I. (1984) *Farm Grants Notifications in National Parks, 1.4.83 to 30.9.83*, Countryside Commission, Cheltenham.

Carlisle, K. (1984) *Conserving the Countryside: A Tory View*, Conservative Central Office, London.

Cox, G. and Lowe, P. (1983a) A battle not the war: the politics of the Wildlife and Countryside Act 1981. In Gilg, A. (ed.) *Countryside Planning Yearbook*, Vol. 4, pp 48–76.

Cox, G. and Lowe, P. (1983b) Countryside politics: goodbye to goodwill? *Political Quarterly*, Vol. 54, 268–282.

Cox, G. and Lowe, P. (1984) Agricultural corporation and rural conservation'. In Bradley, A. and Lowe, P. (eds) *Locality and Rurality*, Geo Books, Norwich, pp 147–166.

Cox, G., Lowe, P. and Winter, M. (1985a) 'Caught in The Act: the agricultural lobby and the conservation debate, *ECOS*, Vol. 6, No. 1, 18–23.

Cox, G., Lowe, P. and Winter, M. (1985b) Agriculture and conservation in Britain: a policy community under siege. Paper presented to RESSG Conference, Oxford. In Cox, G., Lowe, P. and Winter, M. (eds) *Agriculture: Policies and People*, George Allen and Unwin, London (in press).

Cox, G., Lowe, P. and Winter, M. (1985c) Land use conflict after the Wildlife and Countryside

Act 1981: the role of the Farming and Wildlife Advisory Group, *Journal of Rural Studies*, Vol. 1, No. 2, 173–183.

HMSO (1984a) Lords Select Committee on the European Communities 1983–84, *Agriculture and The Environment*, HL Paper 247, HMSO, London.

HMSO (1984b) Lords Select Committee on Science and Technology 1983–84, *Agriculture and Environmental Research*, HL Paper 272 1 and 11, HMSO, London.

HMSO (1985a) House of Commons first report from the Environment Committee, 1984–85, *Operation and Effectiveness of Part II of the Wildlife and Countryside Act*, Vols I and II, HMSO, London.

HMSO (1985b) The government's reply to the First Report from the Environment Committee, HMSO, London.

Lowe, P., Cox, G., MacEwen, M., O'Riordan, T. and Winter, M. (1986) *Countryside Conflicts: The Politics of Farming Forestry and Conservation*, Maurice Temple-Smith, Gower, London.

Majone, G. and Wildavsky, A. (1978) Implementation as evolution, *Policy Studies Review Annual*, Vol. 2, 103–117.

Nature Conservancy Council (1981) *Annual Report*, NCC, London.

Patterson, T. (1984) *Conservation and the Conservatives*, Bow Group, London.

5

MINERALS AND PLANNING: THE SOCIAL BASIS OF PHYSICAL OUTCOMES

Andrew Blowers

PRECONDITIONS AND PROBLEMS OF MINERAL EXTRACTION

Minerals are natural substances which can be transformed into resources providing energy and raw materials — the essential physical bases of industry, transportation and construction in modern society. The extraction of minerals produces fundamental changes in our physical surroundings; it is an expression of the relationship between society and nature. Minerals are won from the rural environment and used mainly in the production of the urban environment. Their use is both destructive and creative involving a cyclical process of excavation, transportation, production, consumption and disposal which continually reconstructs the environment.

The use of minerals depends on a set of *preconditions* (Blaikie, 1985). First, there is the appropriate *technical knowledge*. Natural resources are not naturally resources; minerals in the earth only become resources when social development devises a use for them. Some minerals such as clay for brick-making or iron ore for manufacturing, or coal for the production of energy have long been used. Others, such as oil, uranium or aluminium, have only become resources as technology has advanced. In other cases the uses have changed; for example, tin was originally used for utensils but is now mainly required for packaging, soldering and in chemical and electronic industries. Many minerals are used in combination with others so that demand is derived indirectly from a range of applications. In general, the demand for both established and new mineral uses has increased the pressure for exploitation of existing and virgin sources of supply. The second precondition is *positive identification* of resources (the potential availability of materials under different regimes of technology) and the calculation of reserves (the known levels to meet current rates of demand). This presents a problem for planning in that the extent of proven reserves falls well short of the potential resources which may be discovered by exploration or increased through better exploitation or recycling. The extent of reserves reflects a third precondition — the *comparative utility* of minerals — which depends on factors of location, mining technology, quality and quantity of deposit, accessibility, competition and substitutability. Decision-makers face the difficulty of assessing the need for a specific resource in the context of alternative possibilities. And, fourthly, there is the precondition of *political control* which involves the ownership of land, the right to exploit minerals and the power to control extraction. The relative power of interests favouring extraction and those opposing it varies according to the particular combination of the other preconditions in a specific location. The outcome will represent the social evaluation of the costs and benefits of extraction.

Mineral extraction creates a set of problems for planning which act as *constraints* on implementation. First, there is the constraint of *land use*. Mining is in competition with other productive land uses, particularly agriculture, and minerals are often found in areas of high amenity. For minerals of widespread occurrence it may be possible to avoid conflict with other uses and where extraction is short-lived interference is limited, especially where restoration to a former or acceptable use is feasible. But where minerals are rare and extraction involves long-term or permanent land-use change, acute land-use conflicts will arise. Second, there is the constraint imposed by the *negative externalities* produced by mining. All mining activities create some problems of noise, traffic, fumes, dust and nuisance afflicting local communities. Some impose long-term amenity damage in the form of dereliction, and production processes associated with mining may result in harmful substances polluting water and the atmosphere. And, third, there is the constraint of *restoration and after-use*. Externalities can be mitigated if progressive restoration is accomplished. Mineral extraction is, to an extent, complemented by waste disposal which completes the cycle. But waste disposal may also create its own negative externalities and, as in the example of nuclear wastes, introduces potential risks that are unacceptable to local communities.

The preconditions and constraints describe the context for decision-making; explanation of outcomes reflects the relative power of the *interests* involved in each decision. These interests are conventionally characterized as economic and environmental interests and decisions are explained in terms of a conflict between opposing interests. But interests are not always separable or indivisible but are often intertwined. Thus *economic interests* incorporate a number of components such as jobs, profits, incomes and wealth creation. They have an impact on different groups at different times and in different places. Economic interests may be in conflict, as when workers demanding wage increases conflict with owners concerned to protect profit margins. But, at other times, economic interests may be in concert as when workers and owners have a mutual interest in the exploitation of a mineral resource for the jobs and profits it will yield. *Environmental interests* embrace another set of concerns or issues, defined by Goodin (1976) as amenity, public health, resource depletion and survival. These, too, affect different groups to different degrees and may be conflicting or congruent. Thus, the interest of affluent groups in protecting their amenity by the prevention of mineral working may be in conflict with the interests of poorer, less powerful groups whose amenity and possible health suffer as a consequence of mineral development being diverted to their communities. On occasion, especially when a development threatens widespread risks, the community as a whole may unite to resist it. Thus, conflicts are not simply between economy and environment but involve overlapping and shifting alignments between *material interests* in both the economy and the environment. The implementation of policies for mineral extraction — and for all forms of development for that matter — reflects social conflicts for the acquisition or maintenance of control over land. It is, in short, a political matter.

CONSENSUS OR CONFLICT?

The political characteristics of minerals planning range from consensus, where (visible) conflict is absent to intense and apparently irreconcilable conflict. In the sense used here 'consensus' may be expressed as a general agreement among interests leading to a presumption in favour of minerals extraction or, conversely, the prevention of extraction. 'Conflict' describes the political situation where opposing interests cannot reach agreement and, consequently, outcomes are unstable representing either compromise or the outright victory of one set of interests over another. Consensus and conflict are tendencies rather than mutually exclusive categories. The tendencies can be expressed in relation to the three sets of concepts already introduced — preconditions, constraints and interests — in the form of an explanatory model summarized in Table 5.1.

From the model it can be hypothesized that consensus favouring mineral extraction is most likely to prevail under the following preconditions:

1.   The state of technical knowledge demonstrates a social need for the resource.
2.   The resource has been positively identified.
3.   The occurrence of the resource is restricted and substitutes or alternative sources are unavailable.
4.   Power is concentrated among mineral developers.

In addition the constraints on development will be weak in that:

5.   There is an absence of land-use competition.
6.   The externality effects of exploitation are minimal or highly localized.
7.   Extraction is short term and restoration to an appropriate after-use can be secured.

Lastly, in terms of interests,

8.   Economic interests in jobs, profits, etc. are the predominant concern.

A consensus favouring the prevention of minerals exploitation is likely when the converse set of conditions applies as Table 5.1 shows. In this case the need for the resource may be challenged; the resource may be widespread and substitutable; and political control will be dispersed. The constraints will be severe with clear alternatives to the development, widespread externality effects and long-term or permanent impact on the land. Environmental interests will predominate and be mobilized to resist development.

A tendency to conflict occurs when one or more of the conditions necessary for consensus cannot be achieved. In terms of the model shown in Table 5.1 conflict represents the intermediate possibilities along a continuum ranging from consensus favouring development to consensus favouring conservation. Thus a consensus favouring development may be transformed into a conflict when the social need for the resource is effectively challenged; or the existence of alternative resources or materials can be asserted; or alternative land uses are identified; or the externality effects are shown to increase or become more widespread and so on. Conflict will occur as opposition to any or all of the conditions can be mobilized to provide a challenge to prospective developers. The intensity of conflict and its ultimate resolution will reflect

Table 5.1 The politics of mineral development

Political tendencies	Preconditions				Constraints			Material interests	
	Technical knowledge	Positive identification	Comparative utility	Political control	Land use	Externalities	Restoration and after-use	Economic	Environmental
Consensus favouring extraction	Demonstrable need established	Resource and reserves established	Restricted occurrence. No alternative source or available substitution	Concentration of power in the industry	Absence of competing land uses	Minimal or highly localized	Short-term impact and appropriate after-use	Jobs, profit etc. pre-dominant concern	Absent or passive
Conflict	Social need challenged	Extent of resources and reserves uncertain	Alternatives may be available	Competition between powerful interests	Appropriate land use disputed	Impact of externalities disputed	Prospects for restoration uncertain	Interests in conflict. Intensity varies according to relative power and outcome uncertain	
Consensus favouring conservation	Need not established or challenged	Extent of resources and reserves unknown	Ubiquitous material or alternative sources of available substitutes	Dispersal of power in the industry	Competition from alternative uses	Significant and widespread	Long-term or permanent impact	Absent or passive	Amenity, public health, etc. pre-dominant concern

the relative power of interests. Thus, the demand for jobs may eventually prevail over the desire for amenity; the concern for public health may overcome the need for investment and so on. Where different interests can be aggregated then powerful and cross-cutting alliances can be constructed by opposing sides which intensify and spread the conflict. For example, a major developer may secure the support of dependent workers while conservationists, primarily interested in protecting their amenity, may enlist the support of a broader constituency concerned with the risks to health.

The tendency towards consensus or conflict will vary also within dimensions of time and space. In general over time it appears there has been a shift (at least in developed countries) towards greater environmental concern. This is a product of greater affluence as interests which have secured basic needs begin to prize 'positional goods' such as amenity, goods that are 'fixed in supply and whose consumption is dependent upon one's position in society' (Newby, 1980, p. 202). And there has been growing anxiety about the ecological and social consequences of economic growth. As concern for amenity has begun to embrace other environmental issues so there has been a breakdown of the consensus favouring development leading to increasing conflict and a shift in some cases towards the consensus at the other end of the continuum. But it is not a simple progressive movement since, in times and places where economic problems are manifest, the interests favouring development recover their ground.

Geographical differences also complicate the picture. In the past exploitation of minerals and their impact tended to be localized. Now the spatial scale of mining operations has become regional, national and even international as more areas are exploited and externalities, in some cases, are transmitted beyond local or even national jurisdictions, the so-called 'transboundary effects'. Thus over time and space the issues and interests involved have become more complex leading to greater politicization and conflict.

For each type of mineral development there will be a specific set of preconditions, constraints and interests which change over time and space. The model which expresses the tendencies towards consensus or conflict helps us to understand where and why minerals are exploited and what the outcomes are likely to be in terms of implementation through state intervention by planning. This framework underlies the following discussion of examples drawn from one county in England.

MINERALS IN BEDFORDSHIRE

Bedfordshire is the third smallest English county in area (305 072 acres) but its geology and location in southeast England make it a significant source of minerals used in the construction industry with 2 per cent of its area currently or previously worked for minerals. The county straddles the belts of Jurassic and cretaceous rocks crossing in a southwest–northeast direction. The major minerals are chalk, sand and Fuller's earth (Lower Greensand), clay for brick-making (Oxford clay) and aggregates (sand and gravel from river-bed deposits or construction sands from the Lower Greensand) (Figure 5.1).

Minerals planning is the responsibility of the County Council and policies are promoted through the Structure Plan and elaborated in more detail in subject plans for each mineral. Bedfordshire's first Structure Plan was approved in 1980 and revised in

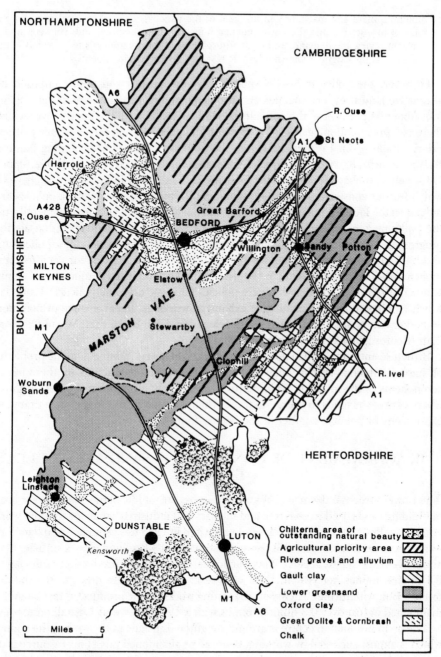

Figure 5.1 Geology and sites of mineral working in Bedfordshire.

1984 though the revised plan awaits approval. The policies for minerals are substantially unaltered and the broad strategy is presented in policy 62 which, as revised, states:

The County Council will determine applications for new mineral workings and associated buildings, plant and machinery in the light of the national, regional or local need for the mineral in question and the environmental impact of that proposal, and will keep under constant review the demand, and likely future demand for the minerals to be found in the County and the extent of known workable reserves. (Bedfordshire County Council, 1984a)

However, the policy is heavily qualified by the various constraints imposed by alternative land uses, externalities and problems of after-use and restoration (policy 63). About 44 per cent of the agricultural land falls within grades 1 and 2 over which there is a presumption against development (policy 49) and in favour of agricultural priority (policy 52). Further, there are the Chilterns Area of Outstanding Natural Beauty (policy 58), Areas of Great Landscape Value (the Greensand Ridge, upper Ouse Valley) (policy 59), woodlands (policies 57, 57a) and wildlife interest (policy 60) which further constrain potential development. In terms of externalities, policies are judged on the local impact of noise, fumes and dust (policy 63) and, more generally, on the pollution created (policy 87). Permissions also require adequate proposals for progressive restoration and must minimize the visual intrusion of workings (policies 63 and 64). These general policies are reinforced by specific policies for each mineral (policies 65–71) and, in the case of Oxford clay, by a subject plan (Bedfordshire County Council, 1984b). In addition there are policies for waste disposal (policies 91 and 92) which emphasize the reclamation of exhausted workings, the avoidance of pollution and other externalities and which are developed in detail in the draft Waste Disposal Plan (Bedfordshire County Council, 1985).

Structure and subject plan policies embody the planners' approach to the problems of implementation. In the analysis which follows the interaction of the various components of the model is explored through different examples moving from those where consensus tends to prevail to those which have given rise to the most dramatic expressions of political conflict in the county (note 1).

THE ACHIEVEMENT OF CONSENSUS — SAND AND FULLER'S EARTH

The Lower Greensand which forms a ridge across the middle of the county is a source of building sands used in concrete and mortars and industrial sands for foundry work and filters. Production of building sand varies and in 1985 was estimated at 0.9 million tonnes per year from 16 pits with reserves estimated at 4.8 million tonnes sufficient for about five years' supply at current production rates. At this rate production would fall to 0.1 million tonnes per year in 1995 with reserves at that date down to 0.3 million tonnes. But, with further extensions to existing workings the production rate could be maintained at just over 0.3 million tonnes with a 1995 reserve of 1.4 million tonnes.

The main production centre is around Leighton-Linslade in the west of the county which is almost encircled by working, restored or abandoned pits. This resource is of regional significance and is regarded by the industry as the best quality sand in the southeast in the area north of the Thames. A survey in 1978 estimated that 815 acres had been worked in this area, permission granted for a further 494 acres with 576 acres unrestored, though in some cases natural reclamation by wildlife was occurring (Bedfordshire County Council, 1978). Elsewhere there are a number of sand pits in the centre and east of the county.

The preconditions for sand working, demonstrable need and lack of available alternatives, ensure a consensus favouring further working. 'It is particularly important for the County Council to be seen to maintain a positive policy towards mineral extraction if we are to be successful in resisting applications on more sensitive areas' (Bedfordshire County Council Environmental Services Committee, 18 July 1985, item 20 A5). The consensus is often reinforced where environmental concern about loss of amenity is passive or can be accommodated by careful planning and tight conditions which overcome the constraints.

Recent applications illustrate the pragmatism characteristic of planning for sand extraction. In the east of the county near Potton and Sandy there were two major extensions to existing workings releasing 600 000 and 3 million tonnes respectively in an area where there were no agricultural or landscape constraints. In one of these, the largest sand pit in the country, restoration would be at low level while, at the other, the area would be progressively backfilled with industrial waste from surrounding towns. The removal of the Council's own landfill and civic amenity waste disposal operations from this site would reduce traffic, noise and dust. These applications were consistent with planning policies and provoked little opposition.

Similarly, in the west of the county around Leighton-Linslade further extensions of sand working have been accommodated with little conflict. In one case a further 600 000 tonnes were released with virtually no local problems. In another, a reserve of 800 000 tonnes north of Leighton-Linslade was located in an Area of Great Landscape Value. However, in the planners' judgement the richness of the seam, its remoteness from residential areas, its unobtrusive nature and the fact that planning conditions could ensure restoration of both the new workings and the more visually prominent unrestored workings nearby ensured a planning gain sufficiently attractive to overcome the notional policy constraint.

These examples demonstrate how a consensus which favours extraction can be sustained by the application of flexibility in planning implementation. Although the operators claim that policies are too restrictive and sterilize reserves, the planning authority counters with a grudging release of land for sand extraction which, they argue, preserves the best features of the ridge, encourages the efficient use of the resource and maintains production. The approach is reminiscent of Micawber. The County Planning Officer explained at the Examination in Public of the Structure Plan in 1977, that the county had 'existed in this sort of hand to mouth manner over a great many years, and that something generally does turn up . . . the door is not and never has been altogether closed to new sites coming forward' (Examination in Public of the Structure Plan for Bedfordshire, 1977, p. 51).

Fuller's earth represents a case where consensus has been restored through reconciliation of conflict. Fuller's earth is a relatively rare mineral with specific qualities of swelling in water and a number of applications as a binding, bonding, dispersing and suspending agent in the foundry, drilling, engineering and chemical industries. One-third of British production (about 50 000 tonnes per year) comes from the Woburn Sands area in west Bedfordshire (Figure 5.1). This case has been fully discussed elsewhere (Blowers, 1980, Ch.4). An area covering 136 acres, worked since 1961 by Steetley Minerals, was becoming exhausted when an application was made in 1975 for a further 138 acres nearby in order to maintain production levels. The preconditions favoured extraction. There was a demand for the mineral from a number of industries and its production could produce export earnings and reduce import costs. Its occurrence was restricted with only one other major producing area, at Redhill in Surrey, though permission had been granted at Clophill in central Bedford-shire in 1952 and at Baulking (Oxon) in 1975 on appeal. By releasing Woburn Sands (and Baulking) the possibility of a monopoly in the hands of Laportes (Redhill and Clophill) would be averted. Substitutes were not available and the national interest in production was clear in the support given by the Department of Industry to the application. Thus the county planners concluded that need 'is a determining issue and must weigh heavily in favour of granting a planning permission' (Environmental Services Committee, 20 February 1976, item 15[10]).

There were, though, significant constraints. The proposal was in an Area of Great Landscape Value, covered by woodlands and used as a recreational area by residents of Woburn Sands and the developing city of Milton Keynes. The workings would impose noise on an area of 'quietness and tranquillity'. As against this the excavation would be short term, about 12 years, with progressive restoration through backfilling of overbur-den and ultimate return to its former use. The problem of balancing conflicting interests was neatly encapsulated in the Structure Plan policy: 'Any future application for the working of Fuller's Earth will be treated entirely on its own merits, weighing national need against environmental and other local considerations' (policy 70). The planners calculated in favour of the application.

However, in an area with an articulate, affluent population, environmental opposi-tion was easily aroused and a local pressure group gained the support of the District Council who doubted the strategic need for the mineral and opposed the proposal on grounds of noise and disturbance. Pressure was applied on the members of the County Planning Committee who, in interpreting the policy, came to precisely the opposite conclusion to their officials stating they were 'not satisfied that the national need for Fuller's earth outweighs the environmental damage which would be caused to this high amenity area' (Environmental Services Committee, 20 February 1976, minute 76/k/54). The company appealed against the decision and at the public inquiry was able to convince the Inspector on the economic case. But he also acknowledged the environmental problem and suggested that working begin furthest from the residential area and not be permitted to come as close to dwellings as the applicants had intended. This compromise was accepted by the Minister. The case of national need had been upheld but local interests had achieved a more acceptable solution. Although the issue had generated conflict it was resolved and a consensus had been forged.

CHANGING CONSENSUS — THE CASE OF AGGREGATES

Sand and gravel are used as aggregate for concrete and for roadstone. Gravel is bulky and cheap and serves local markets. Gravel in Bedfordshire comes mainly from shallow deposits in the Ouse and Ivel river valleys in the north of the county (see Figure 5.1). Production is about 0.5 million tonnes per year. Gravel is a mineral causing 'intense' conflict although there are signs that a consensus preventing further extraction is being established.

The preconditions for gravel extraction nationally point towards further land releases. 'For the economic health of the country, it is essential that the construction industry is provided with an adequate and steady supply of minerals it needs' (Department of the Environment, 1982, para. 3.2). But in the southeast, the region with by far the highest demand for aggregates in England, the constraints on local supplies are becoming so acute as to outweigh the preconditions favouring extraction. Gravel is a high-bulk/low-value commodity and transport costs are high so that sources near demand centres are at a premium to support a 'cheap gravel' policy which 'does not reflect the social costs which workings impose on the community' (Standing Conference on London and South East Regional Planning, 1979, p. 3). Gravel extraction faces severe land-use competition since it often underlies high-grade agricultural land or Areas of Great Landscape Value. Further releases are likely to eliminate land uses with regional or even national importance. Extraction is an extensive activity and there are problems of restoration and after-use such that, in some cases, landscape and land-use change is permanent. A survey of the southeast reported that 9884 acres remained unrestored (ibid.) and a Bedfordshire survey estimated gravel extraction had left 247 acres of wasteland (Bedfordshire County Council, 1978). The problems of restoration include uneven settlement, poor topsoiling, bad drainage, lack of interest by farmers, inadequate planning conditions on earlier permissions or lack of adequate landfill ibid., pp 43–45). By contrast, some old gravel workings have been transformed into new landscapes for amenity purposes and examples in Bedfordshire include a park and marina in Bedford, a country park and a nature reserve in the Ouse Valley.

The increasing pressure from constraints is altering the preconditions for extraction in the southeast. In the 1970s the region yielded 40 per cent of the national total of land-won sand and gravel but met only about 60 per cent (30 million tonnes) of its total needs (note 2). About 17 per cent of needs were provided by imports, mainly of crushed rock from other materials. The government expected the proportion of the region's demand met by land-won gravel to reduce to around 54 per cent (25 million tonnes) by the 1990s (Department of the Environment, 1982, pp 8–9). Imports would account for about 20 per cent and marine-dredged gravel would supply most of the remainder. But there are severe difficulties in finding alternative sources or suitable substitutes to reduce the pressure on land-won supplies. Marine dredging requires capital investment which cannot be covered by the price obtained in competition with cheap land-based supplies. There are also adverse effects on coastlines and navigation, and fishing and technical constraints on marine dredging. The importation of crushed rock faces two problems. One is the lack of capacity of aggregates depots for rail-borne aggregates. The Verney Report (HMSO, 1976) concluded that 'by the early 1990s almost all of the gravel-bearing land in the South East which is not agriculturally valuable or environmentally *precious* will have been worked out' and proposed a total of 200 depots in the region built at the rate of 9 per year, a total that has proved wholly unrealistic. The second problem is the increasing resistance to exports of regions like the southwest and east Midlands as quarrying crushed rock imposes amenity damage and externality effects on National Parks or areas of landscape quality. Furthermore, substitute materials such as colliery spoil, ash, clinker, slag and waste products do not offer significant short-term solutions since they, too, have to be imported and cannot compete with locally produced gravel.

The commercial interest in cheap gravel confronts environmental interests in conserving existing land uses. The dilemma for planning authorities in the region is underlined in the report of the Regional Aggregates Group: 'Those most concerned about continued land working noted the irony that the more that local areas took what might be seen as a realistic and responsible view and agreed albeit reluctantly to further workings then the less the pressure to force progress in these matters' (Standing Conference on London and South East Regional Planning, 1979, pp 1–2). However, there are signs that the balance of political pressures is moving from a presumption favouring exploitation of cheap gravel towards a consensus preferring tighter restraint on working. And, in the absence of effective national or regional policies, this emphasis is being established at the local level.

In Bedfordshire the parsimonious attitude towards further gravel extraction was unsuccessfully challenged at the Examination in Public by the mineral operators who asserted, 'there is not sand and gravel that can be worked in Bedfordshire because it is all overlain by certain constraints. It is a very negative approach' (Department of the Environment, 1978, p. 25). The county produces only about one-half its needs, importing supplies from neighbouring counties and crushed rock from the southwest and east Midlands via aggregate depots in Luton and Elstow, near Bedford, respectively. The County Planning Officer justified this undersupply in terms of the net export of other construction materials:

> Bedfordshire already exports bricks all over the country at great environmental cost to itself. It exports sand all over the region at great environmental cost to itself. The fact that it is getting something for nothing by relying on aggregate coming from elsewhere I regard as farcical in this greater context. (p. 24)

The tight restraint is evident from recent decisions on gravel working. In 1975 permission was refused for 128 acres on grade 2 land in the area of landscape quality at Harrold in the upper Ouse Valley (see Figure 5.1). An appeal was rejected, the Inspector concluding that release of the land would create a precedent and that 'supplies should be obtained from areas and by routes where there would be least environmental disturbance' (Department of the Environment, 1978, para. 117). It was regarded by the planners as a test case reinforcing resistance to futher land releases in protected areas. Further working was not entirely precluded as demonstrated by subsequent decisions in the lower Ouse Valley at Great Barford (35 acres containing 0.25 million tonnes on grade 3b land) and Willington (170 acres, 3 million tonnes on grade 3b and 3c land), and in the Ivel Valley near Sandy (57 acres, 0.7 million tonnes on grade 3b land). Two of these cases were extensions to existing workings with few objections or planning constraints. The large reserves at Willington with an annual production of 0.2 million tonnes provided a major boost to dwindling supplies. The woodland was due for felling in any case and the planning conditions required retention of a tree screen, further planting to conceal the workings and progressive restoration to agriculture with a small area reserved for wildlife. The scheme secured general approval and strengthened the planners' hand in refusing permissions elsewhere. Their opportunity came in 1985 when an extension of 46 acres, which would maintain production for two years in the remaining site in the upper Ouse Valley, was refused on the grounds that it was in an area of landscape quality, would cause local disturbance and loss of amenity and might create a precedent for further working. With gravel working restricted to two major sites in the lower Ouse and Ivel Valleys, environmental considerations had become paramount and Bedfordshire was facing the prospect of the elimination of local gravel extraction before the end of the century unless new areas free from constraint could be found. With the loss of one such site on the Cambridgeshire border near St Neots to industrial use, the chances of the county maintaining its supplies of gravel at previous levels looked distinctly slim.

FROM CONSENSUS TO CONFLICT — THE CASE OF OXFORD CLAY

Oxford clay is by far the most extensive mineral worked in Bedfordshire. The Oxford clay beds up to 98 ft thick cross the centre of the county in the Marston Vale (see Figure 5.1). The clay is used in Fletton brick-making and its combustible qualities enable the production of cheap bricks which can be sold to a national market. The share of national brick production from Bedfordshire and neighbouring counties has declined from one-half to just over one-third and about half this total was accounted for by the county until the closure of one of its major works in 1981. While a consensus exists in favour of extraction for brick-making there has been intense political conflict over the environmental impact of clay extraction and brick manufacture. This conflict reached a climax in the late 1970s and early 1980s and is the subject of a detailed study (Blowers, 1984).

The preconditions favour brick-making in Bedfordshire. The clay constitutes a national resource which is exploited for Fletton brick-making in a belt stretching from Buckinghamshire, through Bedfordshire to the area around Peterborough in Cambridgeshire. The planning permissions for extraction are controlled by one company, London Brick, which is now part of the international conglomerate of Hanson Trust. There is, therefore, a concentration of control over brick-making in the county. London Brick is one of the county's major employers, though with closure of major works and redundancies at existing ones, production in the county is now restricted to the large Stewartby works with around 1200 employees in 1985. The need to retain major capital investment and employment provides the economic case favouring the exploitation of Oxford clay.

The consensus is also supported by the absence of land-use conflict. The landscape and land quality of the area are generally poor. Given the extensive permissions already held for future working and expected to last until well into the next century there is a presumption against further permissions (Structure Plan policy 65) but the significance of the resource is made clear in the Subject Plan which proposes a broad 'consultation area' 'to protect workable deposits of Oxford Clay from unnecessary sterilisation' (Bedfordshire County Council, 1984b, policy 1) and to grant further permissions when necessary 'to ensure that the brickmaking industry can meet the anticipated future demand for Fletton Bricks' (policy 2).

Conflict has arisen over the dereliction and pollution caused by brick-making, thus imposing negative externalities on surrounding areas. Altogether about one-half the total permitted area of nearly 4200 acres remains to be worked. Since virtually all the clay can be used for bricks, extraction creates huge voids in the landscape estimated at nearly 2824 million cu. ft and increasing at over 35 million cu. ft per year with backfilling unable to keep pace. About 1853 acres are unrestored representing 40 per cent of the total unrestored mineral workings in the county. The dereliction is a longstanding problem (Bedfordshire County Council, 1967) although landscaping, tree planting and some reclamation have improved the appearance of the Marston Vale in recent years. Brick manufacture results in air pollution from sulphur dioxide, fluoride and the organic substances in the clay which produce noxious odours (mercaptans). Whereas clay extraction is basically an amenity issue, air pollution involves possible risks to vegetation, crops, animals and human health.

For many years, though the problems gave rise to complaints, little effective action was taken. The early permissions granted by the Minister stipulated few conditions on landscaping or restoration and none on air pollution; there was a lack of landfill capable of reclaiming the voids; and the company was indifferent to its environmental impact at a time when the economic need for brick production was regarded as far more important than environmental issues. These conditions had changed by the 1970s. Brick-making was in decline and environmental pressures were growing to a point where both company and council had to respond. An opportunity came with London Brick's proposals for replacement of its existing ageing works in the Marston Vale by two new 'superworks'. They agreed to submit schemes for landscaping abandoned and working pits, a master plan for the restoration of the Vale, and the dispersal of pollution through tall chimneys. Although the attempt to tackle the problem of dereliction was welcomed, local environmental opposition developed over the air pollution issue and campaigned for elimination of pollutants at source.

The conflict engulfed the County Council for a period of three years (1979–81). Local action groups focused on the impact of brick-making on their localities while an umbrella group, Public Review of Brickmaking and the Environment (PROBE), was formed among influential politicians, businesspeople, farming and landed interests. This group exploited the local and national media and successfully lobbied the County Council so that a pollution control condition was imposed on the application for one of the new works. With the deepening recession the threat to employment became palpable with the announcement of the closure of one of the largest works in Bedfordshire. As economic interests were reasserted the situation was transformed in favour of the company who gained the permission they sought (though at a different site) and the opposition was routed. Air pollution had been the trigger for a conflict which had become, in effect, a struggle for power between implacable opponents. The precise effects of air pollution were unknown and it was this uncertainty that fuelled the debate.

Dereliction was a visible problem and here some headway in cleaning up the environment has been made. Old works have been demolished, water-filled pits have been converted into recreation areas, and three pits receive landfill from within the county and from neighbouring areas and London. But landfill operations are regarded by the company as a commercial proposition and the high costs of transport are likely to vitiate the long-distance transfer of wastes, such as the proposal to move colliery spoil from the developing coalfield in Leicestershire, which might close the gap between future excavation and restoration. There remains a number of abandoned and derelict pits with little hope of restoration through backfilling to original surface levels. In these cases the County Council has proposed restoration at low level for agriculture (Subject Plan, policy 6) following feasibility trials (Land Capability Consultants, 1983; Harrison, 1984). This proposal has been resisted by London Brick who doubt its feasibility and object to the policy being applied to specific pits. Here again, as in the case of pollution control, environmental improvements are likely to be a matter of what the company is prepared to concede rather than what the planning authority can enforce.

In the example of brick-making and Oxford clay there is a condition of continuing conflict. Environmental interests able to mobilize a broad constituency of protest in favour of reducing the externalities produced by brick-making confront a powerful monopoly industry representing local and national economic interests bent on avoiding commercially unacceptable conditions or controls. The conflict manifests itself in different issues at different times and each stage is marked by compromise. The conditions of political stability necessary for consensus have not been achieved.

POWER, POLICY AND IMPLEMENTATION

The fact that 'Minerals can only be worked where they occur, and the degree of locational control that can be imposed must be considered in the light of the need for the minerals concerned' (Standing Conference on London and South East Regional Planning, 1979, p. 22) identifies the fundamental problem for minerals policy-making and implementation. The transformation of natural materials into socially useful resources depends on the relationship between a set of preconditions, constraints and interests over time and space as the model and the preceding analysis have shown. This relationship, in specific circumstances, determines the use of the mineral, the extent of reserves, the feasibility of extraction, the location of production and the controls imposed on working. The extent to which consensus or conflict is the prevailing political context within which implementation takes place must be explained by the relative *power* exerted by the various interests involved.

The power of mineral developers varies according to the national importance and relative scarcity of the resource, the wealth and jobs created and the degree of influence that can be exerted over decision-makers. Thus, Fuller's earth and Oxford clay are, in their different ways, strategic minerals whose exploitation is strongly supported by central government. They are limited in geographical occurrence and, while there is no problem of reserves, there is a presumption in favour of developing proven reserves. Oxford clay provides considerable local employment and cheap bricks, and Fuller's earth has a large number of industrial applications. London Brick, with its monopoly of Fletton brick-making, is able to achieve acceptable permissions in one area by the threat of investment withdrawal. By contrast, it was the desire to avoid a monopoly of Fuller's earth production which encouraged the development of the Woburn Sands reserves. But, in both cases the concentration of power in the industry has provided developers with considerable leverage in their negotiations with planning authorities.

Sand and gravel are more ubiquitous minerals for which there are alternative, if more expensive, supplies. There is, therefore, no strategic need to protect or exploit reserves wherever they occur and the jobs and wealth contributed by these industries are of marginal significance to the local economies. Sand and gravel extraction is a competitive industry with nine companies currently operating in Bedfordshire.

Although most of these are members of associations of operators (note 3) their bargaining power is relatively weak since they have few sanctions to apply and (in Bedfordshire at least) the development of a monopolistic organization seems unlikely. Recognition of their weakness was exposed in the comment made by one operator at the Examination in Public that, 'We are the poor relatives of the family' (Department of the Environment, 1977, p. 16).

The power of material interests in the environment mirrors these relative strengths within the minerals industry. The analysis has shown that certain components of environmental concern, notably amenity, appeal most strongly to those who have achieved the affluence which makes the maintenance of positional values important. But, as concern about hazards to health and even survival have increased, so a greater constituency of protest has developed. On the other hand, the need for production and profit on which affluence rests is also a major concern and accounts for the power of developers to resist controls especially in times of recession. Thus material interests in the economy and environment, though conflicting, are interrelated and interdependent and specific outcomes will vary. For example, concern for amenity and conflict with an alternative productive use in agriculture have led to tighter controls over sand and gravel working and, in the case of aggregates, the prospective elimination of working altogether in Bedfordshire. With Fuller's earth environmental pressures are unable to prevent development but they can mitigate its detrimental effects. Oxford clay working involving possible risks to crops, animals and health as well as amenity has stimulated conflict which rages over a range of issues and interests.

Planning policy is conditional on the power exerted by material interests over specific minerals in the particular circumstances of time and place. These circumstances relate to more general conflicts which connect the local to the regional, national and sometimes international context in which material interests are pursued. Implementation rests on the outcome of these conflicts. That is why planning policies are, of necessity, qualified and flexible requiring interpretation as each case arises. Planning may influence the extent, location, after-use and impact of minerals development. But the planning process is dependent on the social processes which ultimately determine the most basic questions of the use we make of the land.

ACKNOWLEDGEMENT

The author wishes to thank the Bedfordshire County Planning Department for advice and assistance in the preparation of this chapter.

NOTES

1. Chalk is not considered here. Chalk is quarried from the Chiltern Hills for use in cement production. The industry in Bedfordshire is of declining importance as production is now concentrated on Thames-side. Apart from one small local quarry the only remaining output is from Kensworth (Figure 5.2) which supplies 1 million tonnes per year via pipeline to the cement works at Rugby. The main problem with chalk is the number of abandoned quarries which scar the landscape of the chalk escarpment.
2. Production of aggregates in England and Wales rose fourfold between the 1940s and 1970s but has been declining more recently. Production figures were 77 million tonnes in 1955, 225 million tonnes in 1973 falling to 181 million tonnes in 1979 (Department of the Environment, 1982). For the southeast region the Verney Report (HMSO, 1976) forecast

demand at 88 million tonnes per year by the mid-1980s but the likely figure is now estimated at 67 million tonnes (Standing Conference on London and South East Regional Planning, 1979).

3. Six operators in Bedfordshire were believed to belong to the British Association of Construction Materials Industries (BACMI), three were in the Silica and Moulding Sand Association (SAMSA), one was a member of the Sand and Gravel Association (SAGA) and one was unaligned. Two operators had membership of two associations.

REFERENCES

Bedfordshire County Council (1967) *Bedfordshire Brick Field.*
Bedfordshire County Council (1978) *Mineral: Appraisal and Issues*, March.
Bedfordshire County Council (1980) *County Structure Plan.*
Bedfordshire County Council (1984a) *County Structure Plan: Proposed Alterations to Policies.*
Bedfordshire County Council (1984b) *Oxford Clay Subject Plan*, May.
Bedfordshire County Council (1985) *Waste Disposal Plan*, Consultation draft, April.
Blaikie, P. (1985) *Natural Resources and Social Change*, Unit 7, D205, Changing Britain, Changing World, Geographical Perspectives, Open University Press, Milton Keynes.
Blowers, A. (1980) *The Limits of Power: The Politics of Local Planning Policy*, Pergamon, Oxford.
Blowers, A. (1984) *Something in the Air: Corporate Power and the Environment*, Harper and Row, London.
Department of the Environment (1977) *Examination in Public of the Structure Plan for Bedfordshire.* Transcript of Proceedings, 21 December.
Department of the Environment (1978) *Proposed Extraction of Minerals from Land at Harrold Lodge Farm.* Report of the Inspector at the Inquiry, July.
Department of the Environment (1982) *Guidelines for Aggregates Provision in England and Wales*, Circular 21/82, August.
Goodin, R.E. (1976) *The Politics of Rational Man*, Wiley, London.
Harrison, L. (1984) *A Study of the Suitability of Callow for Reclamation.* Joint study sponsored by Bedfordshire County Council, London Brick Company and Imperial College, London.
HMSO (1976) *Aggregates: The Way Ahead.* Report of the Verney Committee. HMSO, London.
Land Capability Consultants (1983) *Quest Pit, Low Level Restoration*, May and *Thrupp End/ Estcheat Pit, Low Level Restoration*, July. Reports prepared for Bedfordshire County Council.
Newby, H. (1980) *Green and Pleasant Land?* Penguin, Harmondsworth.
Standing Conference on London and South East Regional Planning (1979) *Policy Guidelines to Meet the South East Region's Need for Aggregates in the 1990s.* Report by the Regional Aggregates Group, SC 1151R, July.

6

A CASE STUDY IN NATIONAL PARK PLANNING

J. Allan Patmore

THE NATIONAL PARK IDEAL

Though a nation of town dwellers, we retain at heart a romantic vision of rural paradise. In Marian Shoard's evocative words, 'England's countryside is not only one of the great treasures of the earth, it is also a vital part of our national identity . . . For hundreds of years, our English countryside has given us such ideas as we have had of what paradise might be like' (Shoard, 1980, p. 9). To secure the apogee of paradise in the heady years of postwar idealism, the 1949 National Parks and Access to the Countryside Act sought to enshrine, in the prosaic words of legislation, 'the purpose of preserving and enhancing the natural beauty of the areas specified . . . and . . . the purpose of promoting their enjoyment by the public' (Section 5-1).

All too frequently, reality has dulled that purity of purpose. As one observer recently noted, 'it has often been a confused scene with compromise and "fudge", exaggerated claims, political pragmatism, high hopes and faded dreams' (Cherry, 1985, p. 128). Of a wider public perception, 'the paradox remains that in the United Kingdom the title "National Park" has misled visitors and natives alike for more than 30 years, arousing fears that have little justification and expectations that it has not satisfied' (MacEwen and MacEwen, 1982, p. 6). Nor are these reservations the prerogative of independent observers alone. One National Park Committee sadly comments that:

> at present National Parks are working in a vacuum of policy guidance. Government agencies cover all . . . facets of National Park life . . . Each though, tends to pursue its own objectives with little reference and often in direct opposition to the others. This partisan approach may profit some people for some of the time but in the long run the only sure and probably irrevocable result will be the impoverishment and decline of the National Park to the detriment of all. The cri-de-coeur of this National Park is for co-ordinated government policy and appropriate machinery to make it work. (North York Moors National Park Committee, 1984a, p. 88)

In a national context, there is literature enough on the purposes and problems of Britain's National Parks, and there is no intention in this chapter of adding to that tally.

The aim is rather to examine the interpretation of purpose and the resolution of problems at local level, in order better to illuminate the wider generalities of the national scene. It is in consequence parochial and descriptive, for only at this scale do policies come to practical fruition. Further, considerations of space confine attention to a single park, the North York Moors, where the author has been an appointed member of the Park Committee for over nine years.

Such an approach inevitably neglects issues which are high on the agenda elsewhere, either because they are not within the immediate remit of the Park authority or because they have not been a major concern in this particular park. Those more familiar with the Lake District, for example, might well have expected a detailed treatment of the social implications of development control policies, not least in the lack of housing opportunities for local low-income groups, or again might have anticipated a much more positive approach, on a more intensive scale, to recreation provision. Neglect does not belie the importance of these and many other issues, but the chosen balance, within the confines of available space, is, for this observer at least, a fair reflection of the concerns which have dominated the agendas and the thinking of a specific Park Committee. Whether the agendas are balanced or complete is another, different debate!

THE PARK IN PERSPECTIVE

The ten National Parks of England and Wales cover 5250 sq miles, 9 per cent of the total area. The North York Moors National Park, designated in 1952, is very much of average size, being 553 sq miles in area. Its prime characteristics are the wide sweeps of open heather moorland rising to a maximum height of 1490 ft at Botton Head on Urra Moor. Moorland and upland heath occupy some 35 per cent of the Park as a whole. The moors are penetrated by the pastoral landscapes of the dales: these, the coastal fringe and the rich agricultural lands of the southern margin comprise the 40 per cent covered by enclosed farmland together with another 5 per cent of broad-leaved and mixed woodland. The third main land use is the 20 per cent devoted to commercial forestry plantations, by far the majority being the province of the Forestry Commission.

As with all the National Parks, the great majority (81 per cent) of the land remains in private ownership. The biggest public landowner is the Forestry Commission, with almost 17 per cent; the only other landowners of consequence are the National Trust and the National Park Authority, each with less than 1 per cent.

The Park Committee's role in managing the landscapes of the Park is inhibited not only by its lack of direct ownership, but by the restrictions imposed through its inherent powers, its adopted policies and its available funds. Legislation governing the first of these has been the subject of several reviews (Sheail, 1975; Cherry, 1975, 1985; MacEwen and MacEwen, 1982) and though it is the essential background to much that follows it is not considered directly here. The Park's policies in exercising its powers have evolved gradually since designation, but are set out in detail in the *National Park Plan* of 1977 and the *First Review* of the Plan of 1984. The impact of these policies in action forms the core of this chapter, but it must be preceded by a clear understanding of the most limiting factor of all — the amount of funds available to the Park Authority.

By any standards, the Park Authority's budget is modest when it is remembered that the Authority has a responsibility for managing the landscape of almost 1 per cent of

England and Wales. In 1985–86, its estimated *gross* expenditure was £1.2 million (North Yorkshire County Council, 1985) — only 0.4 per cent of that for North Yorkshire County Council as a whole. (Although 5 per cent of the Park lies within the county of Cleveland, and 16.7 per cent of its *net* rate-borne funding comes from that county, it is administered for National Park purposes through North Yorkshire.) Admittedly, the Park Committee has no direct part in the provision of such expensive local authority services as education, highways and transportation, police and social services, but for its prime functions as the local planning authority for the area of the Park and for its role in managing the area for National Park purposes, its funding is little enough.

Table 6.1 summarizes the balance sheet for 1983–84, the last complete year for which figures are available. As with all the Parks, 75 per cent of the *net* income of the North York Moors National Park comes from the national purse through the National Park supplementary grant. The scale of that support is very much in accord with the Park's size: in 1983–84 it received some 9 per cent of the total supplementary grant (Countryside Commission, 1984). The rate-borne support remains modest: £175 000 from North Yorkshire and £35 000 from Cleveland in the year in question. On the expenditure side, staffing is by far the largest single item. In March 1984, 65 full- and part-time staff were in post, and accounted for 53.4 per cent of *net* expenditure. It is against this financial background that the achievements of the Park Authority must, in part at least, be measured.

Table 6.1   North York Moors National Park Committee accounts, 1983–84 out-turn (data from North York Moors National Park Committee, 1985)

	£000	%
Income		
Receipts from users	157.0	15.3
Grants from national exchequer		
National Parks supplementary grant	629.9	61.5
Countryside Commission grants	27.0	2.7
Rates and non-specific grants	210.0	20.5
	1023.9	100.0
Expenditure		
Administration	441.4	43.1
(including development control)		
Field services	168.0	16.4
(including rangers, litter collection, footpath maintenance)		
Management services and grants	184.1	18.0
(including car parks, conveniences, conservation schemes)		
Information services	156.4	15.3
(including information centres and publicity)		
Capital works	74.0	7.2
	1023.9	100.0

THE BUILT LANDSCAPE

Prime tools of landscape management are the normal mechanisms of development control. The limitations of these mechanisms in a rural context are well known and need no detailed rehearsal here. Suffice it to recall that they are concerned largely with the *built* environment, that they can apply only when a change in land use or a major building alteration is contemplated, and that the control is essentially negative in nature. Indeed, the success of a development control policy must be measured more by what is not seen in the landscape than by what is seen.

The Park Committee is the planning authority for the area of the Park. The Park had a total population of 25 253 in 1981, and the total volume of planning applications is, understandably, not large. In 1984–85, out of 522 applications 417 (80 per cent) were approved. In the same year, the results of 32 appeals against refusals were notified: only 7 were allowed.

The landscape impact of development control policies is important at two quite different scales. The first relates to the spread and the pattern of settlement. The basic principles have been clearly articulated (North York Moors National Park Committee, 1980). In essence, there is general support for infilling within existing settlements and opposition to residential development in the open countryside unless required for agriculture. This accepts a generally nucleated pattern of settlement, with farmsteads the only exception to a presumption against dispersal. Such policies are continually under pressure by those not engaged in agriculture who seek to utilize an attractive, and often isolated, site for their dwelling. Few of the more blatant suggestions are pressed to the point of a formally submitted application, but there are frequent attempts to extend defined planning limits around particular villages so as to include a marginal site.

In one particular aspect, the presumption against dispersal is justifiably breached. One legacy of the changing techniques and economics of modern agriculture, even in the more marginal upland areas, is the creation of a surplus of farm buildings, due either to the amalgamation of holdings or the unsuitability of existing buildings. In this context, the conscious planning policy is to value the retention of the basic structure, provided it is not an isolated barn, more highly than the avoidance of population dispersion. Housing policy 13 states in part: 'The conversion of non-residential buildings to residential and other appropriate uses will normally be supported within existing settlements or farmsteads and small groups of buildings. It will be resisted with isolated buildings.' The scope for such conversions is considerable. In the period 1977–81, 135 applications for conversions were approved, of which 103 were for dwellings, 21 being specifically for holiday accommodation (North York Moors National Park Committee, 1981a). It is not known how many of these conversions were outside existing village limits, though the presumption is that the majority were so located. Thirty-five of the buildings in question were already disused.

This emphasis on the visual rather than the functional aspects of the Park's landscape is even more marked at the scale of building detail rather than building location. The use of local stone and red clay pantiles, coupled with traditional building styles which were slow to change, has given strong, readily recognizable forms of local architecture. The policy implications of this tradition have long been seen clearly by the

Committee: 'This strong local architectural tradition contributes much to the character of the settlement in the Park and needs to be respected by new construction' (North York Moors National Park Committee, 1980, p. 71). The problem, of course, is the meaning of 'respect'. The use of traditional materials, despite the cost penalty it involves, is generally accepted, albeit at times grudgingly, by developers. The details of design occasion more debate. The Committee's policy advice notes that 'traditional designs should not merely be copied' for this is 'architecturally somewhat sterile', but goes no further than stating that 'it takes considerable skill to design new buildings which are sympathetic with what is already there and the skill lies in relating elements of the new design to the locality's traditional architecture.'

The publication of a design guide, *Housing in the National Park*, has been a major help, but decisions in the end must rest on the perceptions of the Committee in discussing a particular application. These decisions have tended to be of a fairly conservative nature, and there is always a clear danger of attempting to fossilize the built landscape of the Park. The Committee is often reminded that there are other perceptions. A case in point was the Committee's resistance to the growing practice of installing 'Dutch' canopy-type blinds over commercial premises. One refusal, in Castleton, was taken to appeal in 1980, and the appeal was upheld. The Inspector commented: 'On the question of design . . . the local planning authority would prefer a straightforward retractable blind . . . the canopy shape has, in my opinion, become more usual for cafes and baker's shops . . . In my opinion the colour of the proposed blind is more important in the local context than the shape.' The result, in 1981, was a new policy adopted by the Committee specifically relating to blinds: it retained control over colour, but noted that 'where the principle of a blind is acceptable, then either a suitably coloured retractable or canopy blind would be acceptable'.

MOORLAND LANDSCAPES

Important though the details of the built landscape are in the Park, there are other far more vital considerations where the limitations of the planning process are much more acute. In the context of the North York Moors, this is nowhere more clearly seen than with the moorland itself — the wide, open sweeps of heather-covered plateaux which give the Park its basic character and which were the prime reason for its initial designation.

The exact extent of the moorland has long been subject to change (Statham, 1972; Parry *et al.*, 1982) but the scale of change since designation has not only been threateningly large (Figure 6.1) but shows few signs of abating. In simple arithmetic terms, the moorland covered 47.3 per cent of the Park in 1950, but only 35.1 per cent in 1983: in other words, more than one-quarter (25.9 per cent) of the moorland at the time of designation has disappeared. Conversion has been to both agriculture and forestry, the former accounting for 29 per cent and the latter 71 per cent of the converted area. The pace of conversion seems to have slowed a little, with only 4.4 per cent of the remaining area converted between 1975 and 1983, but the basic threat remains acute. It has been estimated (North York Moors National Park Committee, 1982) that of the remaining moorland, 87 per cent is technically capable of conversion: about 85 per cent could be afforested and 33 per cent could be improved for agriculture.

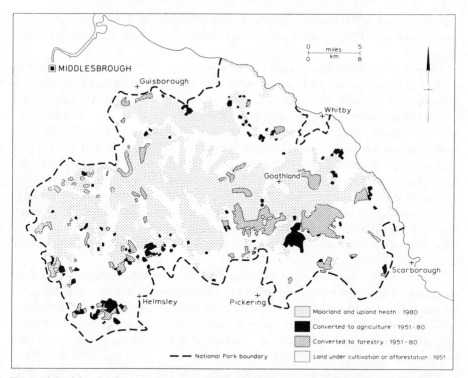

Figure 6.1   Moorland conversion in the North York Moors National Park 1951–80 (data from North York Moors National Park Committee, 1982, map 4).

The threat is not only from conversion. Parts of the moorland are themselves in physical decline. A survey in 1980 highlighted problems of erosion and degradation. It was then estimated that 19 per cent of the moorland, a total of 38 sq miles, should be classed as 'eroded, eroding or degrading', and 8 sq miles were 'in danger of being totally lost'. The biggest single problem was over-aged, undermanaged heather, liable to burn hot and deep, damaging or destroying the peat soils of the moorland. The root of the problem lies in the economic and social changes of the past 50 years, which have resulted in decreased management activity on the one hand and increased recreational use on the other. Reduced labour forces and increasing costs mean that the moorland landowners and the flockmasters can no longer deal with large tracts of vegetation in the traditional ways. Heather is burned less regularly, with an attendant high fire risk from the old, woody plants, and with an increasing incursion of bracken by some 300 acres per year.

All these threats strike at the very heart of the crucial landscapes of the Park, for in theoretical terms at least, no less than 95 per cent of open moorland could be, or is being lost. As the 1984 *Plan Review* makes clear, the Park Committee is fully 'aware of the threats to the continued existence of moorland and upland heath' (p. 12) and declares that 'conversion . . . will almost always conflict with the conservation objectives of the National Park Committee' (p. 11). Awareness and action, however, cannot be coincident if the powers for action are lacking or inadequate. In the context of the present chapter, it is the use of the powers available which is the real concern. Three routes to moorland conservation must be considered: demonstration, consultation and ownership.

The impact of changing management regimes has already been noted, in particular the lack of regular, controlled heather burning by landowners. Part of the problem is the sheer cost of labour, but in some areas this has been compounded by a decline in the number of sheep grazing on the open moor. On moorland adjacent to the main A169 Whitby–Pickering road, sheep numbers decreased from 3976 in 1959 to 2210 in 1981. In the same period, the number of sheep killed on the road increased from 215 per year (5.4 per cent of the flock) to 325 (14.7 per cent). To alleviate this problem, the Committee agreed, despite the opposition of the Countryside Commission, 'to raise no objections to proposals to fence the A169' (policy PP7) though 'it remained opposed to fencing on all other open roads' considering that 'the advantages to agriculture do not outweigh the disadvantages in landscape and recreational terms' (policy PP8). The Commission subsequently changed its position to a stance identical with that of the Committee.

Such measures alone are no cure for the more deep-rooted problems of moorland condition. The Committee obviously has limited powers in this connection, but recognizes the need for changed management regimes. It therefore established a Moorland Management Programme, with the aim of increasing knowledge through experimental work and field trials, as a means of demonstrating to landowners the worth of a range of practical techniques.

The most compelling of demonstrations, however, is no substitute for more positive powers. There have long been those who argue that in such sensitive areas of landscape as National Parks, major land-use changes within the agricultural sector, for example those involved in moorland conversion, should be subject to some form of development control. In the event, no such powers are available. One significant change, however, came in October 1980 when the Ministry of Agriculture, Fisheries and Food (MAFF) revised its capital grant procedures and among other conditions stipulated that within National Parks farmers must consult the Park Authority about their proposals and obtain its agreement before commencing work. Such consultations, of course, relate to the whole of the agricultural area: the vast majority are concerned with normal agricultural operations on cultivated land and no objections are raised. In the period October 1984–March 1985, for example, 154 notifications were dealt with by the Park Authority, and no comments were made on 144 (93.5 per cent). In 8 cases, minor modifications were requested, 6 relating to the colour of buildings. In only 2 cases were objections raised, both relating to moorland — one notification of moorland reclamation, the other of moorland enclosure.

Where objections are raised, the 1981 Wildlife and Countryside Act requires (Section 41) the objecting authority to offer a management agreement restricting the use of the land and paying compensation for the losses involved due to the refusal of grant aid. In the eyes of many observers, this Section 'turned the Act from an indifferent one to a bad one' (Gilg, 1982). Acceptance of the agreement is entirely voluntary for the applicant, the compensation prescribed is relatively generous and the protection afforded only lasts for the currency of the agreement.

Experience has enhanced concern about this provision of the Act, especially where protection of the moorland landscape is concerned. Though objections by the Park Authority under the consultation procedure are few — only 19 in the period October 1980 – March 1985 — a majority (63 per cent) have related to moorland reclamation. In several of these, an agreement has been refused by the applicant and the work has proceeded regardless even if the MAFF grant is not available. Even when agreements are entered into, they involve much time in negotiation and are an expensive drain on the Committee's limited resources without yielding long-term safeguards. Exasperation led the Committee, despite the strong farming element in its membership, in its evidence to the House of Commons Environment Committee in 1984, 'to see no alternative in cases of basic land use change, such as the ploughing of moorland and the draining of wetlands, to a system of control analogous to planning control. This would not only be a less expensive system but a much more efficient one . . .'

One other provision of the Act needs mention in a moorland context. Section 43 requires the production of a map 'showing any areas of moor or heath the natural beauty of which it is, in the opinion of the authority, particularly important to conserve' (North York Moors National Park Committee, 1984b). How effective such a declaration will be remains to be seen, for the designation carries no additional protection.

Demonstration and consultation have evident and worrying limitations as mechanisms for conserving the moorland landscape. The only real security is for ownership to be vested in the hands of a landowner with moorland conservation at heart. In practice, the situation in the Moors is perhaps less gloomy than might at first appear to be the case, for no less than 61 per cent of the moorland has some form of protection against land-use change, though the effectiveness of that protection varies widely (Table 6.2). There is no space to consider these categories in detail, but the role of the Park Committee itself deserves comment. Ownership by the Committee is obviously the highest safeguard which can be offered to any part of the moorland landscape, but any extension of ownership faces two obstacles — the first political, the second the practical issue of resources.

In practical terms, Committee ownership is only an option in the most crucial areas, and the most important has been in the heart of the Park, adjacent to the A169 road at Saltersgate. In 1975–76, the Committee acquired the 2095 acres of Levisham Moor and the Hole of Horcum, an area of outstanding landscape value and heavily used for recreation. Here an unsuccessful attempt had been made by a consortium of farmers to buy out the common rights with a view to ploughing and land improvement, and the

Table 6.2 North York Moors: protected moorland 1983 (data from North York Moors National Park Committee, 1984a)

Category	% of total moorland
National Park ownership	1.6
National Trust ownership	0.4
Yorkshire Wildlife Trust ownership	0.1
Sites of Special Scientific Interest	6.6
Capital Transfer Tax exemption area	12.1
Common land (finally and provisionally registered)	49.4
Total (avoiding overlapping categories)	61.1

Committee's action was largely in response to this threat. A more disputed acquisition was that of the 328 acres of Nab Farm, alongside the A169 northeast of Levisham, in 1980. It was advertised for sale with reclamation potential and, by a slender majority, the Committee agreed to purchase, aided by a grant from the Countryside Commission of 50 per cent of the purchase price (£90 000 at auction). The heated debate led swiftly to a debate later that year (instigated by the County Council) on the whole principle of land acquisition. For the purposes of landscape protection this would only be 'as a last resort', when 'alternative courses of action would not provide acceptable safeguards or would be prohibitively expensive'. It is not clear whether it was this debate or changing attitudes to conservation which resulted in the Committee's purchase of the 908 acres of the adjacent Lockton High Moor in 1985 with little dissent in principle. The prime obstacle was raising the purchase price of £150 000 — well beyond the Committee's means — but this was finally reached with the assistance of grants of £97 500 from the National Heritage Memorial Fund and £7500 from the Nature Conservancy Council. It is interesting to note in this case that if the alternative approach of a management agreement had been pursued, it is likely that compensation would have been of the order of £15 000 per year with no guarantee of long-term landscape security.

FARM LANDSCAPES

While the moorland is, in more ways than one, the heart of the Park, enclosed, cultivated land is not only more extensive but in the dales and fringing lowlands gives the landscape much of its character. Even in what are often marginal farming conditions, that landscape has not been immune to change. In one parish alone, Cold Kirby in the southwest of the Park, 13 per cent of all field boundaries disappeared in the period 1972–79, and smaller sample areas have shown losses of up to 25 per cent.

Beyond normal issues of development control, the Park Committee has little impact on the cultivated land though grant-aid schemes such as those for tree planting, woodland management and wildlife conservation are available. Two further initiatives deserve a more extended mention showing how even modest inputs can have significant landscape impact. The Upland Management Scheme was established in the Park in 1977. Its functions are, first, to help farmers bear the cost of maintaining important landscape features such as stone walls which are not justified by modern agricultural practice and, second, to offset the cost to the farmer of heavy recreational use, causing, for example, eroded field entrances and access paths. The scale of grant is small (only £16 000 in total in 1983–84), but the goodwill generated in the farming community towards Park purposes far outweighs the modest cost.

The second initiative is more recent. In 1985 the Committee instigated a scheme for farm conservation plans. The starting point is individual farmers' own proposals for the management of their land. An assessment is then made by Park staff of the landscape and wildlife values of the farm, and suggestions made as to how these might best be conserved within the context of the farm plan as a whole. Implementation is a matter for the individual farmers, but partnership in planning brings their assent and active cooperation in the basic aims of landscape and nature conservation for the Park as a whole.

RECREATION PATTERNS

Landscape conservation is but one side of the National Park coin: the other is the duty 'to promote the enjoyment of the National Park by the visitor'. In retrospect, it is curious that the 1949 Act used the word 'promotion', with its connotation of positive development, and a seeming lack of recognition that landscape conservation and the promotion of visitor enjoyment might be, on occasion, mutually incompatible. However, the pressures engendered by the growth of countryside recreation in the 1960s and 1970s were scarcely foreseen in the late 1940s. The Act was rather a reflection of the values and patterns of the 1930s, when G.M. Trevelyan could write, in 1938, of the essential need 'to preserve for the nation walking grounds and regions where young and old can enjoy the sight of unspoiled nature. And it is not a question of physical exercise only, it is also a question of spiritual exercise and enjoyment' (Cherry, 1975, p. 15). In practice, it was not walkers but car-borne hordes who came seeking rural pleasuring grounds, their very numbers in danger of 'spoiling what they go to the countryside to seek' (Minister of Land and Natural Resources, 1966, p. 4).

The balance between promotion and protection in providing for recreation has always been difficult to strike for National Park authorities, and the problem is not made easier by budget restrictions. The first essential is a clear picture of the scale and pattern of visitor pressure. In the North York Moors, visitor numbers appear to have reached a peak by the early 1970s and to have remained at approximately the same level since that date (North York Moors National Park Committee, 1981b). In 1973, surveys in the Park suggested an annual total of some 11.3 million visitors, in 1979, 11.1 million. A typical August Sunday in 1980 saw an estimated total of 137 500 visitors in the Park.

Numbers alone, of course, give little indication of pressure. Over the Park as a whole, such daily totals would mean an average of roughly one visitor per 2.5 acres, but in reality patterns show great extremes of pressure. A large proportion (28 per cent) of visitors have Scarborough or Whitby as their prime destination, and simply travel through the Park to get there, albeit enjoying the scenery en route. It is noteworthy in this context that the Park is above all a haunt for day trippers as opposed to holiday visitors (the latter forming only 18 per cent of the total on a typical summer Sunday), and the biggest single contributor of visitors is the county of Cleveland (30 per cent of the total in 1979). Both main routes from Teesside to Whitby and Scarborough (A171 and A174) pass through the Park. Another group of visitors uses the roads of the Park as a scenic drive; and as many as 21 per cent of the total do not stop during their travels. Virtually half of all visitors, therefore, use the road network for movement in the Park, but place little demand on its other facilities.

The other half of the visitor total comprises those who stop in the Park for a substantial period, and for whom the Park Authority may have to make increased provision. About one-fifth of all visitors (21 per cent) arrive by car, but choose to park either on their own or in a small group, whether to relax, picnic or walk. Such visitors who 'seek the quietness of the more open parts of the National Park . . . require few facilities since sophisticated provision would destroy the atmosphere they are seeking' (North York Moors National Park Committee, 1984a, p. 36).

The remaining 30 per cent of visitors pose the greatest potential problem. They arrive by car and make their way towards one of the traditional centres of attraction. This resulting pattern of 'honeypot' concentration is nothing like as marked as in some other National Parks, not least because there are no major urban centres within the Park boundary, but it still causes evident management concerns. This group of visitors is distributed through only 24 locations, and almost one-quarter of all visitors is found in only 14 locations, all of which may expect to have in excess of 100 cars parked on an August Sunday afternoon. The 14 sites are well scattered through the Park: 5 are in open country, but the remainder are concentrated in the villages and small towns. Surprisingly, only 3 sites (Robin Hood's Bay, Runswick Bay and Staithes) are on the coast, but the major resorts and points of access, Scarborough and Whitby in particular, are outside the boundary of the Park.

The spatial concentration of visitors is matched by a seasonal concentration. Some 58 per cent of all visits are in the months of July, August and September, with 25 per cent in August alone.

RECREATION POLICIES

Visitor concentrations are matched by funding concentration. As the 1984 *Plan Review* comments, the Park Committee

> has traditionally provided facilities for all-comers when the circumstances have made it appropriate but now, in a different financial era . . . not all recreational groups can expect an equal slice of the cake, nor even a slice at all, so it is important to establish priorities to guide the limited funds available for recreational facilities. Such priorities cannot be established by an assessment of the relative level of 'enjoyment' of each group because 'enjoyment' is not proportional to the resources needed. (North York Moors National Park Committee, 1984a, pp 36–37)

Current priorities are clearly enunciated:

1. Work in the areas of concentrated recreational activity which will lead to an increased enjoyment by the visitors; improvements to the local landscape; and benefits to local residents and landowners by diverting demand.
2. Restorative work to those smaller areas, often in the open countryside, which are subject to erosion by car parking and visitor pressures.
3. Assistance and promotion of public transport to and within the Park.

It is important to put these policies into practical perspective. In a National Park, there is rarely a need, and even less often a justification, for capital intensive works on an urbanized scale. Modest car parks, toilet blocks and simple interpretative facilities are sufficient. It is not only limited resources which constrain a capital programme. In its 1986–90 capital programme, the Park Committee envisaged no more than the building of two car parks, three toilet blocks, a refreshment bar to expand the facilities of an existing visitor centre, and basic access and landscape works at the recently acquired site of Cawthorn Roman camps. The total sums involved are modest, only £268 000 over the period at 1985 prices. Put in a different way, this is only the equivalent of 0.6p per anticipated visitor!

RECREATION PROVISION

Recreation provision is not, of course, limited to capital works alone, nor is the car-borne visitor the only one for whom there is practical provision. A simple catalogue would serve little purpose, but three other areas of recreational work deserve passing mention.

Perhaps the most passionate concern of the pioneers of the National Park movement was freedom of access to the wilder parts of the country. The legacy of that concern is the Park Committee's responsibility for the footpath network (though technically it is only the footpath authority for those parts of the Park in North Yorkshire). But that responsibility has its own dilemmas. The network is extensive — some 1100 miles — and the Committee's resources are unequal to the task of maintaining the whole network to a high standard. The policy again is one of selectivity. A threefold hierarchy of paths was established between 1977 and 1983, as a practical response to the problem. The available resources for patrolling and maintenance are used most intensively on the first category, and attempts are made to concentrate use on these paths by waymarking and the provision of leaflets.

Even this degree of selectivity brings its problems. The most noted path on the Moors is the Lyke Wake Walk, though much of it has a *de facto* rather than a *de jure* right of access. It runs for some 42 miles across the highest part of the Moors, and by 1981 there were 7681 successful crossings in the year and perhaps three times that number using it in whole or in part. The effect of such heavy visitor pressure on the fragile deep peat surface of the highest sections was severe: parts of the path were more than 300 ft wide in places and the damage was serious in both a visual and an ecological sense. Full remedial works would have been prohibitively expensive as well as visually intrusive, and the alternative course was taken of asking walkers, through intensive publicity, to use alternative routes. While the problem is by no means solved, usage fell by 50 per cent in three years.

A second major thrust of work is through interpretation. Of particular importance here are the two visitor centres maintained by the Committee at Sutton Bank and Danby Lodge. The latter illustrates some of the dilemmas of provision. A former hunting lodge whose grounds are themselves an attractive venue, the house contains a major interpretative display, lecture rooms, bookshop and a refreshment room. To maximize income, an admission charge was made even though such a charge might well exclude (as research suggested) those visitors to the Moors most likely to need the basic information and interpretation 'message' of the exhibition. In practice, this policy meant a substantial subsidy to every visitor who came: in 1981, the net cost of running the centre was £44 500 for some 35 000 visitors, though not all costs directly related to work at Danby Lodge. For 1984, a new policy was adopted of free admission but reduced staffing. The results fully justified the experiment. Visitor numbers increased by 25 per cent against a general decline in visitors to comparable attractions elsewhere in the Park, much more was spent on literature and souvenirs, and the crude subsidy fell to some 14p per visitor. This policy represented a much more cost-effective approach to the interpretation function and, at least as important, removed any financial obstacle to visitors receiving the interpretation 'message'. As part of the package, some of the resources released were used to appoint a youth and schools liaison officer, bringing the interpretation 'message' to a much wider audience both within and beyond the Park.

The recreational aspects of planning need one final comment. The open uplands, with *de facto* access for much of their extent, provide an attractive venue for a wide range of active outdoor pursuits, giving rise to conflicts with other visitors, with the primary agricultural users of the Park and with conservation ideals. The policy again is one of selectivity. The 1984 *Plan Review* is clear in this context: 'the Committee neither can nor should cater for all activities: it has never been part of the National Park philosophy to match, automatically, recreational demands but rather to temper those demands to the ability of the landscape to absorb them' (p. 37). In practice, conflicts have been few, and highly localized. One of the more embarrassing was the impact of hang gliding on the Committee's own land at the Hole of Horcum. As the sport developed in the 1970s, this was seen as an ideal site, and the National Championships were held there in 1976. To provide a measure of control over this adventitious use, planning permission was required (though the need for this was not legally tested): it was granted in 1977 on a temporary basis and renewed in 1980. On the latter occasion, reservations were expressed by conservation interests and it soon became evident that these reservations were justified with serious erosion taking place on the take-off and landing areas on the slopes of the Hole. Options varied from artificial surfacing of the area to a complete ban on hang gliding, however difficult to enforce. In the event, a compromise was adopted: hang gliding was permitted for a further period, but was restricted in location and limited to experienced pilots, avoiding the frequent landings which had been the major cause of erosion. The problem of course remains as to where pilots can gain experience: the solution shifts the problem rather than solves it.

PARK PLANNING IN PERSPECTIVE

This account of National Park planning in practice has been inevitably fragmentary and descriptive. It has been deliberately wide ranging, to illustrate the kaleidoscope of issues which concern the Park Authority, but many issues remain without mention, not least those concerning the economic health of the area. The account has also focused on outcome rather than process. The Park officers work to coherent objectives and with clear policy guidelines, but Committee members can debate only those issues which are placed before them for decision. In this Park at least, the debates are keen but objective and constructive, with overt political considerations rarely intruding. Nonetheless, emphases inevitably change, and while it would be unrealistic to claim complete consistency through the fragmentary process of decision-making, broad concerns are clearly evident. A growing appreciation of the conservation ethic is one such concern, seen not least in a more ready acceptance of the need, in the last resort, for the control through ownership of critical land areas. Another is the recognition that National Park purposes are not always best served by maximizing revenue at the visitor's expense.

The achievements in the Park, however, must not be measured by the consistency or the direction of policy, or even by the effectiveness of planning principles in practice. Rather they must be judged by the quality of the landscape more than 30 years after designation and by the quality of recreational experience still enjoyed by visitors. Park authorities — and Park committees — have many critics but by these measures, however intangible, they have also much of which to be proud. The vision of the progenitors of the 1930s and 1940s is still largely intact, though the threats to it remain no less acute.

ACKNOWLEDGEMENTS

I gratefully acknowledge the most helpful comments of the National Park Officer, Derek C. Statham, on the first draft of this chapter.

REFERENCES

Cherry, G.E. (1975) *Environmental Planning*, Vol. II, *National Parks and Recreation in the Countryside*, HMSO, London.

Cherry, G.E. (1985) Scenic heritage and national parks lobbies and legislation in England and Wales, *Leisure Studies*, Vol. 4, 127–139.

Countryside Commission (1984) *Annual Report: the Seventeenth Report of the Countryside Commission, 1983–84*, Cheltenham.

Gilg, A.W. (1982) *Countryside Planning Yearbook, 1982*, Geo Abstracts, Norwich.

MacEwen, A. and MacEwen, M. (1982) *National Parks: Conservation or Cosmetics?*, George Allen and Unwin, London.

Minister of Land and Natural Resources (1966) *Leisure in the Countryside: England and Wales*, Cmnd 2928, HMSO, London.

North York Moors National Park Committee (1977) *North York Moors National Park Plan*, Helmsley.

North York Moors National Park Committee (1980) *North York Moors Local Plan: a District Plan for the North York Moors National Park within North Yorkshire*, Helmsley.

North York Moors National Park Committee (1981a) *The Management of Enclosed Agricultural Land*, Helmsley.

North York Moors National Park Committee (1981b) *Patterns of Informal Recreation in the North York Moors National Park*, Helmsley.

North York Moors National Park Committee (1982) *The Future of the Moorland*, Helmsley.

North York Moors National Park Committee (1984a) *North York Moors National Park Plan First Review*, Helmsley.

North York Moors National Park Committee (1984b) *Moor and Heath Conservation in the North York Moors*, Helmsley.

North York Moors National Park Committee (1985) *Annual Report*, April 83–March 84, Helmsley.

North Yorkshire County Council (1985) *Budget for the year ending 31 March 1986 and summary of accounts for the year ending 31 March 1984*, Northallerton.

Parry, M.L., Bruce, A. and Harkness, C.E. (1982) *Surveys of Moorland and Roughland Change*, No. 5, *Changes in the Extent of Moorland and Roughland in the North York Moors*, Department of Geography, University of Birmingham.

Sheail, J. (1975) The concept of national parks in Great Britain, 1900–1950, *Transactions of the Institute of British Geographers*, Vol. 66, 41–56.

Shoard, M. (1980) *The Theft of the Countryside*, Maurice Temple-Smith, London.

Statham, D.C. (1972) *Land Use Changes in the Moorlands of the North York Moors National Park*, Centre for Environmental Studies, London.

7

A BIAS FOR ACTION: INDUSTRIAL DEVELOPMENT IN MID WALES*

Paul Pettigrew

INTRODUCTION

Formal development efforts in Mid Wales go back to 1957 with the founding of the pioneering Mid Wales Industrial Development Association (MWIDA). This was a grass roots local authority initiative to 'do something' about the severe loss of the region's population, especially young people, in the context of a backward postwar agricultural economy presenting few job opportunities as capital rapidly replaced labour (Garbett-Edwards, 1972, 1979; Mid Wales Industrial Development Association, 1973). Ever since those early years, development efforts in Mid Wales have consistently emphasized the importance of taking direct action to create and maintain jobs in order to allow people the opportunity of remaining in the region and also attracting people from elsewhere to live and work in Mid Wales (Development Board for Rural Wales, 1979a, 1978–1985).

Any success is all the more remarkable given the modest resources that have been made available by government for development in Mid Wales, and the fact that the region itself contained no intrinsic development potential or history of entrepreneurship apart from farming (Development Board for Rural Wales, 1980a). The region, generally, remains unattractive to private investment without public subsidy in almost every sector.

The purpose of this chapter is to outline briefly the historical influences on recent development efforts in the region, and to provide a flavour of the constant interaction and conflict resolution between the need for action on the one hand, and the exigencies of ensuring that this action accords to a coherent and integrated framework. The recurring theme in development work is 'What development, where, how, for whom and to what effect?' Inevitably the answers to these questions rarely fit neatly into any preconceived notion of tidy strategy or policy implementation. Needs and opportunities both play their part in shaping the type and location of investment. Yet the results of

---

* The views expressed are those of the author and not necessarily those of Mid Wales Development.

some 28 years of industrial development in Mid Wales vindicate and reflect the consistent philosophy of approach and strategic spatial investment policy which have been in operation since 1968.

The evolution of this strategy is considered along with an explanation of the more pragmatic means to achieve it. Alongside the 'nitty gritty' of how the Development Board for Rural Wales (DBRW) carries out the industrial development job, in this chapter an attempt is made to relate this to policy and organizational issues which in turn influence the nature, scale and location of action 'on the ground'. Wherever appropriate, the facts and figures of the DBRW's development success are highlighted in the context of a generalized exposition of the Board's approach to practical industrial development.

HISTORICAL INFLUENCES

The Development Board for Rural Wales (known, for promotion purposes, as Mid Wales Development [MWD]) is the latest stage of an evolutionary process of regional development in Mid Wales in terms of regional economic and organizational development. A full account of the Board's lineage is provided elsewhere (e.g. Garbett-Edwards, 1979; Broady, 1980 a, b) but it is important to pick out some important tenets of policy and action which emerged during this evolutionary process and which are still highly relevant to the way in which MWD conducts its industrial development programmes.

The most important threads to pick up from the region's recent history of economic development are:

1. Development stemmed from genuine *grass roots* concern to promote economic development in order to stem depopulation. MWIDA was an association formed by the region's local authorities.
2. The evolutionary process led to increasing awareness of the region's problems, the realization that structural change was needed, and an increasing impatience to get on with the job of taking action to solve the depopulation problem, the causes of which were well understood.
3. The lobbying of MWIDA led to increasing government recognition that depopulation could be solved only by the application of central government policy and resources. Progress was achieved through the building of advance factories (1964); the designation of Mid Wales as a Development Area (1966); the creation of the Mid Wales Development Corporation (MWDC) in 1967 to develop Newtown under New Towns Act powers; and 10 years later the formation of the current regional development agency, DBRW.
4. The longevity and robustness of the region's development strategy have survived, virtually unchanged in principle, since the Beacham Committee reported in 1964.
5. The increased sophistication since 1977 in the way the job of industrial development is carried out has been remarkable. The pace of development has increased markedly with a highly professional approach to industrial marketing and development. In addition there has been a marked shift in the range and scope of the Board's efforts, undiminished by deep recession in the national economy and the virtual withdrawal of regional policy aids from the area.

6.   The creation of DBRW was the culmination of a steady progression from grass
     roots initiative to state-sponsored agency. The *quid pro quo* was a government
     commitment to far greater resources for the region's development channelled
     through a board responsible for the social and economic development of Mid
     Wales. The benefits thus derived to tackle the region's problems far outweighed
     the consequent requirement of the Board to be answerable to government through
     the Welsh Office.

THE DEVELOPMENT BOARD FOR RURAL WALES

The Development Board for Rural Wales (DBRW) began operations in April 1977. Its
area of responsibility extends to the district of Ceredigion in Dyfed, Meirionnydd in
Gwynedd, and the whole of the county of Powys (Brecknock, Montgomery and
Radnor) (Figure 7.1). The Development of Rural Wales Act 1976 gave the Board
powers 'to promote the social and economic well-being of the people of Mid Wales'.
The Act encompasses and consolidates all the previous economic activity in Mid
Wales, and in many ways can be seen as a New Towns Act adapted for a region. The
scope of the Act does not allow the Board to be directly involved in agriculture or
forestry; it emphasizes the Board's ability to buy land, construct property and provide
services; it provides no power for the Board itself to provide assistance to firms in its
area, but it does include the power to build houses to complement its industrial
factory-building activities. In other words, the Act is very much a product of regional
development thinking of the 1960s and 1970s — with a continuation of factory-
building very much in mind with little reference to the broader powers required of a
modern development agency to carry out wider forms of development in a rural area
(e.g. tourism, agriculture, infrastructure development, etc.). Thus, while the 1976 Act
continues to be of value to the industrial development process, it tends to lend itself to
restrictive interpretation in other sectors.

   With a commitment, therefore, to continue to concentrate on industrial development
following its formation in 1977, the Board devoted nearly all of its resources (then in the
region of £6 million) to the attraction of industry, principally from outside the region.
The Board had inherited 36 empty factories from its predecessors, but within its first
two years had let 71 (Development Board for Rural Wales, 1978, 1979). This
successful beginning has blossomed, despite the onset of recession in 1979, a static
budget and unhelpful regional policy, to the situation where the Board now owns 422
factories (excluding 33 that have been sold) totalling some 1.9 million sq ft. The
factories (and indeed some 85 per cent of Board expenditure) are concentrated in a
number of growth and special towns. This — perhaps unusually in comparison with
structure and local plans — represents a very close connection between Board policy
for the region (Development Board for Rural Wales, 1979a) and the policy's actual
implementation. The estimates of total DBRW expenditure on industrial development
are shown in Table 7.1.

   The Board's success in developing an area with no history of entrepreneurship or
industry is testimony to its commitment to stick to a chosen strategy. The Board has
concentrated on those activities which would best meet its objectives of stemming
depopulation and encouraging repopulation, by providing and maintaining jobs,

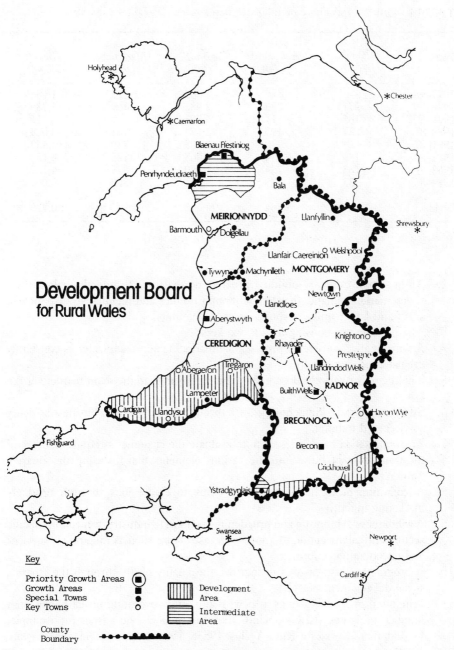

Figure 7.1 Map showing area of responsibility of the Development Board for Rural Wales.

increasing incomes and improving the quality of life.

A number of interrelated factors account for this success:

1. Concentration of resources both functionally and spatially, linked to direct intervention in the local economy.

Table 7.1   DBRW expenditure on industrial development 1977/78 – 1984/85

Year	Land (£000)	Site development (£000)	Construction (£000)	Marketing (£000)	Total (£000)
1977–78	—	50	1,482	125	1,657
1978–79	371	278	2,983	107	3,739
1979–80	165	517	4,703	91	5,476
1980–81	37	193	2,673	121	3,024
1981–82	68	220	2,905	239	3,432
1982–83	130	534	3,365	125	4,154
1983–84	163	734	2,860	425	4,182
1984–85	133	978	3,641	309	5,061
Total	1,067	3,504	24,612	1,542	30,725

2. An imaginative factory-building programme that tries to find the balance between market demand, development opportunities and regional strategy needs; small and larger units; bespoke and advance units.
3. The provision of housing for key workers.
4. An imaginative and highly professional marketing approach which is constantly evaluated against results.
5. The region's relatively close geographical proximity to the main markets of the UK.
6. Strong support for indigenous growth through the provision of business advisory services and training.
7. An emphasis on market research to evaluate the customer's requirements, and the translation of these into the various elements that make up the Board's 'product'.
8. A commitment to help indigenous firms to create jobs through product-marketing initiatives.
9. A willingness to innovate and broaden the support to industry by tackling specific sectors and taking action to improve infrastructure such as rail and air services and telecommunications.
10. A programme of measures to improve the quality of life through the Board's social development powers.
11. Promotion of Mid Wales as a 'new' region and advocating on its behalf on a number of issues (EEC, upland, transport policies etc.) (see, for example, Development Board for Rural Wales, 1983a, 1984a; Countryside Commission, 1984).

It may seem that none of these factors is especially novel. It is true there is no magic wand, no formula that can be applied in any geographical context. Much depends on the nature of the region. In the case of Mid Wales, for example, continuity of spatial policy and the region's close proximity to major markets are very favourable elements supporting the Board's industrial development efforts. The following sections briefly discuss how these activities are organized and implemented in practice.

CONCENTRATION OF RESOURCES

The Board's spatial investment strategy responds to the fact that there must be some degree of concentration of its limited resources if results are to be achieved. Neither the extremes of concentrating all the Board's resources in one settlement (e.g. Newtown) nor attempting to support even the majority of settlements in its area would be politically acceptable or economically rational. The Board's hierarchical system of growth areas, special towns and key towns, where most of the Board's units are built, continues the established strategy for the region and perhaps can best be described as 'dispersed concentration' (Moseley, 1974) (see Figure 7.1).

Policies of concentration have been used in a wide variety of geographical and economic contexts and in pursuit of a wide variety of policy objectives. They are not without their critics. Gilder (1979) has, for example, questioned the merits of concentration policies as a means of achieving economies of scale in the provision of public services. Martin and Voorhees Associates (1980) and Cloke (1979) have also questioned the validity of policies of concentration to achieve widely disparate objectives.

The Board, however, takes a very pragmatic view of the policy in the belief that the existing settlement pattern cannot be fossilized and that the support of *every* settlement in the region is neither cost effective nor practically feasible. As with any other business, local authority or government department, scarce resources have been channelled to the places where growth potential exists or has been perceived to exist. Growth potential encompasses both physical capability and potential attractiveness to industrialists. Thus, while academics might debate the merits and incidence of such arcane phenomena as 'spread' or 'trickle-down' effects, 'threshold attainment' or 'economies of scale' as a model for industrial policy implementation, the Board would be content to defend its strategy on purely practical resource utilization grounds. The author's view (which would appear to be shared by Morgan [1984]) would be that neither the scale of resources nor the degree of concentration has yet been sufficient to attain worthwhile scale thresholds or 'trickle-down' effects, with the possible exception of Newtown, where these effects can be seen in embryonic form.

In fact, DBRW's growth areas and special towns (the top two tiers in the spatial hierarchy) include nearly every town in Mid Wales with a population of at least 1000, and virtually no settlement is more than 12 miles away from one of these designated towns. Thus, the Board's spatial investment policy has probably been less controversial in Mid Wales than perhaps would have been the case elsewhere.

The lowest settlement category, however, the 'key towns and villages', has not proved to be meaningful. Originally, it was hoped that the Board would 'respond to initiative' in these settlements by providing workshop space. In fact, neither the Board's resources nor the demand for such accommodation have been sufficient to pursue this policy, although the Board has consistently grant-aided the area's local authorities to provide workshop space themselves (e.g. Tregynon and Llanbrynmair in Montgomery, Tregaron in Ceredigion). The Board's growth town policy is, therefore, a robust regional strategy and is instrumental in allocating the bulk of DBRW resources. It must be distinguished, however, from the much criticized key settlement policies of many local planning authorities in the UK. Unlike these *planning* policies, the Board's *development* policies are positive in that they do not attempt to restrict development in

Table 7.2   DBRW/County Council spatial policy in Mid Wales

County council structure plan designation	DBRW designation (taken from Board policy statement, 1979)*				
	Priority growth area**	Growth area	Special town	Key town	No MWD designation
Powys County Structure Plan (1983)					
Area centres – main settlements for new housing and employment developments	Newtown (designated New Town) Central Powys: Rhayader] Llandrindod Wells] Builth Wells]	Welshpool Brecon	Machyhlleth Llanidloes Presteigne Ystradgynlais Llanfyllin Hay on Wye†	Llanfair Caereinion Knighton Talgarth Crickhowell	
Dyfed County Structure Plan (1983)					
Main settlements for industrial development	Aberystwyth		Lampeter Cardigan	Tregaron Aberaeron Llandyssul	Adpar/ Newcastle Emlyn
Meirionnydd and Dyffryn County Structure Plan					
Main settlements for industrial development		(Blaenau Ffestiniog (Penrhyn-deudraeth	Bala		
Main settlements for industrial tourism development		Blaenau Ffestiniog	Tywyn Bala	Barmouth	Trawsfynydd Harlech
DBRW-designated settlements undesignated in structure plans			Dolgellau	Felinfach‡ Llanwrtyd Wells	

*   The Board policy statement guides factory development. The Statement was modified in 1982 when Llanfyllin and Presteigne were upgraded from key to special towns, and Knighton was downgraded from a special to a key town and Crickhowell was introduced for the first time.
**   In 1983 the Board decided to give particular emphasis to the growth areas of Newtown, Aberystwyth and Central Powys.
†   Although designated a key town, Hay on Wye operates as a *de facto* special town.
‡   Felinfach and Llanwrtyd Wells act as *de facto* key towns but are not formally designated as such.

non-designated settlements. In fact, the reverse is true — the Board's policy is to actively support job-creating activities wherever they might arise, subject of course to normal planning criteria. The approved Structure Plans of Dyfed, Gwynedd and Powys County Councils all contain policies implying dispersal, yet there are in fact only minor differences from DBRW's expressed policies of concentration (Table 7.2). There is, therefore, a problem of perspective when viewing settlement strategies where differences may be more apparent than real.

INDUSTRIAL DEVELOPMENT

The Board organizes its construction programme under an informal five-year plan. This relates the Board's ideas on future factory-building (advance, bespoke, specialized, size of units) and housing and commercial development to the Board's spatial policy. Budgetary provision is, however, provided annually by the Welsh Office in the form of the National Loans Fund (NLF) for construction in Newtown (and housing outside of Newtown), and Grant-in-Aid (GIA) for factory-building outside of Newtown. These sources of funds are roughly equal and totalled some £10.7 million in 1984–85.

The Board must seek the approval of the Secretary of State for Wales for the construction programme proposed for the ensuing financial year. In recent years the Board's budget has remained broadly static in real terms, although recent government policy would appear to foreshadow a hardening attitude to DBRW's industrial development expenditure, particularly in respect of advance factories:

> [...] factory building will continue to be restricted to levels which will ensure that new factories, on average, remain unallocated for no more than a few months. Priorities will continue to be to build bespoke factories for known developments, to make provision for the high technology industries and for economic and infrastructure developments, particularly where projects could stimulate private sector investment. (HM Treasury, 1985)

Thus, the government has been recently signalling a change in direction away from the provision of advance factories. The Board itself has recently devoted an increasing proportion of its factory programme to provide extra space for indigenous expanding companies, producing new jobs. This only serves to indicate the success of past development policies, however, which have strongly featured both advance factories at market rentals and regional policy incentives. While DBRW is happy to reap a rich harvest from past sowings it would be concerned if its ability to sow seeds for the future were now to be hampered.

In addition, Mid Wales has never attracted significant private funds for the building of industrial floorspace, and would appear unlikely to do so in the future given current rent levels and rental growth prospects — at least with present incentives. Thus, current government policy seems to be moving in a direction which is not conducive to optimism that the scale of resources for advance factory construction, and their deployment, will be to the benefit of Mid Wales. The Board's construction programme will in the foreseeable future continue to depend on the additional funds that can be generated from sale of assets. In 1984–85 sales of assets exceeded £1 million and represented no less than 10 per cent of gross out-turn spend for the year. However, as sales proceed, the opportunity for further sales reduces, and so the opportunity to increase the Board's budget by these means will progressively decline.

The Board has been building up to approximately 135 000 sq ft per year of factory floorspace in recent years. Its current industrial property portfolio is shown in Table 7.3. The normal size range of units ranges from 500 to 10 000 sq ft. Normally, factories over 5000 sq ft are confined to the growth areas, and up to 5000 sq ft in the special towns. The rolling five-year programme takes account of the need to provide factories at sizes which try to anticipate likely 'trading-up' demands from tenants in starter units (up to 1500 sq ft) and general market demand.

Table 7.3   Mid Wales Development industrial property portfolio (December 1985)

Location	Units (including planned and under construction)	Size (sq ft)
Aberystwyth	50	146,246
Cardigan	28	98,204
Felinfach	2	1,400
Lampeter	25	59,264
CEREDIGION	105	295,114
Bala	16	65,909
Blaenau Ffestiniog	9	70,220
Corris	6	6,000
Dolgellau	18	40,513
Penrhyndeudraeth	2	6,000
Tywyn	16	33,750
MERIONNYDD	67	222,392
Brecon	25	138,785
Builth Wells	5	22,215
Crickhowell	1	26,711
Hay-on-Wye	3	12,760
Llanwrtyd Wells	2	2,000
Ystradgynlais	29	398,877
BRECKNOCK	65	601,348
Llanfyllin	8	6,000
Llanidloes	20	33,260
Machynlleth	9	41,227
Montgomery	1	19,377
Newtown	140	1,013,197
Welshpool	22	252,512
MONTGOMERY	200	1,365,573
Knighton	1	16,852
Llandrindod Wells	31	164,192
Presteigne	10	14,916
Rhayader	15	94,491
RADNOR	57	290,451
MID WALES	494	2,774,878

Changes in the political situation, public expenditure policy, regional policy and the national economy itself can all separately or together radically change both the provision and demand for industrial and housing space. The Board closely monitors national and local economic trends in order that its construction programme in any one year matches likely demand. National patterns of investment, output, consumer spending, manufacturing capital expenditure in new building work, CBI investment intention surveys, etc., are all taken into account to ensure that the Board's product — in this case the hardware — is likely to match demand. This information is now published half-yearly by the Board (Development Board for Rural Wales, 1985a). The location of proposed investments responds, within the general strategic framework, to local economic and demographic conditions. Thus, for example, the Board is faced with the constant dilemma of whether to build factories in the places the market demands (generally east of the Cambrians — Welshpool, Newtown, Brecon) or where the local need is greatest (e.g. Teifi Valley area of Ceredigion with consistently high unemployment rates approaching 25 per cent).

There is no magic solution to this dilemma — obviously a balance has to be struck between the two competing demands for resources. The danger, of course, is that either the more successful parts of the region become starved of resources, or the more remote, 'unpopular' areas for manufacturing investment are overprovided with floor-space that remains unlet. It is absolutely essential, nevertheless, to maintain a factory-building programme that will ensure an adequate supply of available factory space of various sizes at various locations. Choice is paramount if the 'customer' is to be persuaded to 'buy' the product.

Recent letting figures for Board factories are shown in Figure 7.2. Encouraging signs

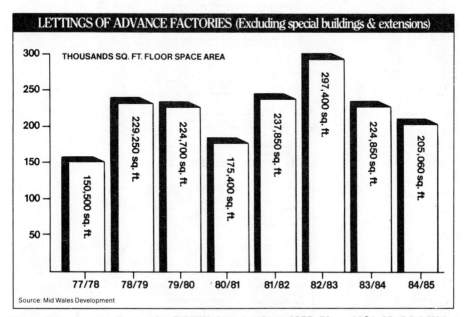

Figure 7.2   Letting figures for DBRW factories from 1977–78 to 1984–85 (Mid Wales Development, *Economic Review*, July 1985).

of a massive increase in lettings during 1985–86 were evident by the fact that lettings in the first five months of the financial year were already higher than in the whole of the previous year. Lettings during 1985–86 should support some 1000 new job opportunities, while the Board's factory vacancy rate at 10 per cent (by floorspace) is among the lowest in the UK.

The factory development process itself is outlined in Figure 7.3. The significant factors relating to this process are that (1) the Board has almost complete control of the whole process and (2) implementation of the programme is *relatively* straightforward compared with non-factory projects.

Again, it can be seen that the continuity of industrial development policy and its widespread support from within the region for a period of almost 30 years have produced a familiarity that feeds the momentum for development. Site acquisition and

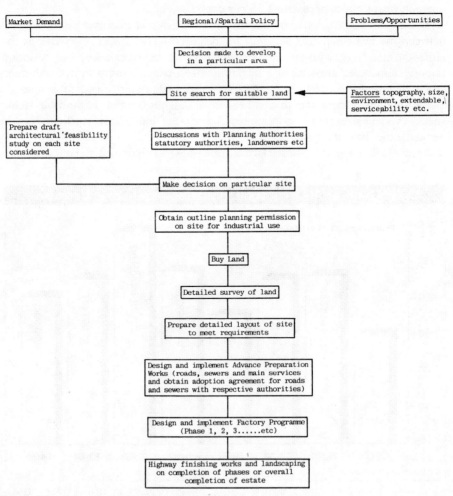

Figure 7.3   Advance factory development process.

liaison with planning authorities and statutory undertakers take place generally without unresolved conflicts. The Board has the powers and resources to meet the requirements of its partners in the development process, but the Board itself is firmly in control. Although frequently received with some scepticism, the Board actually does enjoy excellent relationships with all the local authorities in its territory, and this is reflected at all levels in the organization. Practice, at least in the industrial development process, seems to have made for extremely effective, if not perfect, interorganizational cooperation. This can also be seen throughout the development process, for example consultation on the forthcoming construction programme, local authority help to identify suitable land for development, talks at an early stage with the local authority planning office, etc.

The Board's 1984–85 construction programme, valued at £4.75 million, included factories at Aberystwyth, Cardigan, Lampeter, Dolgellau, Tywyn, Brecon, Llanidloes, Llanfyllin, Newtown, Welshpool, Llandrindod Wells, Presteigne and Rhayader. These units ranged from 750 to 10 000 sq ft and totalled 147 250 sq ft. The precedent and familiarity — the political acceptability of the factory-building programme — ensure that the implementation process tends to be achieved smoothly and uncontroversially (Slowe, 1981). While this may render other forms of development more tricky to achieve because of 'terror of precedent', it is a source of great strength to a continuing, if recently threatened, factory-construction programme.

Construction — on land the Board has previously acquired with the approval of the Secretary of State — is carried out by the Board itself. The Board acquires some 15 acres per year on average to maintain a worthwhile land bank. Land is normally identified in close consultation with the region's planning authorities early in the development process. The difficulties that DBRW has experienced in this part of the process are usually related to owners' unwillingness to sell or physical constraints (e.g. flooding at Builth Wells, shortage of sites in Blaenau Ffestiniog, etc.). Normally, land acquisition relates to existing industrial estates. Problems most often arise during the establishment of new industrial areas, for example recently at Three Cocks (Aberlefeni) in Brecknock where agreement to purchase a suitable site could not be achieved. Generally, however, with these exceptions, the acquisition of land is a generally straightforward process. Physical problems, however, can have a significant effect in modifying the Board's spatial policy. Thus, in 1982, the Board downgraded Knighton from special to key town status since it had proved impossible to identify suitable land for industry in the town which was not susceptible to flooding. The acquisition of land and industrial estate maintenance is carried out by the Board's own estates' surveyors.

Similarly, advanced engineering works — roads, sewers, land drainage, etc. — have to be provided by the Board prior to construction. This work is managed in-house using both the Board's own technical expertise and consultants. Close liaison with the statutory undertakers ensures that the Board's construction programme is rarely delayed severely. Again, the Board manages an increasingly complex building programme using both its own design team and consultants. This programme has become increasingly sophisticated in recent years with more and more bespoke extensions, special factory/retail units and 'high-tech', 'high-spec', and 'science park' projects displacing standard advance units. In 1984–85, for example, significant funds were used for the construction of two industrial parks — at Aberystwyth and Newtown —

which relate to science, technology and research-based industries. As a commitment to growing indigenous companies, the Board gives priority to extensions. The single most important factory project the Board has ever undertaken, however, is the massive 135 000 sq ft factory which is being built for Laura Ashley PLC, in Newtown, the Board having persuaded the company to chose a Mid Wales location in preference to a site in Holland. This single project will tie up a large proportion of DBRW's development budget for Newtown for some two years. Another recent departure from normal Board practice was to refurbish an old station, a listed building, at Llanidloes to provide 13 workshop units of varying sizes.

The Board's construction processes and programmes are, therefore, well tried and tested. Increasingly the projects undertaken are 'special' and innovative although the Board also remains committed to maintaining an advance factory programme. The programme needs to respond to market demand, thus the Board's construction programme for 1986–87 will, in the light of market research, be composed of larger units. Demand for smaller units, particularly 750 sq ft units, is expected to be satisfied by existing empty stock and turnover supplemented by local authority workshop projects which can be grant-aided by the Board.

FACTORY MARKETING

The Board's factory-marketing programme has been crucial to its success in creating a current total theoretical capacity of 7425 job opportunities throughout the DBRW area. The Board's efforts are devoted to both in- and out-region marketing, and are managed on a two-tier basis through (1) generating industrial enquiries (currently around 100 per month) and (2) conversion of enquiries into firm factory allocations utilizing tailored packages of incentives and factual information for the prospective customer. The Board conducts its marketing activities in much the same way as any professional consumer-based product manufacturer using highly cost-effective techniques with the twin objectives of maximum generation of enquiries and 'conversions' (factory allocations) relative to the budget available.

Competition for new industry and new entrepreneurs is now intense. It is impossible for the Board to compete in advertising battles with the big-spending authorities and high-profile industrial development locations, including enterprise zones, urban development corporations, new towns, development areas, local authorities and other development agencies. The withdrawal of regional policy incentives from much of the Board's area has made the job even harder (see Figure 7.1). The Board, therefore, has to attempt to transcend these constraints by devising and implementing imaginative means of marketing its 'product' — which remains strong despite regional policy setbacks. Without divulging details of the Board's 'state secrets', Mid Wales Development operates a policy of achieving face-to-face contact with businesspeople using a mixture of economical media advertising, normally eschewing the politically high profile, but relatively cost-ineffective, full-page adverts in the leading daily and Sunday newspapers. Film shows and specialized event promotions, often at the business community's leisure functions, are among the techniques used.

The Board's marketing programme is never static as new 'sales pitches' are devised to suit both demand and the changing nature of the Board's 'product'. The Board capitalizes on the environmental/lifestyle benefits of Mid Wales as an industrial location, and has found the incidence of non-economic factors (e.g. holiday experience, family connections, etc.) to be highly marketable commodities in compensation for the lack of traditional regional policy tools.

In addition to specific industrial marketing, DBRW also engages in a programme of corporate marketing to 'sell' Mid Wales as a whole. The main thrust of the Board's advertising lies in the promotion of the whole region, but in certain cases specific areas and products are marketed. For example, the Board is currently paying particular attention to the needs of its priority growth areas — Newtown, Central Powys and Aberystwyth — and particular promotions have been aimed at 'starter factories' and the Board's science park and manufacturing/retail units. The Board also operates the Mid Wales Development Centre in London which is used as a focus for promotions, exhibitions and presentations, and provides a convenient London base for contact meetings. 'In-region' enquiries are normally self-generating, coming directly to the Board through its Business Advisory Service. In-region promotion of factories generally has not proved successful in the past, although linked with the Board's entrepreneurial training courses, a much greater level of interest has recently been shown.

A well-researched and coherent marketing strategy is an essential element in achieving success in factory enquiries, and a new strategy has currently been prepared by the Board. Based on meticulous independent market research, DBRW is highlighting Mid Wales's environmental strengths and seeking to reduce misconceptions of the region by potential relocaters with advertising proclaiming 'Mid Wales . . . A New Wales'. The conversion of these generated contacts is the critical phase which turns customer enquiries into firm factory allocations. This is the stage where the hard bargaining begins and ends. As shown in Figure 7.2, the Board let 205 060 sq ft in 1984–85 (excluding new buildings for known customers and factory extensions). The targets for 1985–86 and 1986–87 are respectively 250 000 and 300 000 sq ft. The balance between out- and in-region promotion and conversion fluctuates from year to year according to the level of activity in the national economy and regional policies, but broadly there is a balance in the lettings between indigenous and exogenous companies.

An internal DBRW research study in 1982 showed that some 40 per cent of businesses in Board factories were 'start-ups', half of which were generated from within and half from outside the Board's area. Of the 60 per cent of firms which were already in existence prior to occupation of their factories, 35 per cent were exogenous transfers of branches, and 25 per cent were transfers from within Mid Wales. In total, therefore, 45 per cent of the Board's tenants were based in Mid Wales, and 55 per cent emanated from outside the Board's area.

One feature of Mid Wales's manufacturing industry is that it is now very diverse, with only clothing (Laura Ashley, Tootal, Slimma, etc.) as a conspicuously strong employer, attracted by high female labour availability (low activity rates) and relatively low wages (Figure 7.4).

On the basis of data recently published by the Department of Trade and Industry, Mid Wales has been shown to be a particularly successful region in terms of business fertility relative to 'deaths' (Figure 7.5). In fact Mid Wales has the highest 'starts per stop' ratio in Great Britain, which is very encouraging in terms of the Board's seminal

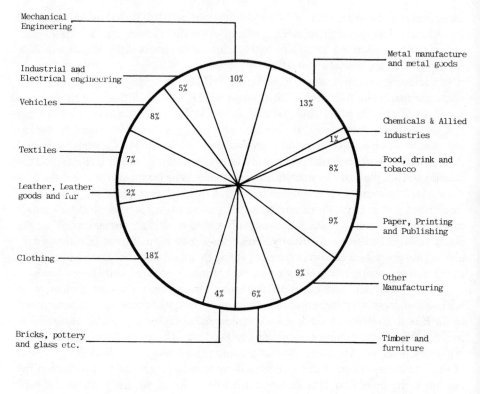

Mechanical
Engineering

Industrial and
Electrical engineering

Vehicles

Textiles

Leather, Leather
goods and fur

Clothing

Bricks, pottery
and glass etc.

Metal manufacture
and metal goods

Chemicals & Allied
industries

Food, drink and
tobacco

Paper, Printing
and Publishing

Other
Manufacturing

Timber and
furniture

10%
5%
8%
7%
2%
18%
4%   6%
9%
9%
8%
1%
13%

Source: Census of Employment

Figure 7.4   Structure of Mid Wales industry, 1981 (Census of Employment, 1981).

and continuing efforts to encourage new entrepreneurship, as well as its efforts to support companies facing difficulties.

Regional policy changes in 1980, 1982 and 1984 have left most of Mid Wales without Assisted Area status (see Figure 7.1). The Board fought hard against the latest changes in area coverage because it has long believed that a strong regional policy was partly responsible for the considerable success in factory lettings achieved by the Board and its predecessors. The Board's criticism of the government's White Paper *Regional Industrial Development* was that it put too much emphasis on indigenous development potential (Development Board for Rural Wales, 1984b). Compared to many other parts of Britain, Mid Wales has a modest industrial base, which itself is a result of inward investment over the past 20 years under the influence of relatively strong regional policy. The Board argued that the base was not yet large enough to provide the basis for spontaneous unassisted indigenous growth. As Table 7.4 shows, however, despite criticisms and accepting that the 'ceteris paribus' criterion is not a practical reality, the Board's annual average factory lettings have continued to increase (to 1.3 per week). These figures are probably due to the very effective Mid Wales Development Grant. This new power was given to the Board to replace the assistance formerly available in the Assisted Areas which in 1982 were downgraded to 'non-assisted' status. In

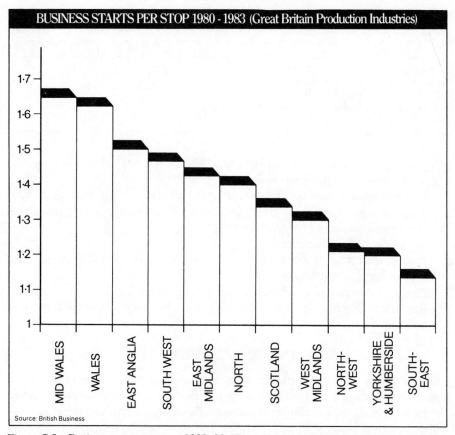

Figure 7.5   Business starts per stop 1980–83 (Great Britain production industries) (Depart-ment of Trade and Industry, *British Business*, 18 January 1985).

November 1982 the Board formally launched the scheme, consisting of a discretionary grant similar in concept and operation to selective financial assistance in the Assisted Areas and provided under the auspices of the Welsh Development Agency Act 1975. Since its introduction the grant has contributed towards a total of £8 million expendi-ture on new plant and equipment and supported 1500 jobs. The fact that the grant is operated and managed by the Board itself, and therefore integrated with other aspects of the Board's promotional and advisory work, is a crucial factor in its success. The grant is neither constrained by the Board's spatial investment policy nor confined to its own tenants. It is interesting to note that some 40 per cent of Mid Wales Development Grant cases have been located in non Board-owned premises.

The other major incentives negotiable with DBRW include rent-free periods and market rentals. The former depend on location and job creation; the latter come in the form of a hidden subsidy since the Board itself bears the difference between economic and market rentals, and market rentals are among the lowest in Britain. The Board marshals these incentives both to entice new industry to the region, nowadays more in the form of starts-up and transfers rather than branches, as well as to encourage

Table 7.4   Mid Wales – government factory lettings

Date	Status	Total let	Annual average
1957–66	Pre-development area	9	1
1967–76	Post-development area	49	5
1977–79	Post-DBRW	107	53
1980–82	Reduced regional policy coverage	119	60
1983–85	Post-regional policy change	244	81

indigenous expansions where appropriate. Other forms of 'softer', but no less important elements of the total 'package', include:

1. Business advisory services (finance, technical matters, pricing, packaging, etc.).
2. Training (e.g. 'Women into Business', Graduate Enterprise, Getting into Business, Small Business Development Programme, etc.).
3. Schools/industry programme.
4. Product marketing (to identify new sales opportunities for Mid Wales businesses both in the UK and abroad).
5. Product research and development (e.g. food, giftware, lamb, etc.).
6. Redundant building grant to encourage small businesses in redundant rural buildings.

INFRASTRUCTURE

The provision of a factory at market rentals, incentives, key worker housing, assistance with training and business development are only part of the regional development job. 'At the sharp end', industrialists are concerned about transport infrastructure, accessibility, transport costs (real) and distance costs (perceived). Research has shown consistently that transport costs in relatively remote areas are as small a fraction of turnover as in urban areas (PEIDA, 1984). Yet the single most important barrier to attracting new industry to Mid Wales is the problem of perceived accessibility and distance costs. The simple reduction of transport costs is not the main reason for promoting transport infrastructure in Mid Wales, but it is essential if negative perceptions by key industrialists of Mid Wales's remoteness are to be overcome. 'Good infrastructure endowment', according to a recent European Community report, 'is clearly correlated with high levels of economic performance. . . Regional disparities are found to be high for . . . transportation' (Biehl, 1982). Experience in Mid Wales has illustrated that regional accessibility and perceived peripherality are critical issues affecting the image of Mid Wales as a location for industrial investment.

A more detailed account of the Board's efforts to reduce accessibility constraints is provided elsewhere (Pettigrew, 1984) but the main ingredients have been:

1. The marshalling of local authority and Board resources to support a major reinvestment in the region's railways totalling some £7 million. Regional accessibility and quality of transport planned will have major positive benefits, including new rolling stock, a loco-hauled through train (intercity standard) making a return journey between Aberystwyth and London Euston daily, and faster times.
2. Advocacy in support of an accelerated programme of trunk road building in the

region, especially the critical east–west links amd those which provide quicker motorway access (Development Board for Rural Wales, 1984a).

3. Progressing a major project to create a Mid Wales aerodrome at Caersws, near Newtown, the planning of which is now progressing well.

4. Establishing a policy and programme of improvements to telecommunications infrastructure in the region by working closely with British Telecom to improve services available to industrialists in an effort to neutralize as far as possible the effects of distance. Major successes have already been achieved with DBRW/local authority grant aid which has persuaded British Telecom to provide local-call access nodes for Packet Switchstream (PSS), allowing cheap access to national and international databases for companies unable to afford or justify dedicated lines.

CONCLUSION

Industrial development in Mid Wales has a long pedigree. Embodied in its present organizational form as the Development Board for Rural Wales, it has displayed a resilience in the face of variable government policy, which has allowed it to maintain an effective cutting edge and worthwhile results.

The co-linearity of the industrial development function with the appropriate organizational form is crucial to an understanding of how policy for the region is implemented. As Gunn (1978) has shown, an important prerequisite for perfect implementation is that 'there is a single implementing agency which need not depend on other agencies for success or, if other agencies must be involved, that the dependency relationships are minimal in number and importance . . .'. The industrial development experience of Mid Wales illustrates the wisdom of this observation, and that the gap between policy and implementation is minimized when responsibility for both are integrated in one organization. The Development Board for Rural Wales shares this characteristic with its sister organizations, the Welsh Development Agency, Scottish Development Agency and Highlands and Islands Development Board. The discordance between policy and implementation happens when a break occurs between those responsible for policy- or plan-making and the organizations responsible for implementation. The classic example is, of course, the structure plan.

The corollary of this argument may be arrogated that this somehow implies a lack of cooperation, coordination or integration with other bodies. The success of DBRW, however, has stemmed from having clear policies to solve a well-understood problem with the necessary powers and resources to tackle it. In this respect, the region's local authorities, having spawned the progenitor of the Board in the first place, have acknowledged the Board as a resource and means by which the region's economic and social problems can be solved. Coordination as a general policy aim is a weak concept, usually implying, in those who seek it, a greater degree of control. It is often used also as a commodity to have more of when the chances of obtaining greater resources — which is usually the real issue — are constrained. However, coordination at *project* level with the region's local authorities has certainly been crucial in making a success of DBRW's industrial development programmes. The indications are that as DBRW involves itself in other sectors of the economy, these relationships will take on even greater significance.

Finally, it is as well to recognize that agencies such as DBRW would not be able to survive the political roller-coaster unless they could point to real results. As Rose (1984) suggests: 'In practice, the test of the performance of policies is whether they shape decisions and actions which change the real world in line with the objectives'. This sums up the political reality. DBRW will be judged by this very criterion — its ability to translate policy into worthwhile results on the ground. As has been shown in this chapter, the Board's industrial development performance so far has been highly successful in creating new jobs, and thus its reputation established. It will be interesting to see whether in the future we will see the DBRW model repeated or adapted for other parts of rural Britain. On the evidence of experience in Mid Wales it deserves to be tried.

REFERENCES

Beacham Committee (1964) *Depopulation in Mid Wales*, HMSO, London.

Biehl, D. (1982) The contribution of infrastructure to regional development. Reported in *The Regions of Europe, Second Periodic Report on the Social and Economic Situation of Regions of the Community (1984)*, Com 84 40 Final/2, European Commission.

Broady, M. (1980a) Rural regeneration: a note on the Mid Wales case, *Cambria*, Vol. 7, No. 1, 79–85.

Broady, M. (1980b) Mid Wales: a classic case of rural self-help, *The Planner*, July 1980, 94–96.

Cloke, P. (1979) *Key Settlements in Rural Wales*, Methuen, London.

Countryside Commission (1984) *A Better Future for the Uplands*, Countryside Commission, Cheltenham.

Development Board for Rural Wales (1978–1985) *Annual Reports*, DBRW, Newtown.

Development Board for Rural Wales (1979) *Board Policy Statement*.

Development Board for Rural Wales (1980a) Memorandum to House of Commons Select Committee on Welsh Affairs. In *The Role of the Welsh Office and Associated Bodies in Developing Employment Opportunities in Wales*, Session 1979–80, HMSO, London.

Development Board for Rural Wales (1983a) Memorandum to House of Commons Select Committee on Welsh Affairs. In *Wales and the European Community*, Minutes of Evidence 23 February, 1983, Session 1982–83, HMSO, London.

Development Board for Rural Wales (1984a) *Trunk Roads Policy Statement*, DBRW, Newtown.

Development Board for Rural Wales (1984b) Memorandum to House of Commons Select Committee on Welsh Affairs. In *The Impact of Regional Industrial Policy in Wales*, Minutes of Evidence 7 March 1984, Session 1983–84, HMSO, London.

Development Board for Rural Wales (July 1985a) *Mid Wales Economic Review*, DBRW, Newtown.

Garbett-Edwards, D.P. (1972) The establishment of new industries. In Ashton and Long (eds) *The Remoter Rural Areas of Britain*, Oliver and Boyd, Edinburgh.

Garbett-Edwards, D.P. (1979) Development in Mid Wales. In *New Agencies in Wales — Portents for the Future*, Proceedings of a Regional Studies Association Conference at the Joint Students Union, Park Place, Cardiff, 10 March, 1979, Regional Studies Association, London.

Gilder, I.M. (1979) Rural planning policies: an economic appraisal. In Diamond, D. and McLoughlin, J.B. (eds) *Progress in Planning*, Vol. 11, Part 3, pp 213–271, Pergamon, Oxford.

Gunn, L.A. (1978) Why is implementation so difficult? *Management Services in Government*, November 1978, pp 169–176.

HM Treasury (1985) *The Government's Expenditure Plans 1985/86 – 1987/88*. Cmnd 9248. HMSO, London.

Hodge, I.D. and Whitby, M.C. (1979) *New Jobs in the Eastern Borders: An Economic Evaluation of the Development Commission Factory Programme*, Monograph 8, Agricultural Adjustment Unit, University of Newcastle upon Tyne.

Martin and Voorhees Associates (1980) *Review of Rural Settlement Policies 1945–1980*.

Mid Wales Industrial Development Association (1973) *Development in Mid Wales*, Sixteenth and Final Report, Newtown.

Morgan, R.H. (1984) Population trends in Mid Wales: some policy implications. In Williams, G. (ed.) *Crisis of Economy and Ideology: Essays on Welsh Society, 1840–1980*, pp 88–102, BSA, Sociology of Wales Study Group.

Moseley, M.J. (1974) *Growth Centres in Spatial Planning*, Pergamon, Oxford.

PEIDA (1984) *Transport Costs in Peripheral Areas* (on behalf of European Commission, Industry Department for Scotland and Department of Economic Development, Northern Ireland), Planning, Economic and Industrial Development Advisers, Edinburgh.

Pettigrew, P.J. (1984) Mid Wales: a Development Board for Rural Wales perspective on transport and regional development. In Cloke, P.J. (ed.) *Wheels Within Wales*, pp 78–100, Centre for Rural Transport, Lampeter.

Rose, E.A. (1984) Philosophy and purpose in planning. In Bruton, M.J. (ed.) *The Spirit and Purpose of Planning*, Hutchinson, London.

Slowe, P.M. (1981) *The Advance Factory in Regional Development*, Gower, London.

8

IMPLEMENTATION AND THE ROLE OF THE WATER INDUSTRY
Philip Bell

INTRODUCTION

As the various water services usually constitute one of the most basic elements of any housing or other development in rural areas as elsewhere, reconciliation of the aims and activities of county and district planning authorities with those of the regional water authorities (RWA) in particular becomes more than usually urgent. A number of studies (Gilg, 1978; Glyn-Jones, 1979; Hickling *et al.*, 1979; Winter, 1980; Blacksell and Gilg, 1981) have illustrated a severe mismatch between these agencies, which became manifest as the actual pattern of development diverged ever more sharply from that projected in formal planning documents. At first sight, this suggests the existence of an 'implementation gap', and certainly in some rural examples coordination between these two functional agencies would appear to have been almost non-existent. For example, half of the key settlements in Devon, designated for some growth in the county's *Development Plan Review* of 1964, were found subsequently to be subject to various water restrictions which could prevent them from fulfilling such a role (Devon County Council, 1977; Gilg, 1978). With development in such places blocked, pressures for growth in other settlements became almost impossible to oppose, especially if spare capacity in services existed there (Blacksell and Gilg, 1981). Despite the gloomy picture painted by these examples, some commentators (e.g. Cherry, 1982) have noted the emergence of comparatively good and harmonious working relationships, as arrangements for liaison have been allowed to consolidate and develop over the period since 1974, when both local government and the water industry were reorganized. Any problems which can be identified are unlikely to be static, but instead will be subject to change both in their scale and nature, and therefore the temporal dimension is a crucial one.

In this chapter we examine how the relationship has worked out in practice in a particular rural area in the southeast, the extent of conflict that arose there and the degree of distortion to planning aims that resulted. Some general principles are then discussed, and lastly the role and influence of development interests and the central state are considered. It is shown that these two latter agents are of major and growing significance, and that a focus on questions of coordination alone will not provide a comprehensive picture of all the factors influencing the relationship between land-use and water planning.

A number of considerations are important in any examination of this particular interrelationship. One of these concerns the stage at which objectives are negotiated. In the Devon case, it is apparent that there was little coordination over the preparation of the original development plan review, so difficulties became manifest only at the implementation stage. As an alternative, plans could be drawn up incorporating the various constraints imposed by the water services into formal policy. In this case, implementation could appear relatively harmonious although the actual influence of the RWA would be no less strong. A second point relates to the root cause of any discrepancy or disagreement, whether it arises during the implementation process or earlier. This could be attributed to simple difficulties in coordination, at its simplest perhaps due to a basic lack of contact and the consequent absence of flows of information. Such a situation might be rectified quite easily with improved interorganizational links. Other influences are at work too, one of which derives from the differing attitudes held, individually and collectively, within the two organizations. Gray (1982) has stressed the importance of the engineering background of many professionals in the water industry in determining the latter's planning strategy, and this is likely to lead to conflict with local authority aims. Influences from outside are also likely to be strong, notably the private housebuilding industry and central government, as mentioned above. The aims of the former have been afforded even more complete primacy by the actions of central government in recent years. Of particular importance to the water industry are Circulars 22/80 and 22/83, the first of which advocates negotiation and the use of Section 52 agreements if water services are inadequate in preference to outright refusal of an application, and the second seeks to set the boundaries of the works it is reasonable to require of developers in such arrangements (Department of the Environment, 1980, 1983). Central government has also been limiting, to an increasing degree, the levels of direct investment that both water and local authorities can undertake. In view of the strength of these outside pressures, there may be definite advantages to both water and local authorities in standing together, or at least not engaging in direct public conflict.

Other commentators have considered general principles pertaining to this interrelationship (Hawkins, 1981; Penning-Rowsell, 1982), and so these are not elaborated further at this stage. In the following section an assessment is made of how this liaison has been reflected in policy and practice in a specific rural location in East Sussex.

POLICY IMPLEMENTATION AND RWA INFLUENCE IN LEWES DISTRICT

In common with most parts of the outer southeast, the area covered by Lewes District Council (Figure 8.1) is subject to heavy pressure for development. Most villages are concentrated on the Low Weald area in the north of the district, and along the Ouse River valley as it cuts through the South Downs (Figure 8.2). The Downs themselves carry an Area of Outstanding Natural Beauty (AONB) designation, and have little

Figure 8.1   District councils in East Sussex.

settlement apart from isolated farmhouses. The northern villages in particular come under pressure for development emanating from the adjacent Mid-Sussex District, notably from the towns of Burgess Hill and Haywards Heath. The four larger, urban settlements in the district itself are Lewes, the county town situated at the north end of the Ouse gap, and Seaford, Newhaven and Peacehaven/Telscombe on the coast. General policies of restraint operate, but some points within the area are planned for growth, so there is at least the potential for undermining the former and stifling the latter, if the Devon evidence is replicated.

Water services are provided by the Southern Water Authority (SWA) based at Worthing, and now operating with four divisions (Isle of Wight, Hampshire, Sussex and Kent). The Sussex division, based at Falmer on the outskirts of Brighton, is responsible for most services supplied to Lewes District. The District Council declined to exercise their option to retain a sewerage agency arrangement in 1974, so the SWA has direct control of this aspect in addition to sewage disposal, land drainage and other services. The private Mid Sussex Water Company, however, supplies water to most of the area.

RURAL AREAS — THE BASIC POLICY FRAMEWORK

Lewes District Council has prepared no specific local plans for the more rural areas in its charge, which are therefore subject to the general village policy of East Sussex County Council (ESCC). This came into operation just at the commencement of the study period (1976–1982). In its original form (East Sussex County Council, 1975a) it named six villages where modest growth would be allowed, though this was quickly reduced to four (East Sussex County Council, 1975b). After further modifications, this upper tier was deleted entirely in 1979 (East Sussex County Council, 1979). All the

Figure 8.2   Settlements in Lewes District.

original six villages had in fact been in the other two rural districts (Wealden and Rother), so Lewes was only directly concerned with the more numerous second-tier villages where infilling would usually be permitted. After the removal of the upper tier, this secondary category was widened to incorporate 'small-scale development', which was not quantified. The rest of the county, including those smaller settlements not included in either first or second tiers as well as the open countryside areas, was subject to very strict restraint, with developments only being permitted for proven agricultural or forestry needs (Bell, 1986).

Many county council attempts to nominate settlements for particular levels of growth have been thwarted by the deletion of such specifications by the Secretary of State, as in Kent and mid-Hampshire. Rather unusually, East Sussex has been allowed to retain its village list in the Structure Plan and its numerous modifications, but the County Council was instructed at its examination in public to provide a more reasoned justification for this selection. When submitted, this contained a strong service-based rationale, with water services being dominant within this category. Lists of spare capacity in treatment works and sewerage systems were usually supplied to the counties during their plan preparation, and so the SWA was able to exert, via these lists, an influence over where development was to take place. However, it was evident that the county's wish to preserve the appearance of the countryside constituted an imperative at least as strong (and probably more so) than that of servicing costs, and led to the concentration of development into the larger urban settlements and into the larger villages within the rural group. Such a pattern was well suited to SWA wishes for the most part, but despite this the SWA hesitated to endorse these plans and strategies positively. It preferred a stance of apparent neutrality, not wishing to be seen as dictating to the local planners, and so the Authority's usual practice in such cases was to state merely that it had no objections.

POLICY AND PRACTICE

Given this policy framework, the broad findings of the study in the rural areas can be stated simply: the SWA appeared to have very little influence in modifying the desired development pattern. In the open countryside, refusals of applications for planning permission were made basically for policy reasons. The two standard ones stated, first, that the site was not in a listed second-tier village, and second, that it was indeed outside any village, and therefore constituted scattered development. The second element was played down if the proposal was clearly within one of the small settlements not included in the list rather than in the countryside proper. A third reason was usually applied to sites in the South Downs AONB, stating that its visual amenity would suffer if development was allowed. Water authority involvement in these applications was limited, as even in the absence of mains drainage, the SWA was usually quite prepared to accept an alternative method of disposal. Its only stipulation was that septic tanks were unacceptable in defined water-gathering grounds. Certainly, SWA opposition in such instances never prevented a development that the District Council was otherwise minded to approve. Occasionally, the District Council attempted to reinforce its policy reasons by stating either that mains drainage simply was not available, or that such a situation could imperil water-gathering grounds despite the fact that the SWA had not lodged a formal objection. Indeed, in one or two cases they had not been consulted! The significance of this was marginal, however, as this reinforced rather than replaced the basic policy arguments.

In those villages in the district where some development was to be allowed (infilling only at first, but after 1979 small-scale development as well), the influence of the SWA again appeared to be fairly marginal when compared to the basic policy issues. Development in two villages close to Lewes — Ringmer and Kingston — had been rapid during the 1960s and this had relieved the pressure on Lewes itself, which was subject to a variety of constraints. The process and effects of growth in Ringmer have been documented elsewhere (Ambrose, 1974). As a result of this rapid development, in the preparation of the local plan for Lewes (Lewes District Council, 1977), it was accepted that these communities should now be allowed to settle down, and their rate of growth slowed considerably. Ringmer was still the clear leader among the villages in the district in terms of the number of houses built over the study period, but development proceeded on land already allocated there with very few problems. Only on one site, involving about 30 houses, did water services impinge significantly. The disposal of surface water created problems both on and off site, the nearby highway drain being considered inadequate to cater for the extra run-off expected. Detailed negotiations were required between the various parties involved, but agreement had been reached and a permission was issued six months after the initial application had been submitted. Even though this case proved problematic, a delay of only four months resulted. Overall sewerage and sewage treatment capacity had been able to cope with the growth in Ringmer, although this capacity was nearly exhausted by the end of the study period, so it could not be claimed that development in this location had been seriously impeded. The desire to slow growth to avoid overstraining the community may have owed something to the cost of providing extra capacity in services, but the wish to maintain social cohesion seems to have been a stronger factor.

The most dramatic challenges to stated policies arose in the northern villages, such as Newick. It is here that the SWA might have been expected to object most strongly to development, as many of the proposals here were of considerable size, at least in the rural context, and therefore most likely to breach barriers of service provision. For example, a series of appeals was made in Newick over the study period, mostly by one developer. Several of these involved over 100 dwellings, and the largest envisaged 840. The SWA seemed prepared to accept most of these proposals, as its works were felt to have sufficient capacity to deal with the load, although these schemes could pre-empt further development within the village on land already zoned for residential purposes. More specifically, although the sewerage network in general, and a pumping station in particular, were inadequate for the flows envisaged, the SWA was still unwilling to lodge a formal objection, even though it seemed to have major reservations about the extent of improvements required and their financing. The County Council, commenting on the reasons for refusal suggested by the District Council, advised them that it was hard to persuade the SWA to provide evidence that could stand up at an appeal to support any initial objections. More generally, the County Council felt that any refusals should be justified on basic policy grounds rather than by technical objections, and ultimately it was on the former criteria that the District Council fought and won the appeals here.

In general, the SWA seemed tolerant of developments which threatened to overload treatment works or sewerage systems although, at least in rural areas, such applications were usually of a small scale. Water supply could almost always be provided (if at great expense on occasion), and while land drainage was a source of trouble on two particular rural sites, these were resolved after negotiation.

CONCLUSIONS FROM THE LEWES AREA STUDY

The overall impression arising from the analysis of the case study is that the SWA's influence on the outworkings of rural policy was almost always marginal. The basic policy of general restraint in the countryside areas certainly suited the Authority well, as rapid growth would be likely to entail the crossing of many expensive barriers in service provision. The SWA was able to avoid having to argue for such a pattern, however, as its concerns ran largely in parallel with those of the district and county authorities. The policy stance was partly justified by the wish to avoid incurring large expenditure commitments on services, but also in order to preserve the appearance of the countryside. There is no evidence to suggest that the former reason was invoked purely as a cover for the latter, or indeed that the reverse was true; both were genuine concerns. Limiting expenditure on services forms a recurrent theme in the policies of many shire counties, and although water services have been removed from local council jurisdiction, the trends in many other relevant services under their control are similar.

Liaison between the County Council and the SWA over the plan and its subsequent modifications was extensive, and the SWA's influence was pervasive, running as it did in tandem with the other factors mentioned above, but this did not determine policy absolutely. The overall picture which emerged from a consideration of the whole SWA area was that service thresholds acted as a basic constraint, which was breached in a selective, considered manner when other factors pointed in such a direction. The Authority never argued against the levels of rural development which were acceptable to the district planning authority, and because of its acceptance of alternatives to mains drainage, plus some works overloading, the SWA seemed unlikely to act as a significant constraint. More usually, the District Council sought support for the effective implementation of rural policy, specifically in refusing those applications contrary to its provisions. In virtually all cases, the SWA was very wary of lending such support, with the result that arguments were based on policy grounds alone. Neither were these justifications undermined by the provision of water services in locations where it was not intended that development should take place, a situation that seemed likely to persist in view of the close liaison between Lewes District Council and the SWA. Whatever spare capacity had once existed was now largely exhausted, and unless a major rural development were to be completely aborted at a late stage, the creation of considerable new capacity was highly unlikely. This aspect is elaborated later. It would seem, therefore, that it was rarely possible for developers to argue that the existence of spare capacity should favour their development. Provided that the basic policy held, few difficulties would arise for the SWA, or be passed on subsequently to the planners. Despite the increased latitude given to developers under central government advice to planning authorities,the basic policy has become well established and has so far resisted any challenges made to it.

A major change of emphasis in favour of rural development, however, could create more difficulties, although SWA officers felt that even such a shift could be accommodated if sufficient warning was given. In the light of local council and central government attitudes, the SWA appears to be justified in assuming that the present state of affairs is likely to continue. A change of emphasis to promote more rural development certainly would encounter many barriers far more significant than any

SWA opposition. General studies of infrastructure (Thring, 1977; Standing Conference on London and South East Regional Planning, 1981) have concluded that spare capacity in various services usually correlates well with the intentions of formal planning policy. This makes a change of emphasis ever more expensive, as the remaining spare capacity available, particularly in rural areas, is not replaced after its erosion by the small amounts of development permitted there.

This situation would appear to run counter to that uncovered by Gilder (1979) in his examination of the economic rationale for key settlement policy. It is true that some development could still be accepted in most locations, and it is difficult to define precisely at what stage limits have been reached. However, the consequences of improved liaison and basic economic pressures to use investment to the full, are the progressive elimination of spare capacity and new provision only in areas planned for growth. A one-off, temporary period of dispersed growth policy indeed would speed up this process. A change of direction is possible, but would require a commitment to new investment, and as is illustrated later, this could well be at the expense of the developer involved, especially if the returns from development are high. If liaison with other services has been less satisfactory, and their pools of spare capacity are larger, then a policy of strategic dispersal to use this may be cheaper overall than one of provision only in selected growth areas, although this ironically might be more expensive for the SWA itself. The dominant impression emerging from the SWA study, however, was that spare capacity was sparse in rural areas, and very rarely did that in different services come together in one location to cause any reassessment of the basic policy. The service case was not convincing, and had little effect on the environmental argument.

The picture, therefore, is one of a basically harmonious relationship, where both sides have a good appreciation of the conditions and constraints under which their colleagues operate. The liaison arrangements that have developed since 1974 have been of great assistance, neither the local authority nor the SWA having new proposals made to it entirely out of the blue, but instead both are acquainted with future plans at an early stage. Great care has been taken to cultivate good working relationships, and this has paid handsome dividends. This, however, does not provide all of the explanation. The wishes of both agencies are already running largely in parallel, and seem likely to continue to do so, both in the SWA's area and elsewhere. Planning strategy usually matches SWA preferences fairly well, and so restricts the commitments required of the latter. On those occasions where a clear conflict can be identified, the SWA has proved unwilling to press objections to general strategic matters, rather as it has done over individual applications. The clearest example of this is Ashford in Kent, whose primacy as a growth point has been defended by both district and county councils despite considerable SWA unease over the possible cost of sewerage, sewage disposal and flood prevention. Again, fuller analysis is provided elsewhere (Bell, 1986). In summary, then, a largely fortuitous background has been fostered by deliberate efforts to improve contacts, with planners giving full consideration (though not primacy) to SWA comments, and with the latter being prepared to alter its capital investment programme to support planning aims.

GENERAL ISSUES IN RELATIONS BETWEEN WATER AND LOCAL AUTHORITIES

In a general case study of SWA involvement in planning throughout its region, as in the specific district considered above, there is clear evidence that relations were usually good, a point which was stressed by officers of both organizations. Much liaison was routine, and applications proceeded with few problems at the development control stage. There were certain recurrent concerns; the SWA officers wanted planners to defend their basic policies more strongly rather than seeking justification on the basis of water services criteria, whereas the planners complained that they received insufficient support from the SWA technical experts in opposing harmful proposals. The SWA's reluctance to sustain objections could be attributed merely to professional pride, and a wish not to trespass onto planning authority responsibilities. However, a more likely cause of the SWA's reluctance is the perceived difficulty of pinpointing the exact stage at which a previously satisfactory situation becomes unsatisfactory following a particular development. This factor is crucial when any objection has to be sustained at a legally based public inquiry, so in most cases of uncertainty the SWA tended to err on the side of leniency. It also subscribed to a specific philosophy, enshrined in its formal documents, that development should be assisted, not resisted. This seems to derive above all from the SWA's basic duty to support various production interests and functions (Saunders, 1983), reinforced especially by the private business background of senior management, although this issue deserves fuller attention than can be given here (Bell, 1986).

A number of embargoes have operated in the SWA's area, though none of these affected Lewes District. In some cases, as at Teynham in Kent, these were not of great concern to the planning authorities involved. Others were recognized specifically in the planning authority's plans, for example at Bexhill and Hastings, and few challenges were made once these situations were made known. One of the most longstanding and significant embargoes affected Polegate near Eastbourne, where development interest was considerable, and which indeed was identified for some growth. This has been delayed by an embargo imposed on foul drainage grounds, which operated between 1976 and 1984. Only 11 applications had to be refused over this period as this constraint was accepted, but when its removal became imminent, development proposals began to proliferate. Some development frequently was permissible in such cases, although at Polegate the District Council considered a total embargo to be safer and less confusing.

Most of the difficulties in this regard arose in South Hampshire following the reduction in size of a projected regional sewerage network based on Peel Common treatment works, near Gosport (Kirkaldy, 1975). This forced the retention of several overloaded works, at the very least on a temporary basis, one of those affected being Budds Farm, near Havant (Hickling et al., 1979). The most severe problems arose at Bishop's Waltham, where a sizeable (although unspecified) development allocation had not been opposed by the SWA or its predecessors, in the expectation that the local works would close when the Peel Common scheme came into operation. When this particular dream faded, an embargo was imposed, temporarily lifted to allow an extra 100 units when some spare capacity was identified, and then reimposed until improvements to the sewerage works were implemented. Once again, technical uncertainties were apparent on the part of the SWA, coupled with its wish not to be seen to be restricting development. Pressure from developers had also acted as a considerable spur, however, with appeal decisions, or at least the threat of them, worrying both agencies. It was perhaps fortunate that the number of units bid for during the temporary relaxation had been very close to the number the SWA was prepared to allow.

Another charge that has been levelled at the RWAs in general concerns their unwillingness to back more speculative strategies on the part of district and county councils, as noted by Ellis (1981). At a time of retrenchment in public spending, local authorities will become increasingly anxious to attract any industry which offers the prospect of increasing employment, and often see advance, serviced sites as a means of encouraging this. At the same time, restrictions on RWA investment make the latter increasingly reluctant to provide for such schemes, which may well never be taken up. In adopting this strategy, however, the RWAs stress that once development is certain and an application has been made, they would act immediately and complete their schemes before the development could be occupied. Some scepticism was evident about local authority estimates in this regard which, as in the case of overall population figures, tend to display extreme optimism for the future. The early structure plans were identified as particularly bad offenders in this respect by several RWAs, and there were past histories of resultant wasting of resources. Although local authority worries should not be dismissed outright, considerable caution, therefore, should be exercised before condemning the RWA as the one clear villain of the piece.

THE DEVELOPMENT FACTOR

The previous discussion has noted the increasing latitude and encouragement given to negotiations over infrastructure works at several points, although in the case study of Lewes, at least, the floodgates for rural development have not been opened by the growth of this phenomenon, despite its apparent potential for undermining written policy. In conjunction with the requisitioning procedure, however, these mechanisms do offer an opportunity to facilitate development in line with policy, but which might otherwise be prevented. This applies as much to public authorities as to private developers, although the need for a financial commitment can still discourage a sizeable programme of service provision. Use of the formal Section 52 agreement has been growing in all RWAs. This mechanism can be utilized both for positive purposes — to secure contributions for works carried out (e.g. sewer provision at the expense of the local authority) — and for negative ones — to restrict the occupation of new development until necessary works have been completed. Direct negotiations between developers and the SWA were commonplace, and often preceded the actual submission of an application, even in the days before the introduction of planning fees.

It is hardly surprising that the actual contributions could be a contentious matter. The Housebuilders' Federation (HBF), in its document *Land for Housing* (Housebuilders' Federation, 1977), advocated that all works should be financed from general RWA funds, but in practice most developers have come to accept, if a little grudgingly at times, that the RWAs are tightly constrained and that if development is to proceed in difficult cases, then some initial financing is necessary. Indeed, many plans now reflect this situation. For example, in 1983 East Sussex County Council introduced a specific policy stating that the developer should bear infrastructure costs (East Sussex County Council, 1983), having first tried out this approach in a few specific growth locations. With better liaison, developers felt that they often were able to identify any likely problems before land purchase, and reduce the price offered to take account of the expenditure needed, and as a double safeguard it usually was possible to raise house sale prices to cover any excess. The representative bodies of the development industry, the Housebuilders' Federation and the Federation of Master Builders, both considered their members' dealings with the RWAs generally to be very smooth. There was partial support for the contention that larger developers were more likely to find the new arrangements favourable, but this is a complex issue which is not discussed further here. Overall, therefore, such arrangements will tend to smooth out difficulties which might otherwise be encountered at the development control stage. This may be at the expense of the eventual housebuyers, however, and at a time when alternatives to house purchase have become increasingly unattainable, this will hit those at the lower end of the market particularly hard.

Development pressure is a crucial factor affecting the interrelationships between local planners and the water authority. If pressure is minimal, the existence of an embargo or of spare capacity will be of little significance, whereas definite development interest in an area can permit the alleviation of any problems there via the contribution system. Some RWAs, notably South West and Wessex, have made contributions a central feature of their planning. South West Water Authority has recently dropped the terms 'embargo' and 'restriction' from standard usage as they were considered too negative, and now looks to developers' contributions to unlock certain areas of the region for development. Wessex Water Authority tends to be even more aggressive in its contributions policy, which operates along similar lines but includes the expectation that the servicing of all new development can be financed by this method. This enables all RWA investment to be diverted towards the refurbishment of the existing system, and meeting the growth in demand from current consumers.

Both RWAs acknowledge some adverse reaction from local councils. South West Water Authority considers this to result from some council-sponsored development areas remaining unserved, whereas for Wessex Water Authority the main problem is the local councils' fear of undermining restraint strategies. This approach does provide the potential for widening the policy choice for rural areas if the political will existed. It also provides an opportunity to alleviate implementation difficulties, notwithstanding the possible weakening of restraint strategies. Finance is the key to such possibilities, however, and leads us finally to a consideration of central government influences, particularly on the water industry.

THE ROLE OF CENTRAL GOVERNMENT

Central government influence on the town and country planning system has come under increasing scrutiny as the pendulum has swung increasingly in favour of the private development lobby (Herington, 1982). Although this has obvious implications for the RWA/local authority relationship, the reduction of the significance of RWA objections via such devices as Circular 22/80 does not appear in itself to have greatly distorted planners' wishes, so far at least. This is certainly the case in Lewes District, and seems to hold for the rest of the SWA area, and indeed in other RWAs as well (Bell, 1986). The effect of central control of the RWAs has been rather less visible, but currently the RWAs find themselves in the limelight to a degree that is highly unusual for them. The full complexities and ramifications of financial control from the centre are examined elsewhere (Bell, 1986), so as a final component of this chapter, an attempt is made to illustrate the likely direct effects of this control on the local planning link.

Regional water authority spending has been reduced to about one-half the level enjoyed just after the 1974 reorganization and the effect of the various controls imposed has been to dictate almost entirely the levels of investment and charges permissible. Some of the detailed controls may have been relaxed, but the only real discretion left is in the construction of the capital programme, whose basic financial limits have already been set. Increasingly rigorous schemes for defining priorities have become ubiquitous as a response to this. High priority is accorded to the servicing of new development, whether industrial or residential, so it is unlikely that the effects of cutbacks will become noticeable in this sector as rapidly as in those of lower priority, such as improvements to river, estuarine and coastal water quality. In view of Saunders' regional state thesis (1983, 1984), it is perhaps not surprising that those parts of RWA activity more directly linked to production should be dominant. No large-scale rash of additional embargoes has broken out as a result of the restrictions, partly due to improved liaison and technical appraisal, plus the latitude in works consent conditions. Some RWAs have worried that more restrictions will have to come eventually, though there is no likelihood of a blanket policy of allowing more to develop unresisted. Such statements, however, seem to be intended for central rather than local government consumption, as part of the process of bidding for finance.

The RWAs became newsworthy towards the end of 1984. This arose because, after a long history of pressure to keep consumer charges down (with the result that any cutbacks fell on the capital investment programme if borrowing was restrained as well), central government suddenly ordered the RWAs to raise their charges well above the prevailing inflation rate. Superficially this move would seem to have safeguarded capital programmes, although it is unlikely to permit their massive expansion. The opposition of many RWAs therefore was rather muted, as their levels of desired spending were not threatened. However, although the realization that the infrastructure system would be jeopardized by further cuts may have constituted a subsidiary motivation, the wish to reduce the level of borrowing was far stronger. Thames Water Authority, which is already self-financing and repaying its accumulated debt with a view to clearing it entirely in the near future, was by far the strongest in its opposition to these changes. Although it had to raise charges by 10 per cent instead of the 3 per cent originally intended, a cut in its capital programme was still necessary to satisfy the level of profit that it was required to achieve. This acts as a warning that capital investment levels are still not likely to be secure against outside influences and restraints, and we cannot be entirely sanguine about the spectre of privatization which has started to hover over the water industry, both in respect of integrated water management and new 'social' investment.

CONCLUSIONS

The variety of evidence reviewed in this chapter suggests that clearcut implementation difficulties in planning policy caused by the water services are now rare. Improved liaison has eliminated most of the relatively straightforward problems of coordination and, coupled with an inherent tendency for the aims of the two sides to be in harmony (particularly in rural areas), this change has played a major role in reducing conflict over development. Some difficulties can still arise, but now are more likely to relate to the coordination of development on larger sites than to the acceptance or rejection of applications. Troublesome issues usually have been resolved, or at least fought over, before the plan is produced. Local authorities have been advised formally to take account of spare capacities in services, so it is not surprising that most aspects of policy work within the constraints imposed by water and other vital services. These can be breached and indeed have been, but in a selective and considered way, in that costs and opportunities have been weighed carefully, and large investments programmed for selected growth locations alone. Water authorities are also charged to have regard to local policies operating in their area, and generally have appeared willing to alter their programmes to do this.

The introduction of a degree of latitude via negotiation in the provision of water services for development might remove one prop from local authority arguments against a particular application. Now that formal and relatively recent plans exist, however, which in large measure incorporate the various water constraints, this need not matter. The real battles are fought over the degree to which such plans will affect development generally. Recent proposals for new villages in the southeast, most notably at Tillingham Hall in the Essex green belt, have included provision of infrastructure totally at the developer's expense, so the basic arguments will centre on the scheme's desirability in broad policy terms, in this case in relation to the green belt in particular. There is potential here for local authorities to encourage development in areas that they would prefer as well, but this is subject to two caveats; the general restrictions on spending to which these authorities are subject, and lack of will to promote alternative rural patterns of development to the generally restrictive ones which are currently almost universal (Cloke, 1983).

At the moment, such arrangements are more likely to benefit private developers in their pursuit of the goals dictated by the unrestrained operation of the market. The cost of reducing implementation difficulties could now well be deterioration in environmental standards, or at least an additional delay in their improvement, plus possibly higher housing costs both for those owning and renting property, or more general underwriting of some of the costs of new schemes if all of this cannot be recovered from the developer. Of relevance to the first charge is the fourfold relaxation of consent conditions on their works permitted by North West Water Authority (Pearce, 1982). The cost of government ideology in this sector is a regressive reorientation of the costs of providing water services from general taxation to a specific tax on water usage, calculated by the amount used rather than any measure of need and ability to pay. Great efforts over time have reduced simple tensions resulting from poor coordination and differing individual and organizational perceptions. The nature of this particular implementation problem has changed, but not vanished, and despite some attempts to divert attention away from this, the pressure of more basic controls and influences has become increasingly obvious.

REFERENCES

Ambrose, P.J. (1974) *The Quiet Revolution: Social Change in a Sussex Village 1871–1971*, Chatto & Windus, London.

Bell, P.J.P. (1986) The implementation of planning and resource agency policies in rural areas. Ph.D. dissertation, Department of Geography, St David's University College, Lampeter.

Blacksell, M. and Gilg, A.W. (1981) *The Countryside: Planning and Change*, George Allen & Unwin, London.

Cherry, G.E. (1982) Rural planning's new focus, *Town and Country Planning*, Vol. 51, 240–243.

Cloke, P.J. (1983) *An Introduction to Rural Settlement Planning*, Methuen, London.

Department of the Environment (with Welsh Office) (1980) *Development Control — Policy and Practice*, Circular 22/80, HMSO, London.

Department of the Environment (with Welsh Office) (1983) *Planning Gain*, Circular 22/83, HMSO, London.

Devon County Council (1977) *Devon County Structure Plan: Report of the Survey*, Devon County Council, Exeter.

East Sussex County Council (1975a) *County Structure Plan 1975: A Consultation Draft*, ESCC, Lewes.

East Sussex County Council (1975b) *County Structure Plan 1975*, ESCC, Lewes.

East Sussex County Council (1979) *County Structure Plan — 1979 Review: A Consultative Draft*, ESCC, Lewes.

East Sussex County Council (1983) *County Structure Plan — 1983 Review: A Consultative Draft*, ESCC, Lewes.

Ellis, P.J. (1981) Planning in an interorganizational context: the relationship between planning and water authorities. M.A. thesis, Department of Town and Country Planning, Trent Polytechnic.

Gilder, I.M. (1979) Rural planning policies: an economic appraisal, *Progress in Planning*, Vol. 11, 213–271.

Gilg, A.W. (1978) *Countryside Planning: The First Three Decades 1945–76*, David & Charles, Newton Abbot.

Glyn-Jones, A. (1979) *Rural Recovery: Has it Begun?* Devon County Council/University of Exeter, Exeter.

Gray, C.J. (1982) Professional ideologies and planning in water authority–local authority relationships. Paper presented to the Political Studies Association Urban Politics Group Conference on Non-local Urban Services, University of Birmingham, 4 December 1982.

Hawkins, J.K. (1981) Don't panic — or how to get the most out of your water authority. Paper presented to the Town and Country Planning Association Conference on Planning and Water, Coventry, 1981.

Herington, J. (1982) Circular 22/80 — the demise of settlement planning? *Area*, Vol. 14, No. 2, 157–166.

Hickling, A., Friend, J.K. and Luckman, D. (1979) *The Development Plan System and Investment Programmes: Final Report to DoE*, HMSO/Tavistock Institute Centre for Organisational and Operational Research, London.

Housebuilders' Federation (HBF) (1977) *Land for Housing*. A discussion paper prepared by a working party of the Housebuilders Federation, HBF, London.

Kirkaldy, I.D. (1975) Sewerage and sewage disposal, *Journal of the Institution of Municipal Engineers*, Vol. 102, 219–221.

Lewes District Council (1977) *Town of Lewes District Plan: Report of Survey*, Lewes District Council, Lewes.

Pearce, F. (1982) *Watershed: The Water Crisis in Britain*, Junction Books, London.

Penning-Rowsell, E.C. (1982) Planning and water services: keeping in step, *Town and Country Planning*, Vol. 51, 150–152.

Saunders, P. (1983) The 'regional state': a review of the literature and agenda for research. Working paper no. 35, University of Sussex, Department of Urban and Regional Studies.

Saunders, P. (1984) We can't afford democracy too much: findings from a study of regional state institutions in south-east England, Working paper no. 43, University of Sussex, Department of Urban and Regional Studies.

Standing Conference on London and South East Regional Planning (SCLSERP) (1981) *Infrastructure and the Regional Strategy: A Report by the Resources Working Party of the Regional Monitoring Group*, SCLSERP, London.

Thring, J.B. (1977) *The Costs of Changing Plans*, Building Research Establishment Planning Directorate, Watford.

Winter, H. (1980) *Homes for Locals*, Community Council of Devon, Exeter.

9

TRANSPORT AND HIGHWAYS POLICY — A DEAD END?

Gareth Edwards

> The first point to note about roads and traffic in post-war Britain is that, for the most part, governments had a positive policy towards them. That is to say, there was a basic idea of where policy was leading and what was being aimed for. (Starkie, 1982, p. 145)

Starkie's summary of road transport planning in Britain presents a picture of efficient and effective resource development for the nation's benefit. Indeed, the 1950s and 1960s with their traffic studies, scientific road plans and major investment schemes do appear to have had a cohesion and unifying purpose leading to positive policy implementation. However, even at the height of its success the seeds of downfall were being sown for transport planning. The economic recession of the 1970s ruthlessly exposed the inadequacies of the system, dispelling the optimism of the preceding decades and leading to the confusion characteristic of the 1980s. The present situation represents a stagnant pool of policy decisions with few opportunities for new innovative proposals and even fewer for the implementation of effective measures.

This condition has received little attention in either the academic or planning press where discussions have continued to focus on immediate economic and social priorities in transport (see, for example, Maltby and White, 1982; Bell et al., 1983; White and Senior, 1983). As such, policy development within transport and highways has remained a much forgotten and neglected area of the overall planning system of Britain. It is hoped to redress this imbalance to some small degree in this chapter by examining how policy development and implementation have been undertaken in the areas of highway maintenance for minor rural roads and rural public bus transport. This is done mainly in the light of research undertaken in a number of specific case studies throughout Mid Wales. Research carried out between 1979 and 1981 forms the basis of the examination of road maintenance in three case study areas, one in each of the counties of Dyfed, Gwynedd and Powys (Figure 9.1). The discussion of public transport policy is based on an analysis of bus services in the Central Powys area (Figure 9.2) undertaken in 1983. Before entering these detailed examples, however, it is important to examine the general environment within which transport planners in Britain are operating.

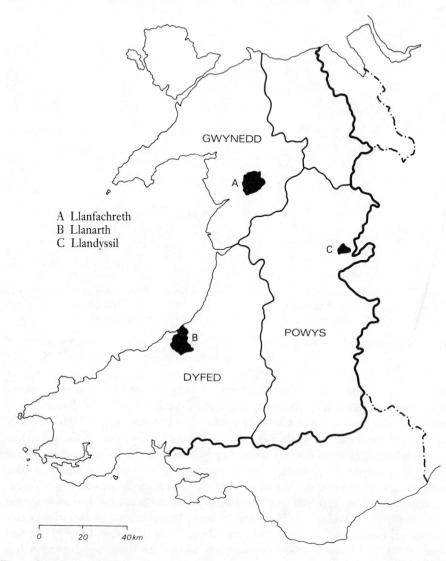

Figure 9.1   Location of the three case study areas.

As with the other aspects of the rural environment covered in this book, attention is beginning to focus within transportation planning on what is termed the 'policy–implementation gap'. Levin (1981) defines how this involves the detailed examination of: 'commitment-carrying statements of policy and . . . the process of implementing them and the extent to which the policy actually gets implemented in the form specified' (p. 11). In response to such examination it is suggested that it is becoming increasingly difficult for policy-makers to put their proposals into action. A number of factors and constraints has contributed to this situation.

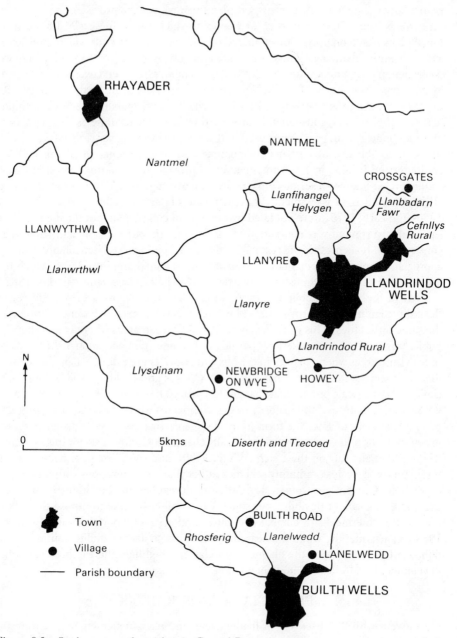

Figure 9.2   Settlements and parishes in Central Powys.

THE NATURE OF TRANSPORT PLANNING

By nature, transport planning involves long-term problem-solving in a constantly and frequently changing environment. This situation often results in policy statements being out of date before any attempts at implementation have taken place. This is particularly so, since much of transport planning involves the provision of infrastructure (roads, railways and airports for example) which cannot be easily altered from initial plans based on projections founded on socioeconomic trends which themselves are constantly changing. Thus, the lead-time involved in, for example, highway construction programmes often means that the schemes have been overtaken by events by the time they are ready to be implemented. This is seen in the road policies developed during the 1960s based on forecasts of car ownership (see, for example, Tanner, 1962) which subsequently proved to be wildly inaccurate as the population and economic growth projections used in the forecasts were never realized. Even with the shift to the use of cost-benefit analysis and the introduction of the COBA-computerized routine in 1973, the inability to provide an accurate forecast of future traffic levels remained a serious drawback which was highlighted by the Leitch Report (1978) on trunk road assessment. As a result many of the road schemes advanced in the 1960s and early 1970s were outdated by the time of completion, but the die had been cast and government was committed to its programme of motorway and trunk road construction. It seems that the reaction to these past failings has been a more cautious approach to policy implementation today at both national and local levels which has fitted in well with the administrative inertia of Whitehall civil servants (Starkie, 1982).

Even in the area of public transport, which obviously enjoys a greater degree of flexibility than highways provision, the long-term development of systems is subject to the same difficulties. This is especially so in major urban areas where comprehensive public transport systems take long periods to become fully operational. At the same time in rural areas where 'in principle, a bus and its driver are a flexible pair of resources that can meet a wide range of trip purposes' (Moyes and Holding, 1984) the path to achieving large-scale operational changes has proved hazardous. This is mainly due to the restrictive nature of the majority of bus companies whose reliance on charter and private hire work dictates the form of their stage carriage services. Furthermore, the use of mini- or midi-buses does not radically change operation costs for bus operators who traditionally rely on the coach (White, 1980), and so efforts have been concentrated on small-scale community schemes rather than on innovations within networks as a whole. Current government legislation to deregulate the bus industry may help overcome this lack of flexibility but some fear it will only serve to expose the lack of readily available means to combat declining rural accessibility (Cloke and Edwards, 1984). Consequently, while the search for robustness and flexibility continues, the failings of the past haunt the planners of today and highlight the gap between policy development and effective implementation.

FINANCIAL CONSTRAINTS

Concurrent with the discovery of inadequacies in policy implementation during the 1970s, the economic recession also began to exert its influence as seen in the national financial crisis and governmental spending cuts. Thus from 1973 onwards national and local transport budgets, along with those of many other public-sector activities, were steadily reduced by successive governments of both major parties, so that by the end of the decade investment in new road schemes was a little more than half its 1973–74 level, while at the height of the crisis in 1976–77 a complete moratorium on new road

Table 9.1 Public expenditure on inland surface transport 1975/76–1980/81 (£million at 1980 prices) (Wistrich, 1980)

		1975–76	1979–80	1980–81
1. Roads				
Motorways and trunk roads	– Construction/improvement	635	352	320
	– Maintenance	93	114	102
Local roads	– Construction/improvement	540	342	*
	– Maintenance	623	558	547
2. Payments to transport operators				
Central government	– BR passenger subsidies	496	449	454
	– BR other payments	349	201	112
	– New bus grant	37	34	34
	– Other	14	16	13
	– BR subsidies	28	32)	225
Local government	– Bus, Underground, etc. subsidies	288	197)	
	– Concessionary fares	113	118	110
	– Public transport investment	255	188	*
3. Other expenditure				
Driver and vehicle licensing		83	51	57
Research and other services		43	12	13
Roads and transport administration		30	26	26
Other local expenditure and administration		215	195	*
Total expenditure		3,860	2,887	2,724

*For 1980–81 the amount of capital expenditure in these areas by local authorities is aggregated to give a total of £544 million.

construction contracts was imposed for nine months (Starkie, 1982). The result was that policy implementation became increasingly difficult as resources were withdrawn not only from road building programmes but from road maintenance and public transport activities as well (Table 9.1).

These expenditure cuts are continuing and are affecting policy implementation. For example, British Rail in its 1984 Corporate Plan assumes that its grant receipts will fall from £935 million in 1984–85 to £690 million by 1989–90 while at the same time declaring its desire to retain its provincial sector (its major loss-maker, which includes all of Britain's rural lines) substantially in its present state. It would seem that British Rail's ability to achieve the latter within the context of the above figures would be a major accomplishment and is somewhat contradicted by a joint report between the Association of County Councils and British Rail (1984) which notes:

> The availability of finance may lead BR to consider the future of certain services. This questioning may also be prompted by the need for expenditure on specific works such as a bridge or a viaduct. An offer of additional finance from a County Council could alter the balance in favour of retaining the service. (p. 3)

Consequently, it appears that the practical implementation at local level of British Rail's general policy in the provincial sector is going to be difficult without extra finance being available.

The operation of rural bus services has for some time been under pressure as less and less money is allocated to local government for revenue support purposes. The revenue support money is now included in the general rate support grant, following the removal of the transport supplementary grant system, and is consequently less secure from diversion to other areas of a county's spending. Thus Moyes and Holding (1984) note: 'What the counties claim for bus subsidies, what they are prepared to allocate, and what the operators need, will become more and more divergent' (p. 75).

It is in the light of this that the government's policy initiative on deregulation has at its core the increase in competition between operators in order to reduce demand for revenue support. It is hoped that the elimination of licensing restrictions and the introduction of a system of tendering for those services which a county council wishes to see retained, but would not be provided without revenue support, will increase efficiency and cut down on unnecessary wastage. Thus, in the Hereford trial area where these policies were experimentally introduced it is stated that service levels were maintained without any substantial increase in fares and with a 38 per cent saving in revenue support (Hereford & Worcester County Council, 1983). However, it is feared that such policies, dictated by financial considerations, will have serious ramifications for the quality and quantity of rural bus services (Moyes and Holding, 1984). This is especially important in the remoter areas where potential savings in revenue support will not be as readily available as they were in Hereford because of the absence of profitable routes and a history of non-competition between operators. Indeed, Cloke and Edwards (1984) conclude:

> [. . .] whilst it is acknowledged that the tendering procedure may well reduce the demands made on revenue support there is evidence from the Hereford area to suggest that the savings might not be as great as claimed. Indeed, it is probable that the savings were influenced by events unrelated to deregulation in that the integration of school contract and stage carriage services and the results of Midland Red's Market Analysis Project were beginning to bear

fruit. If savings do not in fact reach government expectations as reflected in subsequent Rate Support Grant allocations, then pressure on revenue support will substantially increase. (p. 140)

POLITICAL STRUCTURES

A further complication in examining policy implementation in transport planning is Britain's political structures, in particular the relative responsibilities of central and local government. In general, the responsibility for the implementation of policy rests with local government (other than in the case of trunk roads) under what was considered to be discrete pressure, usually through the issuing of memoranda, from Whitehall (Starkie, 1982). However, in recent years with the growing conflict between central and local government over policy statements and the subsequent strengthening of central direction of affairs, it has become increasingly difficult to obtain a consensus on which implementation may proceed. Among the number of clashes between central and local government over transport policy probably the best publicized was that of the Greater London Council's (GLC) introduction of a 25 per cent reduction in fares on London Transport services in 1981. The implementation of this policy, which was included in the ruling Labour group's election manifesto, brought the GLC into direct opposition with the Conservative government who retaliated by withdrawing grant aid to London Transport. In return the GLC proposed to raise a supplementary rate to meet the cost of its policy but the validity of this was challenged in law by Conservative councillors, which resulted in the now famous House of Lords decision against the GLC which was then obliged to raise fares by 100 per cent. Nor have these clashes been restricted to Labour-controlled metropolitan authorities, as recent government proposals for the deregulation of the bus industry have come under heavy criticism from the Conservative-dominated Association of County Councils. This divergence in perspectives between those who in the main finance transport programmes and those who operate them obviously presents major difficulties for effective policy implementation.

Much of this criticism has centred on the impact the proposals will have on safety levels. It is presumed that the new proposals will favour independent operators against the National Bus Company (NBC) subsidiaries as the former tend to have lower running costs. However, in many instances lower maintenance standards contribute to this difference in running costs with the result that independent operators have a poor safety record. Thus, three operators who took advantage of the Hereford experiment to introduce new services were found to be operating defective vehicles. Concern has also been expressed over the continuing integration and coordination of bus networks under relaxed licensing arrangements. Again experience in the Hereford trial area seems to support these concerns as buses tended to lack clear markings and destination boards and did not keep to declared schedules. At the same time it is suggested that while there may be an initial expansion in services, in the long term there may well be an overall decrease as the economic realities of running services overtakes the initial excitement of greater competition. These fears are reflected in the discussions of the Welsh Counties Committee (1984) which, while acknowledging the possible financial benefits of greater competition, concentrate on the need for safeguards to ensure the

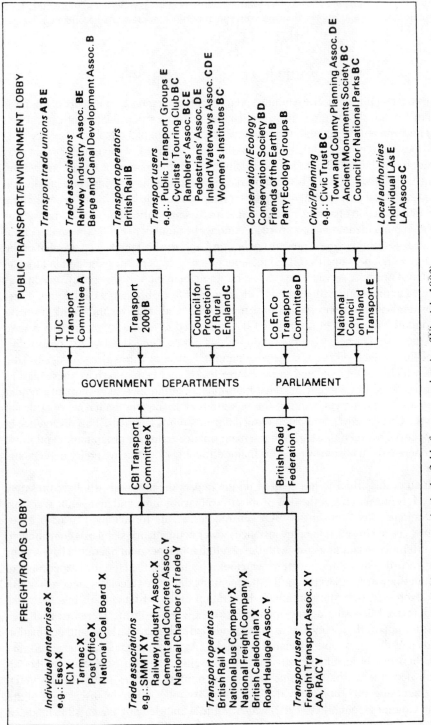

Figure 9.3   Pressure and lobby groups active in the field of transport planning (Wistrich, 1983).

safety, coordination and financial security of stage carriage services.

PRESSURE GROUPS

Within transport planning various pressure and lobby groups are active at both the development and implementation stages of policy-making (Figure 9.3). This is particularly evident in the case of environmental pressure groups whose ability to organize themselves effectively in the 1970s turned many a public inquiry into a battleground. However, the domination of the Department of Transport by road engineers (Levin, 1979; Plowden, 1980) and the strength of the road lobby have led some to dispute the effect of any opposition to existing road policy. This is seemingly supported by the example of the 'Peeler memorandum' of 1978 which spoke of achieving a conclusion to the debate on weight limits for lorries in accordance with the Department of Transport's views seemingly without reference to public opinion or Parliament. Nevertheless, pressure groups did have some notable successes (for example, the indefinite adjournment of the Arredale trunk road inquiry in 1976) and Starkie (1982) notes that at least their activities inevitably delayed the implementation of policy so that the time-lag between the first stages of any road scheme and the start of construction took anything between 10 and 12 years.

In a similar fashion pressure groups have also exerted influence on other areas of transport policy. Again drawing from the case of rural bus services it is possible to see how such national organizations as the National Council of Voluntary Organizations (NCVO) and the Council for the Protection of Rural England (CPRE) and local groups, such as Women's Institutes and residents' associations, do alter public transport policy in their favour in much the same way as the stronger environmentalist lobbies. Although there are clearly differences between 'road' and 'bus' lobbies, not least that the former tend to be negatively environmentalist while the latter seek positive socioeconomic provision, they are similar in their basic objective of altering policy away from a commitment to roads to statements in favour of public transport, and employ similar methods to that end (Wistrich, 1983).

Thus it is clear that transport policy implementation has become a process fraught with complications as the interaction of central and local government with pressure groups, the balancing of professional judgement and financial limits, and the difficulties of long-term planning in a rapidly changing environment all influence the ultimate form of transport measures. Furthermore, this is evident not only at the national scale but also at the local level, where planning is at the 'sharp end'. This is seen in the example of road maintenance and public transport planning in rural Wales.

MINOR RURAL ROAD MAINTENANCE IN WALES

Research carried out between 1979 and 1981 into the problems of maintaining minor rural roads in Wales revealed that the deterioration of these roads stemmed principally from their structural inability to cope with modern-day traffic conditions (Edwards, 1984). Nevertheless, studies in three areas showed that the political and professional decisions made over the allocation and utilization of funds for maintenance exerted considerable influence over the structural condition and state of maintenance of the roads. Within the hierarchy of decision-making three levels of policy formulation are identifiable, each having a different impact on maintenance but all three interacting to shape the pattern of maintenance expenditure seen in the case study areas.

NATIONAL LEVEL OF POLICY

The national level of policy formulation influences implemented programmes through the allocation of crucial resources for road maintenance from the Treasury to local government by means of the rate support grant. However, successive governments have reduced expenditure on roads as part of a general reduction in public spending. These cuts resulted in a 23 per cent decrease in the maintenance budget of Welsh authorities between 1972–73 and 1978–80 (at 1976 prices), and the present government has further reduced the amount spent each year. At the same time this reduction in expenditure has coincided with increased demand on the road network as a result of vehicular trends, and consequently Ellis (1980) sees governmental policies leading to the 'horrendous' prospect of the irreversible deterioration of the road network, while the British Road Federation (1978) more generously describes these policies as being 'short-sighted'. The actual effect of these cuts on implemented maintenance programmes is manifested in different ways.

1. Less effective maintenance

In response to the financial constraints imposed by central government, local authorities have had to rely on cheaper but less effective measures in their attempts to maintain the structural integrity of minor roads. Thus there has been an increasing emphasis on surface dressing and minor repairs within programmes, as resurfacing and reconstruction measures have become expensive relative to available financial resources. However, as early as 1978 Dyfed County Council was showing that surface dressing work as well as resurfacing were falling well behind preferred standards, particularly on unclassified roads (Table 9.2)

2. Reduction in manpower

One of the main ways in which governments have required local authorities to restrict

Table 9.2   Resurfacing and surface dressing cycles in Dyfed, 1978–79 (Dyfed County Council, 1978)

	Cycle based on 1978–79 budget		Preferred cycle	
	Laid (km)	Cycle (yrs)	Laid (km)	Cycle (yrs)
Resurfacing				
Principal	22.8	24.5	37.0	15.0
Non-principal	133.2	29.0	184.0	22.5
Unclassified	23.1	138.0	128.0	25.0
Surface dressing				
Principal	81.1	7.0	110.0	5.0
Non-principal	523.1	7.5	499.0	7.5
Unclassified	260.5	12.0	318.0	10.0

Table 9.3   Dyfed County Council, Highways Department manpower figures 1974–80 (Edwards, 1984)

	Drivers	Craftsmen	Manual labourers	Total
1974	100	118	915	1,133
1975	113	91	855	1,059
1976	188	102	711	1,001
1977	186	104	656	946
1978	181	120	640	941
1979	180	119	635	934
1980	176	155	559	850

their expenditure has been through the reduction and restructuring of their labour force. Again this is illustrated by the example of Dyfed which has reorganized its labour force into mobile gangs (hence the increase in drivers in 1976) in order to cope with the reduction in the total number of its manual workers (Table 9.3).

As the cuts have continued and the workforce has been further reduced, the workload of each 'gang' has increased to the extent that many minor roads are now inspected only once a year, thus limiting the early diagnosis of carriageway defects. Even then there are not always sufficient maintenance workers to carry out remedial work quickly once a defect is noticed.

3.   Increased hazard of accidents

Commentators such as the British Road Federation (1978) and Read (1980) have expressed concern that as road surfaces deteriorate due to lack of maintenance there will be an increased danger to road users, especially from skidding. As a local authority is liable to prosecution by an injured party if lack of maintenance is proved to have contributed to an accident, pressure is again placed on highway authorities to spread their resources thinly over a wide area in the form of surface dressing to maintain road-holding qualities, rather than tackle long-term structural problems.

Thus the influence of the national level of policy formulation should have the effect of limiting maintenance programmes implemented on minor rural roads and doing little to help avert their long-term decline and deterioration.

COUNTY LEVEL OF POLICY

The county level of policy formulation exists to direct and attract maintenance investment. As such, county level policies normally consist of two broad areas of strategy: issuing a statement of interest giving guidelines to local surveyors and highlighting maintenance problems in the county in submissions to government as an attempt to gain increased financial support. Such strategies are normally best expressed by the counties in their annual 'transport policies and programmes' (TPP) documents. An example is seen in Powys County Council's 1978 submission to the Secretary of State for Wales, which drew attention to the adverse climatic and topographic conditions in the county. The Council pointed out that special financial aid is given to some Scottish areas in recognition of their prevailing climatic conditions and that Powys appeared to merit similar consideration as over 80 per cent of its area lies at altitudes above 656 ft, where the average rainfall is between 590 and 984 inches per year. In the light of the resultant winter maintenance and drainage problems, additional financial allocations were requested to meet the claims on resources made by these special factors in the county.

At the same time the counties also have to translate the present national decisions on public expenditure into practical cuts within local road networks which are under the control of the various local surveyors. This entails the statement of priorities and standards to be observed within the county, normally directing the concentration of resources into specific measures, as finance allows, to respond to those local factors influencing maintenance in the area concerned. Consequently, Gwynedd County Council (1978) has formed a policy of concentrating resources on surface dressing, in preference to reconstruction and resurfacing works, as the best means of dealing with its climatic and drainage problems during a time of public expenditure cuts. In contrast Dyfed County Council (1978) has endeavoured to retain a programme of resurfacing and strengthening works to meet the demands placed on its minor rural road network by bulk milk tanker movements in what is a predominantly dairying county.

Thus the county level of policy formulation acts as a link between central government and the local surveyor. The latter's degree of flexibility in implementing maintenance programmes on the ground depends on the degree of creativity at the county level in securing and allocating resources gained from central government within the limits of practical constraints.

LOCAL LEVEL OF POLICY

Policy implementation is substantially affected by the local level in its own right. Lack of adequate methods of assessing the maintenance requirements of different areas means that the allocation of funds, and subsequently implemented programmes, are often based on the quality of representations made by local surveyors to the county authorities. Despite attempts to introduce standardized maintenance rating systems (see Marshall, 1970, for example) much still depends on the interpretation of suggested standards by local surveyors and their staff in the field. However, the local surveyors are responsible not only for the differences in the perceived needs of their areas but also to a large extent for the different levels of investment each area receives. The translation of 'needs' into requests for funds is a specialized skill requiring a high degree of astuteness and experience. The local surveyor collates the projected costs of the maintenance needs of the area and forwards them to the county administration which normally reduces the scale of the schemes submitted according to resources made available by central government. The extent of this pruning operation depends on the surveyor's ability to justify the requests made and to press home the area's needs. Thus, the allocation of funds between local areas reflects the character, ability and experience of the various surveyors as much as the area's relative maintenance needs.

Once funds have been secured the surveyor's skill in utilizing them becomes extremely important. Within their areas local surveyors have a high degree of autonomy in the way they dispose of their resources as long as the broad strategy and standards of the county are enforced. Thus the allocation of resources to different roads and the type of measures employed within a given area are decisions basically taken by local surveyors. Their ability to maximize the use of available resources has an important influence on maintenance policies implemented in their area. A further aspect of this local level of policy implementation is the approaches made to surveyors by local councillors. The presence of a particularly vociferous and influential councillor in an area or village may often result in a greater maintenance investment as the councillor brings pressure to bear on both the local surveyor and the county administration. Thus, the local level has considerable control over the acquisition of funds and the utilization of resources which dictate the final form of the policies implemented in any one area.

The end-result of the interaction of these three levels of policy formulation with their competitive and frequently contradictory aims is that implemented programmes for the maintenance of minor roads show little or no cohesion and certainly no priority evaluation based on the real needs of the different areas. Thus, there was no evidence between the three case study areas (Figure 9.1) of a consistent implementation of a strategic maintenance policy but rather an *ad hoc* reaction to events within each level of the policy hierarchy.

AREA A: LLANFACHRETH

The distribution of resources in the Llanfachreth area is primarily influenced by national and county level decisions with little input in this instance from the local level. The impact of public expenditure cuts is clearly evident in Llanfachreth, where no major carriageway work (resurfacing or reconstruction) has been carried out since 1978–79 and there are no plans to reactivate such schemes in the foreseeable future. These works accounted for 36 per cent of the area's maintenance commitment prior to 1978–79 and, although it is likely that some of the money saved has been directed to other forms of maintenance in the area, the loss of these works represents a significant reduction in the area's maintenance effort. The national level of policy formulation has also led to a reduction in the workforce available for maintenance schemes in the area. In 1974 the Llanfachreth District, of which the case study area is a part, was served by its own roadgang but by 1979 the labour force had been reduced to one full-time roadman who could call on mobile gangs from adjoining areas for assistance. This reduction in both expenditure and the labour force has resulted in a programme of once-yearly surface dressing and minor repair measures.

In this particular case the local level of policy formulation has been considerably weakened and exerts little influence on the final form in which maintenance policy is implemented. The increasing centralization of decision-making in the county has reduced local input to the system. Although the County Council expressed the desire that mobile gangs should 'operate in localised areas where they are familiar with local conditions' (Gwynedd County Council, 1977, p. 22), it is clear from the Llanfachreth area that financial constraints have forced it to modify this principle. It is clear, therefore, that policy implementation in the Llanfachreth case study area has been constrained by the national level of policy formulation passed on through county council decisions with no input at the local level.

AREA B: LLANARTH

The Llanarth case study area has also been heavily influenced by government policy decisions with again no major carriageway works carried out since 1978–79 and the workforce declining in accordance with that of the county of Dyfed as a whole (see Table 9.3). However, in Llanarth the use of surface dressing has also declined, unlike in Llanfachreth, so that by 1979–80 only 9 per cent of the area's roads were being surface dressed annually compared with 18 per cent in 1974–75. However, while maintenance expenditure rose by 12.4 per cent between 1975–76 and 1979–80, expenditure on basic maintenance (drain clearing, hedge cutting and verge maintenance) rose by 197 per cent during the same period. The hedges and verges lining the Llanarth area's roads require heavy maintenance investment in the form of labour-intensive cutting and clearing works in order to conform with environmental and safety considerations. Dyfed County Council stated in 1978 that these measures had been reduced to their minimum and thus cuts in expenditure could only be met by the works carried out on the roads themselves. This is in contrast to Llanfachreth where basic maintenance is not a priority and reductions in expenditure were met by a shift of emphasis within carriageway works. Thus the differences in maintenance programmes between Llanfachreth and Llanarth are mainly a reflection of a difference of policy at the county level, albeit that the divergence is a result of varying physical conditions. However, there is also a difference at the local level as the surveyor of Llanarth was able to concentrate resources to specific road sections, which he perceived to be important links in the local bulk milk tanker collection network, whereas such actions were absent in the Llanfachreth area. Consequently, although the main differences in policy implementation between the two areas are the result of different approaches at the county level, there is also a difference related to local-level acquisition and utilization of resources.

AREA C: LLANDYSSIL

Of the three case study areas Llandyssil appears to have been the least affected by expenditure cuts in that it retained a programme of major carriageway works, costing £34 000 in 1980–81, when such works were no longer financially possible in the other two areas. During the same period Llandyssil had also retained its local 'lengthman', a member of the maintenance team removed in the early 1970s in the other two areas. This is in stark contrast with the Llanfachreth area where the emphasis is on mobile gangs visiting the area once a year whereas Llandyssil has a resident worker to carry out basic maintenance measures and report road defects all year round. It therefore appears that public expenditure cuts from the national level of policy formulation are affecting the other two areas more than Llandyssil. This is probably due to the fact that Llandyssil, as the area of lowest spending (£632 per mile/per year, compared with £799 in Llanarth and £854 in Llanfachreth), has been able to avoid the scrutiny of the political surgeons, which has been concentrated in areas of higher spending. As a result of this reduced impact of changes at the national level policy formulation at county level has also been mitigated in the area as Powys has had to provide few directives to the local surveyor on maintenance reductions.

Table 9.4   The influence of the levels of policy formulation on implemented maintenance programmes in the three case study areas

Area	Level of policy formulation		
	National	County	Local
Llanfachreth	Influential	Active	Insignificant
Llanarth	Influential	Influential	Active
Llandyssil	Active	Insignificant	Influential

Therefore, in this instance, the local level has become a very important determinant of maintenance policy implementation in the Llandyssil area. The ability of the local surveyor to acquire sufficient funds for the area prior to 1975 allowed a positive approach to maintenance. A combination of his own individual skill and the commitment of senior county officials to Powys's road programme resulted in the systematic improvement in drainage of roads in the area which were subsequently resurfaced, thus providing sound carriageway structures which have been periodically strengthened by surface dressing. Thus it appears that as the influence of the national level of policy formulation declines the influence of the local level increases. In summary the interaction of the three levels of policy formulation is given in Table 9.4.

Thus implemented maintenance programmes in Llanfachreth are determined predominantly by national policy decisions; in Llanarth by a combination of national and county decisions; and in Llandyssil essentially by local policy formulation. The result is that maintenance put into effect does not reflect any one set of policy constraints but is essentially a compromise worked out between competing interests according to their relative strength and within the specific conditions of various road environments. Generally, government policy decisions, particularly in the case of expenditure cuts, take priority in this process of compromise. However, the Llandyssil case study shows how, given favourable circumstances and astute management, national policy directives do not influence implemented maintenance schemes to the same extent in every area. The degree of influence exerted depends on circumstances which afford local discretion and on the skill of local technicians in taking advantage of any favourable circumstances. This ability to withstand governmental pressure is seen on a wider scale in the inability of the Department of Transport to secure agreement from local authorities for the introduction of a standardized maintenance rating system which would make financial allocations to authorities easier to assess. The conclusion to be drawn from this examination of minor rural road maintenance in Wales therefore appears to be that there is no coherent and unifying policy implementation but rather a series of reactions to the confrontations between the three levels of policy influence identified above. It seems that the end-result in terms of roads treated and the methods used bears little resemblance to the notion of planned maintenance programmes in line with some guiding principles of set policies.

PLANNING RURAL BUSES: THE RADNOR CIRCLE EXAMPLE

As with road maintenance, the planning and provision of rural bus services are a complicated and often confusing area of local government responsibility. Again there appear to be few instances of coherent policy development and implementation but rather a series of 'trade-offs' between the interested parties, which in this instance include not only central and local government but also the bus operators, either NBC subsidiaries or independents. This brings an added dimension to our discussion of transport policy implementation as it now requires the cooperation of organizations beyond the direct sphere of governmental institutions. Thus, even when a policy consensus is achievable between central and local government its implementation may still be thwarted by, or vary considerably according to, the operator involved. The difficulties inherent in this process are illustrated by the example of the bus service provided in the Central Powys area (Figure 9.2) and the desire by planning agencies to introduce a frequent and regular service to be called the Radnor Circle.

In response to their statutory duty 'to promote the provision of a co-ordinated and efficient public passenger transport network' (Local Government Act 1972) local authorities in the area have formed a rather nebulous policy stating that: 'The District Councils will wherever possible pursue the maintenance and improvement of existing levels of public transport' (Powys County Council, Brecknock Borough Council and Radnor District Council, 1983, CP34). The practical outworking of this policy relied on increased revenue support or the limited introduction of unconventional services. However, it was clear to planning agencies in the Central Powys area that such steps could not support the provision of a frequent and regular bus service connecting the three towns of the area. Such a proposal was incorporated in discussions on the development of the area and a preliminary feasibility study concluded that:

> existing patterns of employment and service provision in the area indicated a modest level of demand for a public transport service linking the three centres and their surrounding villages. In addition, the introduction of such a service would appear to be in sympathy with future plans for the area. (Edwards, 1985)

However, it was also acknowledged that the introduction of such a service would take place against the backdrop of existing service provision and policy implementation problems and would require the commitment of substantial financial and political resources.

EXISTING PUBLIC TRANSPORT PROVISION

Figure 9.4 shows the existing public transport routes operating in the area and reveals a complex arrangement of 13 separate bus services, many sharing the same route and only two providing a direct link between Builth Wells, Llandrindod Wells and Rhayader. However, seven of these services (including the two that link the three towns) are restricted by their scheduling or by regulation, and do not allow the transfer of passengers within the area. In effect, therefore, local public transport in the area is provided by five services operated by Crossgates Motors and the Post Bus which runs between Llandrindod Wells and Rhayader. This reflects one of the major obstacles to policy implementation in that licensing arrangements have favoured existing operators and have inhibited the introduction of new services. In the past, opposition from an existing operator in an area to an application for a route licence by another operator has often swayed the traffic commissioners in refusing the application. Thus, in this particular instance, Crossgates Motors have successfully defended their position as the main provider of stage carriage services in the study area and have retained a powerful veto on any policy development they perceive to be against their interests. The result has been to fossilize the network of services through the restriction of any new services

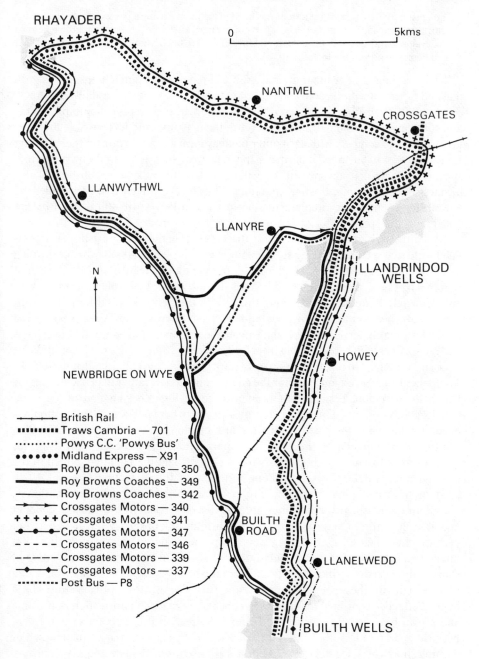

Figure 9.4 Services in the study area.

in terms of their picking up or setting down of passengers. Of course, present government legislation to deregulate the bus industry is based on an awareness that the old licensing system has had this negative effect. The Department of Transport notes:

> The result of these worthy intentions has been to maintain a pattern of services developed for a different age and to neglect the best parts of the market. There has been too little incentive to develop markets to woo the customer. Operators have been hampered by a philosophy that is defensive and inward looking. (p. 1)

The government hopes that deregulation will remove this public transport stagnation and replace it with flexible and vibrant networks as operators are allowed to freely compete with each other. However, under these new arrangements policy implementation still remains substantially at the mercy of the operators and it is possible that they may not wish to compete with each other but may form a cartel to protect their existing routes and overall business. This may happen in areas such as Central Powys where it appears unlikely that anyone will be willing to take the risk of establishing a new business in opposition to existing operators. Thus it is very likely that even under the new arrangements policy implementation in Central Powys will still depend on the reaction of the area's major operator to any proposals made.

Nevertheless, Figure 9.5 shows that spatial coverage of the area by existing services is good with each settlement being served. However, this picture is somewhat misleading as the routes in question are used by an infrequent and irregular service as seen in Figure 9.6. The strength of the Builth Wells–Llandrindod Wells route is evident, with an adequately frequent service along this link in the network. Elsewhere, however, services are less frequent with the Builth Wells–Newbridge-on-Wye section being particularly poorly served and revealing an obvious absence of integration between bus and rail services in the area. People from Builth Wells wishing to use the Central Wales Line and who need to reach a station by bus are forced to travel to Llandrindod Wells, where they often have a long wait for the connecting service, rather than use the nearby Builth Road station. Similarly, there appears to be little coordination of local and non-local bus services. This again identifies an area where policy implementation has been problematic in the past. Despite the introduction of the Public Transport Plan (PTP) system, initiated by the 1978 Transport Act, which included a provision for '[. . .] District Councils and operators to co-operate with the County Council in the co-ordination of Public Passenger Transport services' (Powys County Council, 1979, p. 2), there seems to have been little progress towards achieving it in Central Powys. This is for two reasons: first, obtaining information on services from some independent operators has proved very difficult, not because of any obstinacy on their part but because they themselves do not always keep the required information. It is not unknown for the operators to be unaware of the schedule or even the exact route of some of their services which have been left in the hands of the drivers, many of whom have been driving these routes for many years. Such a haphazard approach affords little hope of effective coordination of services. Second, even when information is available and a plan has been formulated for better coordination it is difficult to implement because operators lack the flexibility to change their stage carriage timetables. For example, buses used for stage carriage duties are also used for contract and private hire work and any suggested changes which would require them for stage carriage services when they are normally used for other duties is likely to be rejected. At the same time

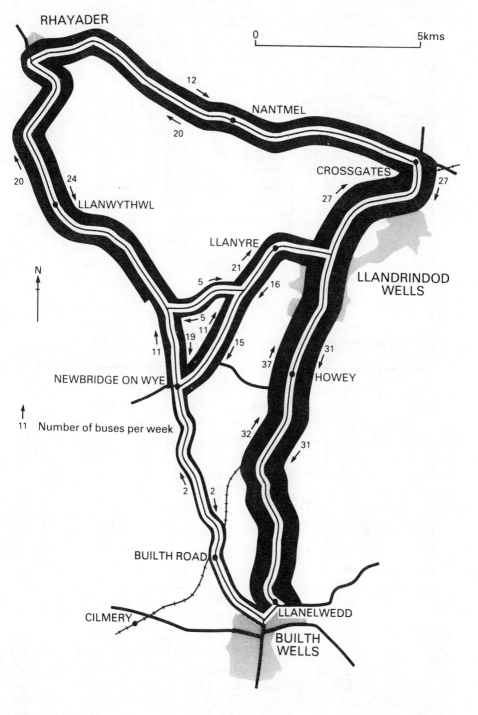

Figure 9.5   Weekly bus flows in the study area.

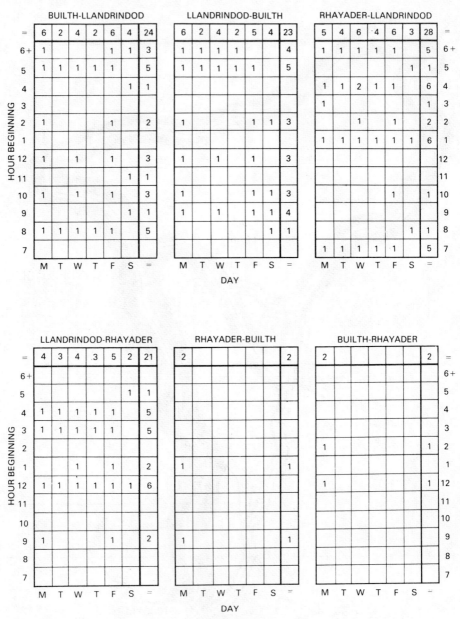

Figure 9.6   Time and day of local bus services in the study area.

many drivers work on a part-time or split-shift basis outside of which they pursue another career which restricts their availability for any new schedules. Indeed, the operations of many bus companies resemble a house of cards: remove one of the cards and the whole intricate system collapses. Again, present deregulation proposals offer little hope of altering this situation as they rely on the operators to coordinate services in their own self-interest and even remove the framework of the PTP while leaving local authorities with their responsibility to coordinate services. These problems are less acute when dealing with NBC subsidiaries who are dedicated to stage carriage operations and employ full-time drivers but in areas such as Central Powys where independent operators predominate coordinating a network of services is often very difficult.

In addition the irregular nature of services in the study area is illustrated by the details of the day and time of each journey shown in Figure 9.6. The increase in public transport activity on Mondays and Fridays reflects the fact that these are the market days of Builth Wells and Llandrindod Wells respectively, but outside of these two days the services provided are extremely irregular and trip-making by public transport is difficult. Even in the case of those buses operating between Builth Wells and Llandrindod Wells, which provide a reasonable journey-to-work service, there is no convenient mid-week shopping service and no provision for evening leisure trips. Services between Rhayader and Llandrindod Wells only allow journey-to-work usage if passengers working in Llandrindod Wells finish work before 5.00 p.m., which is often not the case for retail and service workers, but mid-week shopping trips are feasible by virtue of the presence of the Post Bus. However, that service only allows for one hour's stay in Llandrindod Wells and therefore represents a limited opportunity for using its facilities. Again, no evening service is available. The service between Rhayader and Builth Wells is virtually non-existent with only two return journeys to Builth Wells on market day.

Therefore, the public transport system in the area may be described as a combination of uncoordinated, infrequent and irregular services. Those services do reflect demand in that they concentrate on linking Rhayader and Builth Wells to Llandrindod Wells. However, existing levels of patronage, averaging below 0.5 passengers per mile for Crossgates Motors services, mean that the costs incurred in running the services are far greater than the revenue received and thus they are heavily dependent on revenue support from Powys County Council, which leaves little money available for implementing new policy initiatives. The Council (1983) notes: 'There is thus no likelihood of any increase in provision, and over the last two years there has in fact been a small percentage reduction' (p. 4). This is in accordance with current government policy to reduce public expenditure, which is also at the centre of its deregulation proposals. As noted above it is hoped that the introduction of a system of tendering will decrease the demand for revenue support which will continue to be reduced in anticipation of the projected savings. However, there is concern that in such areas as Central Powys savings will only be minimal thus increasing pressure on revenue support and continuing to restrict the possibility of new policy implementation.

In addition the transport supplementary grant has been phased out in Wales and provision for public transport is now included within the rate support grant system where it faces competition from other areas of local authority spending. Even within transport budgets priority often goes to highway spending, thus for Powys in 1984–85 £7.4 million was spent on highway maintenance, £1.7 million on capital projects and only £322 000 on revenue support. This reflects the importance of Powys's road network in terms of both its agricultural economy and its strategic situation astride numerous important trunk roads. However, it also reflects a general bias within the county's administration where only two people are employed on public transport matters. Thus, the ability of revenue support to resist pressure from other sectors of Powys's statutory responsibilities is limited, especially given the belief that the highway needs are not fairly reflected within the fixed formula of the rate support grant (Powys County Council, 1984). In such circumstances it is clear that securing finance for new public transport initiatives is very difficult and has probably contributed substantially to the present stagnation of services in the area.

Thus existing public transport provision in Central Powys reflects the inability of policy-makers to implement coherent and effective proposals in much the same way as the ineffectiveness of road maintenance policy discussed earlier. Again the question of financial commitment by both central and local government is an important factor in determining policy implementation. However, it is also notable that the influence of the local level of policy implementation, this time in the form of the operator, is equally, if not more, important in shaping the actual provision of services as it was in the case of road maintenance.

RADNOR CIRCLE: THE PROPOSAL

Set against this backdrop of existing services and policy implementation problems the research undertaken by the author offered an example of how a frequent and regular service could be introduced to connect Builth Wells, Llandrindod Wells and Rhayader and integrate with British Rail services. This would obviously be best achieved by a circular route with two vehicles operating in opposite directions around the circuit to allow return journeys along the shortest route between the three centres. However, a simple circular route would leave Llanyre unserved and so a detour to take in Llanyre was suggested as represented in Figure 9.7. This route has the added advantage of taking the service through Llandrindod Wells twice during each complete circuit and doubling its frequency between Howey and Llandrindod Wells, probably the busiest section of the service. The length of the circuit is estimated to be 40 miles and journey times between Llandrindod Wells and any other point on the route should not exceed 35 minutes while journeys between Builth Wells and Rhayader (the two points furthest apart) should not exceed 65 minutes. Although this latter journey time is substantially longer than the direct journey time of 35 minutes it was felt that the greater coverage of the area provided by the proposed route is more than adequate compensation. Furthermore, it is anticipated that the majority of passengers will wish to make journeys to and from Llandrindod Wells. At the same time the ability to make a journey between Builth Wells and Rhayader would be an improvement on existing services even given the length of time needed. However, the implementation of such a policy would face considerable difficulties in line with the above-mentioned difficulties of existing service provision.

FINDING AN OPERATOR

The logistical requirements for operating such a service in terms of bus and driver availability would place a considerable strain on a private operator already committed to school contract and tour work. In the light of this, and the general resistance to change from the major operator in the area noted above, it may prove difficult to attract an

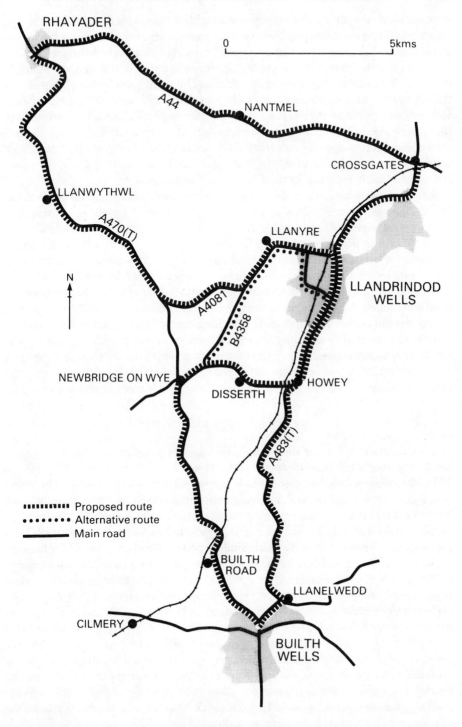

Figure 9.7   Route of the suggested circular service.

operator to run the service. New government legislation provides the framework within which competing operators may tender for the opportunity to provide such a service but it is probable that at best only two existing operators (Crossgates and Browns Motors) have the capability to meet the above specifications and then only if they are willing to drastically restructure their current operations. The service would be better suited to the operational characteristics of an NBC subsidiary but their costs are higher than independent operators and it is unclear whether in the post-deregulation environment they will be able to expand into an area where they have no tradition of service. Indeed, the ending of cross-subsidies whereby NBC subsidiaries have in the past supported their rural services with the profits from some of their urban routes, is likely to lead to a reduction in their presence in rural Wales, not an increase.

A further alternative lies in the possibility of the local authority itself running the service. The existence of buses adapted to cater for disabled people and operated by Powys Social Services Department may provide the basis for the service while allowing greater access to public transport for the disabled and the elderly who have physical difficulties in using conventional stage carriage services. However, the availability of these vehicles, and the purchase of others, for a regular service would require the cooperation of the various departments involved, something which has traditionally been difficult to achieve. In addition the political will to allow the county to provide such a service is unlikely to be forthcoming from local councillors who are in the main very conservative in attitude and include representatives of independent operators who would be unhappy to face competition from a council-run service. Thus, implementation of the scheme would appear to rest on the reaction of the two main operators in the area to its details which they would probably accept in a more modified form.

FINDING THE FINANCE

Overall, the operation of the above route and schedule would involve buses undertaking approximately 100 000 miles per year at a cost of somewhere between £50 000 and £95 000 (based on 1983–84 cost per mile figures for operators in Powys). The actual cost of the service will depend on the operator involved while the cost to the local authority will depend on any tendering arrangements, but it is probable that revenue support of between £12 000 and £25 000 may be required (based on 1983–84 payments to operators in Powys) which would represent between 5·6 and 11·7 per cent of the 1983–84 budget for revenue support to stage carriage services in the county. Consequently, the introduction of the service would require a substantial commitment of resources, although it should be remembered that revenue support for certain existing services may no longer be required. In addition the cost to the local authority may be reduced by introducing a less frequent service, by exploring the possibilities for the carriage of goods as well as passengers and flexible driving arrangements by the operator involved. Nevertheless, the securing of financial aid for the service would require an increase in revenue support in the county, a situation that neither local nor central government representatives are able to foresee happening. There is little evidence that county officials would press for such finances to be made available for the scheme as their attention is predominantly directed towards highway expenditure while the government is equally unlikely to release additional funds given its drive towards reducing revenue support. Thus, again implementation may be expected to flounder on the rocks of inadequate financing.

FINDING THE COOPERATION

A further implementation problem would be gaining the cooperation of all operators in the area to allow the coordination and full integration of the new service. Although the suggested schedule would allow integration with British Rail services the coordination with bus services linking the area to nearby centres would also be important. Such services, however, have their schedules and routes dictated by factors external to the Central Powys area and cooperation with their operators is likely to be hindered. Cooperation with other operators is also essential if the circuit as a whole is to remain intact. It is feasible that under the new licensing system other operators may compete with the new service over its more profitable section (Builth Wells to Llandrindod Wells), thus severely prejudicing its financial position and possibly leading to its collapse. Such a scenario would return bus services in the area to their current unsatisfactory position. The cooperation of all operators in the area would therefore be extremely important to the successful provision of a Radnor Circle service. Once again, unfortunately, past experience would suggest that such cooperation is not easily achieved.

In summary it is possible to suggest that the example of the proposed Radnor Circle bus service confirms the seeming impossibility of effecting any positive large-scale policy implementation. Current government initiatives seem doomed to fail to halt the decline of services in this and other areas unless substantial financial resources are released in support of the proposals. Even then it is difficult to project how such areas as Central Powys would respond as so much depends on the attitude and willingness of local operators to change their traditional operations. At the same time the attitude of local authorities towards rural public transport varies considerably and Powys is not alone in giving low priority to its bus services (see Transport 2000, 1984) which is again an important determinant of the exact form of policy implementation. We therefore return to the same conclusion as reached by the examination of road maintenance; that there is no coherent and unifying policy implementation but a series of local reactions to the confrontation between the various levels of policy influence. It is consequently to be expected that the future of rural public bus transport will be as much characterized by *ad hoc* small-scale changes as it has in the past 20 years.

OVERVIEW: IS THERE ANY POLICY?

It is quite clear from the above discussions that in the specific cases of minor rural road maintenance and public transport in Wales, and in the wider realm of transport planning, there is at present a lack of confidence in the ability of institutions to implement declared policies. The inability of national transport planning to produce the tools to develop realistic and effective policy initiatives further erodes confidence. In the case of road maintenance this is seen in the absence of any standardized maintenance rating system and in the case of rural public transport by a seeming unawareness of the range of social and economic environments facing operators. In such conditions policy becomes more educated guesswork rather than scientifically derived appraisal; the success of the policy being dependent on the experience, or lack of experience, of those doing the guessing. Similarly, the financial constraints which have dominated the public sector for the past decade have also inhibited the implementation of policies developed by local authorities to meet their maintenance and public transport needs. This has been further complicated by the political struggle between local and central government with added confusion being provided by the plethora of highly individualistic contributions from councillors, highway surveyors and bus operators.

There is apparently little prospect of any improvement in the current climate of recession, political confrontation and professional inertia, all of which militate against positive action in pursuit of declared policy goals. Current government legislation regarding the deregulation of the bus industry has already faced difficulties in its passage through the House of Lords, which amended some of the government's main aims as a result of concerted attacks on it by local authorities, the National Bus Company and other public bodies. Furthermore, it is likely that when implemented the expected benefits seen by the government to be so desirable will not materialize as local authorities and operators each pursue their own interests (Cloke and Edwards, 1984). This all serves to raise the question as to whether there are within transport planning at present any attainable policy initiatives or is every idea set to be sacrificed on the implementation altar? Evidence would seem to suggest that at best the planning system is struggling to maintain the status quo in the hope of better times ahead when there will be some sort of policy consensus and finance to put it into effect. At present, however, it must be concluded that transport and highways policy in Britain finds itself at a dead end.

REFERENCES

Association of County Councils and British Rail (1984) *Review of Rural Railways*, Association of County Councils, London.

Bell, G., Blackledge, D.A. and Bowen, P. (1983) *The Economics and Planning of Transport*, Heinemann, London.

British Rail (1984) *Corporate Plan*, British Rail, London.

British Road Federation (1978) Road maintenance, *Roadtalk*, Vol. 1, No. 3, 10–15.

Cloke, P.J. and Edwards, G.W. (1984) Changing need and provision: what future? In Cloke, P.J. (ed.) *Wheels Within Wales*, Centre for Rural Transport, Lampeter.

Department of Transport (1984) *Buses*, Cmnd 9300, HMSO, London.

Dyfed County Council (1978) *Transport Policies and Programmes*, Dyfed County Council, Carmarthen.

Edwards, G.W. (1984) *Minor Rural Roads in Wales*, Centre for Rural Transport, Lampeter.

Edwards, G.W. (1985) Rural public transport alternatives in Central Powys. In Cloke, P.J. (ed.) *Rural Accessibility and Mobility*, Centre for Rural Transport, Lampeter.

Ellis, N. (1980) Horrendous prospect of cumulative cuts, *Municipal Engineer*, Vol. 157, 155–158.

Gwynedd County Council (1977–79) *Transport Policy and Programmes*, Gwynedd County Council, Caernarfon (annual).

Hereford & Worcester County Council (1984) *Public Transport Plan*, Hereford & Worcester County Council, Worcester.

Leitch, (Sir) G. (1978) *Report of the Advisory Committee on Trunk Road Assessment*, HMSO, London.

Levin, P. (1979) Highway inquiries: a study in governmental responsiveness, *Public Administration*, Vol. 57, Spring.

Levin, P. (1981) Policy-making processes. In Banister, D. and Hall, P. (eds) *Transport and Public Policy Planning*, Mansell, London.

Maltby, D. and White, H.P. (1982) *Transport in the United Kingdom*, Macmillan, London.

Marshall, P. (1970) *The Marshall Committee's Recommendations for Standards of Highway Maintenance and for a Maintenance Rating System*, Transport Road and Research Laboratory, Crowthorne.

Moyes, A. and Holding, D. (1984) Running rural buses. In Cloke, P.J. (ed.) *Wheels Within Wales*, Centre for Rural Transport, Lampeter.

Plowden, S. (1980) *Taming Traffic*, Andre Deutsch, London.

Powys County Council (1978–84) *Transport Policies and Programmes*, Powys County Council, Llandrindod Wells (annual).

Powys County Council (1979) *Public Transport Plan*, Powys County Council, Llandrindod Wells.

Powys County Council, Brecknock Borough Council and Radnor District Council (1983) *Central Powys Local Plan*, The Councils, Llandrindod Wells.

Read, M. (1980) Does poor maintenance increase accident risk? *Municipal Engineer*, Vol. 157, 160–161.

Starkie, D. (1982) *The Motorway Age*, Pergamon, Oxford.

Tanner, J.C. (1962) Forecasts of future numbers of vehicles in Great Britain, *Roads and Road Construction*, Vol. 40, 263–274.

Transport 2000 (1984) No go zones, *Transport Report*, Vol. 7, 1–8.

Welsh Counties Committee (1984) Notes on the *Buses* White Paper, unpublished memo.

White, H.P. and Senior, M.L. (1983) *Transport Geography*, Longman, Harlow.

White, P.R. (1980) Alternative public transport: the real costs, *Motor Transport*, Vol. 117, No. 3918, 40–44.

Wistrich, E. (1983) *The Politics of Transport*, Longman, Harlow.

10

IMPLEMENTATION OF RURAL HOUSING POLICY

Tom Rocke

INTRODUCTION

The contemporary provision of housing in rural areas is increasingly a product of interrelationships between planning authorities and private developers. Public-sector housebuilding has become sporadic and unable to respond to needs. Hence, greater responsibility has been placed on rural planning authorities in this respect, but crucially an accompanying restructuring of powers has not occurred. Conversely, central government curbs on public expenditure have tended to militate against rural areas because of relatively poor cost-benefit ratios.

Policies of development concentration have been widely adopted in rural environments (Cloke, 1979; Martin and Voorhees Associates, 1981). These have attempted to reconcile economic and socio-political concerns in the provision of infrastructure and services and housing for rural needs. They are also sympathetic to the fundamental planning ethic of protection of countryside amenity and agricultural land. However, successful implementation of 'countryside' policies has not been matched by that of 'settlement' policies. Martin and Voorhees Associates (1981) attribute this to the social and economic objectives underpinning many settlement policies being less amenable to achievement by planning authorities. This ensues from their reliance on the cooperation of many other agencies, the incompleteness of information on social and economic aspects, and because planning policies can rarely counteract forces of economic and social change. Local government reorganization in 1974 exacerbated the difficulties by further fragmenting both the planning system and responsibility for the functions on which implementation of the social and economic objectives of settlement policies are dependent. The lack of national objectives and of a national strategy for rural setttlement reconciling the large number of different issues with which settlement policies must deal (Blacksell and Gilg, 1981), compounds the difficulties in rural environments. It has contributed to perpetuation of both the protectionist stance of development control in rural areas regardless of the socioeconomic implications, and the belief that regulation of mere physical order will attend to the latter (Harrison,

1972). Thus, Rogers (1976) notes that land-use regulation is less concerned with fulfilling social objectives related to housing need than planning objectives related to landscape quality, thereby emphasizing separation of the material from the human.

Increasingly it appears that resource policies, eliminating open competition with urban areas and planning procedures specific to rural areas are a necessity. The urgency for change is enhanced by economic and social changes resulting in the most pervasive and potentially pernicious of contemporary rural housing problems, the conflict between housing 'demand' and 'need':

> 'Demand' in reality entails the ability to lay claim to sufficient resources to be able to influence the supply of housing in the private market. 'Need' is a socially defined standard setting out the amount and quality of housing that ought to be provided in relation to the perceived housing conditions of a given population at any point in time. (Avon County Council, 1976, p. 8)

Rogers (1976) recognizes this dichotomy — between those groups whose position in the countryside is a direct result of employment, birth or force of circumstance, and those who have entered the rural housing market in both a conscious and well-equipped way. In rural areas, competing social groups are found in pursuit of the same housing opportunities in a way which is far less common in towns and cities. The implications of this in both 'pressured' and 'remoter' rural areas have been well documented (Connell, 1974; Pahl, 1975; Shucksmith, 1981).

The distinctive feature of contemporary rural housing requirements is the unprecedented level of 'demand' both relative to 'needs' and in absolute terms. This must be considered in conjunction with the earlier discussion of, first, the current predominance of the private sector in rural housing development, and second, the concern of development control authorities merely with physical order. As Rogers (1976) observes, much private development is of a type, and consequently at a price, which effectively excludes many of those people who have the greatest need for housing. While strategic (county) planning authorities may schedule development potential on the basis of a socially defined standard of need, development control is preoccupied with its material physical state while realization of that potential is increasingly demand oriented.

Deeper understanding is, therefore, required of the implementation of rural housing policies. This must embrace constraints on the 'availability' of land for residential development. However, non-implementation of social and economic objectives would seem increasingly as much a result of unconstrained forces of land and development markets invading the existing dwelling stock and, more significantly, appropriating the supply of new rural housing. The operation of planning control and its interrelationship with other agencies involved in not only the regulation, but also the development of housing schemes in rural areas must therefore be considered in unison.

RURAL HOUSING POLICY AND DEVELOPMENT PRESSURE IN THE CASE STUDY AREA

THE CASE STUDY AND RESIDENTIAL DEVELOPMENT PLANNING POLICIES

The case study reported here attempted an analysis of residential planning and

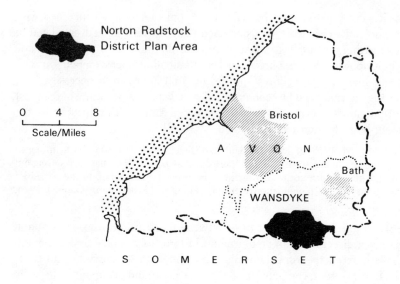

Figure 10.1   The location of the district of study (Wansdyke District Council, 1979, p. 1).

development activities in the district of Wansdyke in the county of Avon. This comprises an interesting variety of rural settlements under development pressure from the cities of Bristol and Bath (Figure 10.1). Table 10.1 depicts the policy history of the study area. Political wrangles of both central and local origin delayed statutory approval of the Structure Plan. Table 10.2 denotes the policy categories for the main settlements of the parishes analysed (Figure 10.2), while Table 10.3 summarizes the policy provisions for settlements in each category.

The secondary centre of Norton Radstock and the two local centres of Paulton and Peasedown St John were expected to accommodate the majority of residential development serving the area's housing needs. The six first-schedule villages were intended to contribute to satisfying the area's housing needs but to a lesser extent than the afore-mentioned centres and with less expansion of their existing developed areas. The nine second-schedule villages were not expected to make a significant contribution to accommodating housing requirements but could accept residential development within their existing developed areas where it was considered appropriate. Outside those settlements in the above categories only development considered essential for specific rural needs would be permitted. The Structure Plan largely reiterated the relative status of settlements in terms of their scheduled potential to receive residential development, although it incorporated a number of notable alterations (Table 10.2).

APPLICANT PRESSURE AND PLANNING DECISIONS

The interrelationship between the local planning authority (LPA) and private developers is of fundamental importance in the implementation of rural housing policies and decisions. Applications by the local authority for residential development for its own

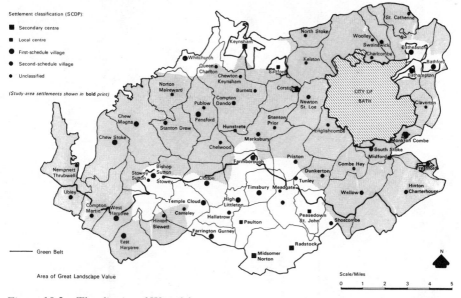

Figure 10.2   The district of Wansdyke.

purposes amounted to a mere 0.85 per cent of all planning applications (1977–82) and comprised 1.5 per cent of all development approved. Table 10.4 demonstrates that the basic policy of channelling development to the larger centres has met with some success. However, there are important differences between settlements both 'within' and 'across' the particular policy categories in terms of both applicant pressure and planning decisions. Wellow, for example, exhibited a high volume of applicant pressure and rate of approval relative to other second-schedule villages and the majority of first-schedule ones. Of special significance is the poor rate of approval of applications in Peasedown, a centre scheduled to accommodate development for general housing needs in the area.

Development pressure from the private sector was considerable throughout the area studied. Both developers and estate agents considered most land to be 'marketable' given that it could be acquired at a reasonable price and freed from constraints. Hence, the most fundamental constraint of land 'marketability', purported by developers to be ignored by planning authorities, was largely absent. Its absence was in spite of the basic policy to push development to the least attractive areas of the district, and even subareas within settlements ensuing from land allocation criteria engaged in the Norton Radstock and Environs District Plan (NREDP) (Wansdyke District Council, 1980). The latter plan in effect was attempting to coerce development of the less attractive land 'available' but remaining undeveloped under the Somerset County Development Plan (SCDP). Hence, the marketability of development land owed little to deliberate effort by the LPA to ensure it. Rather, it resulted from a combination of development pressure and planning restraint which limited development opportunities. However, it effectively increased the power of the LPA to implement its, predominantly physical, planning objectives.

Table 10.1 Planning policy background

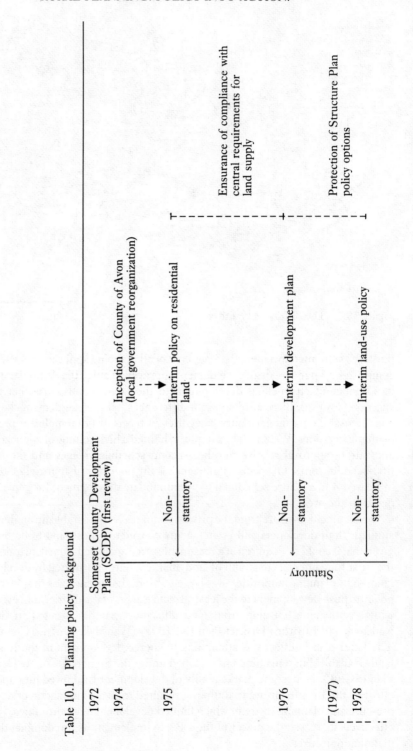

	Strategic (county) planning policy	Local (district) planning policy
1980 (May)	Draft Structure Plan (published)	
(Aug)		Draft Norton Radstock and Environs District Plan (NREDP) (published) ⎫
(Nov)	Amended draft submitted to DoE	⎬ Embraces main area for residential development in south of district beyond green belt
1981 (Jan)		NREDP adopted by District Council as 'informal' local plan ⎭
(June)	Structure Plan withdrawn by incoming Labour-controlled council; reversion to May 1980 draft	
(Nov)	Revised consultation draft (published)	
(1982)		
1984 (June)	DoE modifications	
1985 (July)	Statutory approval of amended Structure Plan	

Study period

Table 10.2 Policy categorization of main settlements of study area parishes

Settlement/parish	Classification in SCDP (first review)	Policy category in (draft) Avon County Structure Plan	Settlements in NREDP area	Other denotations
Norton Radstock	Secondary centre	H.4	*	
Paulton	Local centre	H.5	*	
Peasedown St John			*	
Farmborough	First-schedule village	H.6	*	
Farrington Gurney			*	
High Littleton			*	
Temple Cloud			*	
Timsbury		H.5	*	
Monkton Combe				GB; AGLV; >AAV
Camerton	Second-schedule village	H.7	*	GB; AGLV
Dunkerton				GB; AGLV; >AAV
Freshford				GB; AGLV; >AAV
Hinton Charterhouse		H.6		GB; AGLV
Marksbury				GB; AGLV
Priston				
Shoscombe		H.7		
Southstoke				GB; AGLV; >AAV
Wellow			*	GB; AGLV
Combe Hay	Unclassified			GB; AGLV; >AAV

Key: GB, Green belt.
AGLV, Area of great landscape value.
> AAV, Settlement of more than average amenity value (SCDP).

PLANNING ACTIVITY AND INFRASTRUCTURE AGENCY CONSTRAINTS

Although chance of circumstances meant that indiscriminate allocation of development potential on the basis of physical planning criteria did not in this case compromise the developers' ability to use the sites concerned, the same fortunate coincidence did not abound in other respects. Indeed, it effectively enhanced the restraint necessarily exerted by the water and highway authorities, notably in Peasedown. Substandard infrastructure combined with the potential for development scheduled by the LPA to compel these authorities to raise objections even to small-scale development proposals as an objection to the 'potential' for all similar proposals.

CHANGING WATER AUTHORITY CONSTRAINTS AND THE IMPLICATIONS FOR RURAL PLANNING CONTROL

The constraint exerted by the water authority relented during the study period. However, this again resulted from a fortunate coincidence of its own and central government activities rather than of specific effort by the LPA. Investment in a new sewerage scheme alleviated problems in many of the settlements connected to mains sewerage where the majority of development in the study area was to be accommodated. The Cam Valley scheme intercepted sewage from part of Peasedown and the village of Timsbury. Because the latter formerly drained to the Paulton sewage treatment works its interception created additional capacity for the village of Paulton itself and, with the exception of Farmborough, for the other first-schedule villages which also drained to the Paulton works. The green belt restraint policy, which intensified the concentration of development potential into a confined area, enabled an integrated scheme serving many settlements and with potentially widespread benefits. It thus commanded investment priority. Second, evidence of the Department of the Environment's unwillingness to give continued support to the water authority's policy of objecting to one or two houses only — an attitude later endorsed in Circular 22/80 (Department of the Environment, 1980b, para. 11) — led to a redefinition of policy. Rather than placing a complete embargo on development draining to overloaded sewage treatment works, as previously, this enabled development within certain limits appropriate for particular works. Third, impending legislation giving the public rights to monitor water quality and to prosecute if unsatisfactory, shifted the investment priority in the five-year programme from serving areas of development potential to alleviating existing problems. This seemed more favourable to rural areas. It compensated for the difficulties caused by their otherwise low investment priority, problems enhanced by public expenditure cuts and the removal of investment in sewerage infrastructure from local authority control in 1974.

Nevertheless, the limit of three dwellings per year in Farmborough, for example, implied slow development of the site allocated for residential development in the NREDP. Further, limits were placed on development draining to the Norton Radstock sewage treatment works to prevent it falling into the new investment priority category. They implied a shortfall of 170 of the 800 residences provided for on 'identified' sites in the NREDP alone, regardless of the 500 scheduled from the development of small

Table 10.3 Summary of strategic policy provisions for residential development (Somerset County Council, 1972; Avon County Council, 1980)

Somerset County Development Plan (SCDP)	Draft Avon County Structure Plan
Secondary centre:	*Policy:*
Local centre: Centres where general development may reasonably be anticipated	H4: Housing land to be provided within the capacity of existing or firmly committed infrastructure provision
First schedule: Favourable consideration of satisfactory proposals for development. Amount of development permitted will depend on character of village; local physical features; accessibility; need for economy in use and provision of public services. (Special concern to safeguard established character of villages of >AAV; adherence to green belt policy for villages therein.)	H5: Proposals for residential development in and immediately adjoining rural settlements will normally be approved, provided that the development is not precluded by green belt policies, character of the settlement is maintained and public services at time of proposals are adequate for proposed development
Second schedule: Suitable for more limited development in form of infilling consistent with established character of village and with such essential public services as exist or can reasonably be anticipated. (Proposed to permit only limited infilling in green belt villages of Combe Hay, Hinton Charterhouse, Marksbury, Priston, Tunley, Wellow.)	H6: Proposals for residential development within the limits of rural settlements will normally be approved provided that character of settlement is maintained and public services at time of proposal are adequate for proposed development
Unclassified: Sympathetic consideration of development needed for livelihood of any established rural community. New houses will not normally be permitted in open country except where required for agricultural or other local need. Resistance to expansion of isolated groups of houses and ribbon development	H7: Limited residential development will normally be approved where: (a) meets need of local community for support of (i) a local service; or (ii) local employment, and (b) within existing limits of settlement, and (c) existing public services are adequate for development proposed, and (d) character of settlement is maintained, and (e) cumulative total number of new dwellings built in settlement in plan period does not exceed about either 20 dwellings or 15% of the number of dwellings existing in April 1979, whichever is the less
	H8: New dwellings in the countryside, isolated from existing settlements, normally will be acceptable only where essential for the efficient operation of the rural economy
	H9: Distribution of land proposed for residential use in period 1979–91: Norton Radstock — 1300 dwellings Rest of Wansdyke — 1500 dwellings

Table 10.4 Formal applicant pressure and rates of approval 1977–82

	No. of applications	% of all applications over period	Approvals	% of all approvals	Refusals	% of all refusals	Approval rate (%)
Norton Radstock	171	29.1	110	33.1	61	23.8	64.3
Paulton	52	8.8	35	10.5	17	6.6	67.3
Peasedown St John	44	7.5	11	3.3	33	12.9	25.0
Total — Local centres	96	16.3	46	13.8	50	19.5	47.9
Cameley (Temple Cloud)	24	4.1	14	4.2	10	3.9	58.3
Farmborough	27	4.6	17	5.1	10	3.9	63.0
Farrington Gurney	21	3.6	15	4.5	6	2.3	71.4
High Littleton	49	8.3	28	8.4	21	8.2	57.1
Monkton Combe	9	1.5	3	0.9	6	2.3	33.3
Timsbury	42	7.1	23	6.9	19	7.4	54.8
Total — First schedule	172	29.2	100	30.0	72	28.0	58.1
Camerton	17	2.9	4	1.2	13	5.1	23.5
Dunkerton (Tunley)	16	2.7	5	1.5	11	4.3	31.3
Freshford	18	3.1	4	1.2	14	5.5	22.2
Hinton Charterhouse	22	3.7	13	3.9	9	3.5	59.1
Marksbury	13	2.2	9	2.7	4	1.6	69.2
Priston	8	1.4	4	1.2	4	1.6	50.0
Shoscombe	9	1.5	3	0.9	6	2.3	33.3
Southstoke	10	1.7	5	1.5	5	2.0	50.0
Wellow	29	4.9	23	6.9	6	2.3	79.3
Total — Second schedule	142	24.2	70	21.0	72	28.2	49.3
Combe Hay	7	1.2	6	1.8	1	0.4	85.7
Total	588		332		256		56.5

sites, over the Structure Plan period. Without a change in policy, therefore, additional capacity was dependent on developer contributions.

HIGHWAY CONSTRAINTS AND INDISCRIMINATE PLANNING ACTIVITY

The highway authority exerted the greatest constraint on development within the planning policy provisions for it. The effect of central government curbs on highway expenditure was compounded by the low status of this rural area for attracting it. The latter was, in part, a function of the ordering of county council investment priorities. Necessary highway works in the area were essentially of 'local' benefit rather than yielding advantages for the county as a whole. Hence, substandard access roads contributed to the refusal of 21 development proposals in Peasedown and 12 in High Littleton. In those locations where it was physically possible to alleviate the problems, the scale of development possible did not permit a viable scheme for a developer. Further, insistence on any such solution was probably *ultra vires* since the problems tended to relate to considerable lengths of the service roads and their junctions with classified roads rather than the mere points of access with potential development sites. Thus, a combination of substandard roads and small-scale development opportunities (but in sum comprising a significant development potential) enhanced the restraint necessarily exerted by the highway authority.

On consultation in respect of policy proposals in the NREDP the highway authority stipulated requisite highway works in accordance with the proposed scale of development, but did not allocate responsibility for their implementation. Further, the authority noted that the scale of development could determine whether or not the problem materialized. However, planning activity tended not to avert highway constraints. On the contrary, a fundamental concern of the District Council was to extricate maximum planning gain for the local environment, and highway schemes of 'local importance' befitted this criterion. Hence, where larger sites specifically allocated in the NREDP were associated with highway difficulties, and it seemed that the latter sometimes pre-empted the former, development of the land depended on the alleviation of such difficulties. The larger scales of development to be accommodated on such sites were considered to legitimate this action since the problems could be deemed to arise wholly or substantially from the development itself.

Characteristically, however, commercial viability was not a material consideration when stipulating development contingencies. In Paulton, for example, the largest area of land specifically allocated for housing in the NREDP (9.1 of 12.1 acres) was undevelopable because of the potential developer's inability to comply with the access requirements of the planning authority, supported by the highway authority, for this area. The proposed access would coincidentally form a new alignment for a relief road for the central area of the village, long recognized as 'desirable'. Defined as objective physical planning criteria in a plan document, development control adhered indiscriminately to the requirement for comprehensive development with coincident implementation of the new access. A similar requirement to complete a new road alignment in conjunction with development of a site (7.2 acres) in Norton Radstock, at an estimated cost of £2 million to provide bridges across a floodplain, threatened to thwart the development. However, a compromise was being negotiated because the land was in Crown (Duchy of Cornwall) ownership, planning permission, therefore, only being sought out of 'goodwill', although with commercial benefits to the Duchy.

Under the old-style development plan specific problems became apparent in relation to particular development initiatives and solutions were thereby 'negotiated'. However, in the district plan land was allocated, and contingencies on its development stipulated, formally and specifically, according to local politico-planning objectives and remote from considerations of the feasibility and practicalities of development. At a time when increasing flexibility was necessary to assist increasing privatization of essential infrastructure and housing provision on more difficult sites, the combination of local planning and development control by the District Council was working to the contrary. Infrastructure, notably highway, constraints were intensified and curtailed the residential development potential conferred, *prima facie*, by policy. However, pressure on development land meant that developers would bear the costs, and thereby implement physical planning desiderata, if at all possible.

'PHYSICAL' AND 'OWNERSHIP' CONSTRAINTS ON LAND 'AVAILABILITY'

'Physical' and 'ownership' constraints were further components of the DoE's concern for the 'genuine availability' of housing land deemed available by LPAs (Department of the Environment, 1980a, para. 5) in addition to 'marketability' and infrastructure constraints. Again, however, they were not material considerations for the LPA, and potentially forestalled development and exacerbated planning constraints. Physical constraints were not unduly problematic, the most significant being the reduction in capacity, because of geological faults, of a large area of land in Norton Radstock with residential notation in the SCDP. However, abundant land was available under the less rigid stipulations of that plan and accordant control of development. Further, development pressure again largely enabled 'abnormal' costs of development ensuing from physical site difficulties to be offset against land prices and profit margins.

Development pressure and consequent high land prices induced most landowners to release sites with development status. Further, 'abnormal' costs ensuing from physical and infrastructure constraints could to some extent be offset against land prices and still provide favourable inducements to landowners because of development — relative to existing — use values. However, requirements stipulated in the NREDP for the development of sites, notably in respect of access formation, often involved land under several different ownerships generating difficulties (primarily of delay) with 'ransom' strips. These comprise parcels of land often small in area but essential to development schemes (for example, because access is to be derived across them), the owner thereby being able to 'hold the developer to ransom' and ask a very high price for the land relative to its area. Fragmented ownership of the central development area in Paulton was compounding planning restraint and precluding comprehensive development of the area and any possibility of a developer achieving a viable scheme of access as required by the DPA. It was further prejudicing any likelihood of highway authority funding. Characteristic of rural councils where elected representatives are in close contact with the electorate, use of compulsory purchase powers to surpass such constraints was vehemently resisted because of the political implications.

However, ownership constraints did seem potentially more severe in the future. First, greater abnormal costs of developing the more difficult sites necessitated greater concessions on land prices, requiring owners to accept less than the 'expected price' (McNamara, 1982) for development land. Second, a Ministerial ruling (May 1983) threatened to preclude the Duchy's practice of establishing the development status of land prior to its disposal. A gentleman's agreement (7/77) with the LPA to the effect that planning permission agreed informally would be formally ratified when the land was sold to a private developer, meant that the Duchy had started to release much land, being able to command development prices for it. Since much development land was in Duchy ownership, any reversion to the situation prior to the 7/77 agreement, when the Duchy released no land, had severe implications for the genuine availability of residential development land in the study area.

THE DEVELOPMENT OF RESIDENTIAL LAND

THE DEARTH OF SOCIAL CONTROL OF DEVELOPMENT

The physical attributes of development proposals were the criteria of concern to the DPA. There was little attempt or commitment to exert control to ensure housing provision for particular groups. Occasionally, the specific needs of a *specific applicant* would induce a more liberal interpretation of 'infill' by the Committee, in a settlement where it was permitted, than by the conservative, technical planning definition of officers. However, no commitment was discerned to influence developers to provide for specific needs.

This ensued from a combination of factors. First, there was no statutory provision for anything other than the control of physical order. Second, the splitting of strategic and local planning functions between authorities led to the assumption that strategic requirements and accordant local plan provisions for development and its physical control would accommodate needs without requiring further action. Third, again relating to the interauthority split of functions, (increasingly) prevalent local restraint interests in development control have a focal point for pressure (the application) on the LPA. Further, the voice of needy groups is generally more diffuse insofar as the District Planning Committee is concerned, those not accommodated by private development being the responsibility of the Housing Department and Committee, on which pressure in this respect tends to be concentrated. A fourth factor was the political complexion of the DPA, a Conservative administration favouring private ownership and minimal intervention. Hence, policy change enabling conversion of redundant buildings to residences was promoted, but waiving of standard planning conditions requiring the provision of garages to enable the development of low-cost starter homes did not command such political support.

High and low rates of approval respectively in Wellow and Freshford (Table 10.4) were a result of different attitudes of the parish councils towards development and a vociferous protectionist lobby in Freshford. Political expediency dictated refusal in such areas in the green belt where development was not strategically important. The physical attributes of a scheme in such settlements contributed much to the assessment of whether or not it constituted 'acceptable' infill. The needs criteria of policy H.7

(Table 10.3) seemed immaterial. Indeed, concerns levied by the Wellow Parish Council that the LPA should exert control to provide low-cost housing to restore the social balance of the village and bolster support for ailing services, were ineffectual. As a token gesture the DPA rejected a revised scheme on a site where an earlier approval included semidetached instead of detached units, but justified this decision on grounds of physical amenity. However, elsewhere in the village, physical acceptability of a scheme for which no alternative was presented enabled no such concessions to similar parish council concerns.

In effect, the only needs specifically recognized were those defined, and for which development control procedures were outlined, in statute, namely dwellings for agricultural workers. However, this involved merely responding to forthcoming development initiatives according to standard technical considerations. If the Ministry of Agriculture renounced either the need for a dwelling or the current viability of the holding based on their particular assessment criteria, regardless of any future potential the proposal was immediately refused. Despite purporting to allow for other essential rural needs, in effect this was the only form of development permitted outside settlements selected for infill. The DPA adhered to the premise that adequate development opportunities were available within the villages to accommodate other needs. In a pressured rural area the difficulties of discriminating between, and controlling, indefinite forms of development were acute. However, the implications of this were becoming increasingly profound as the drawing of housing development boundaries (HDB) in the NREDP rationalized development control, and development of available sites seemed increasingly demand oriented. Hence, for example, the exclusion of an HDB for Shoscombe effectively restricted development to that essential for agricultural needs despite its previous acceptability for infill and parish council concern about its stagnation. Although the redundant buildings policy created another exception to normal planning restraint, thereby increasing the housing stock in rural areas, the intentions and benefits of that policy were essentially physical planning ones.

THE PRIVATE DEVELOPMENT INDUSTRY AND RESIDENTIAL DEVELOPMENT

The determinants of the market orientation of development schemes within the study area were, therefore, largely the responses of developers to housing markets within the planning provisions and constraints for the area. In the small, high-amenity settlements close to the urban centres and protected by the green belt, a well-established and intensifying demand-oriented development market was displacing any likelihood of low-cost housing provision. This was enhanced by the dearth of social planning control and the influence of commercial agents involved increasingly in the sale of land and marketing of development schemes for clients. Predominantly local developers were involved in developing small, up-market schemes of high amenity, which were compatible with physical planning concerns in such areas. High profit margins compensated for the limited number of sites available.

South of the green belt, where the majority of the study area's development was to be concentrated in direct and inverse proportion, respectively, to scale and amenity of existing settlements, development activity seemed to be in a state of transition. In the latter stages of the SCDP, development of the larger sites by local and regional developers maintained its characteristics of predominantly terraced and semidetached estates of functional housing for a local population. However, the transition to the new development plan system seemed to mark a change in development markets beyond the green belt resulting from a combination of market pressures, planning activity and upheavals within the housebuilding industry. The commercial expansion of Bristol and physical amenities of the city of Bath, combined with planning restraint within and around these centres, began to direct increasing development pressure beyond the green belt. Initially, this comprised those forced out by high house prices, because of high proximity to employment and services, high environmental amenity and scarcity of housing, within and adjacent to the urban centres. However, it seemed that an increasing executive demand was appending itself to housing markets and influencing the supply of housing, even in Norton Radstock which was considered to be the cheapest housing area in the county.

This change in development markets coincided with diversification within the housebuilding industry because of the nationwide slump in residential markets in the late 1970s. National housebuilders tended to diversify their activities both 'vertically' (developing for a wider market range) and, partly as a consequence, 'horizontally' (seeking a greater range of sites in a greater range of locations). Further, such housebuilders were interested in acquiring sites with clear planning status and developing for established markets close to urban centres, making heavy use of development plans in their searches. The provisions of the structure and local plans thus directed their attention towards the study area. Indeed, such 'transient' volume housebuilders were closely associated with land allocated in the NREDP. Further, they introduced a new form of development, that specifically for lower- to middle-executive markets comprising commuters to the urban centres.

The interest of transient volume housebuilders in smaller sites, and hence the Norton Radstock area, displaced some local developers unable to compete successfully against them in open land markets. Developers previously building for local markets but with interests other than housebuilding showed a tendency to turn towards the latter, and to sell their residual sites to transient volume housebuilders engaged solely in housebuilding. This reflected the precariousness of the local housing market because of a general demise of local economic activity. Only local developers with well-developed land banks and with well-established mechanisms for acquiring land away from the open market (through local contacts, estate agents, and so on) were able to survive. One local developer benefited from a close relationship with the DPA, buying land without clear planning status and hence minimizing the price away from open competition. The company maintained a large land bank, several sites within it subsequently being allocated in the NREDP. It is significant that this developer had a reputation with both the DPA and local purchasers for building an acceptable standard and quality of development. With a well-established land bank (approximately 350 dwellings), land prices were not a constraint at the time and hence the company continued developing for local markets (from first-time buyers through to retirement bungalows, upholding planning policy by concentrating the latter close to services). The main difficulty was that the land bank of this developer, incorporating a number of sites allocated in the NREDP, was subject to slow development (20–30 houses per year) dependent on the state of the company's contracting operations rather than the intensity of need.

PLANNING AND THE PUBLIC HOUSING SECTOR

As already discussed, development by the public housing sector was very limited, a complete embargo having been placed on development between 1978 and 1981. Indeed, the predominant activity of the local housing authority was disposal of land surplus to its requirements in accordance with Regulation 5 of the Town and Country Planning General Regulations 1976. This was despite the housing department's waiting list (July 1983) of over 900 persons, only half of whom had points. The main emphasis was on rehousing those suffering from overcrowding, young, single people having little chance of obtaining accommodation. In addition, the two housing association schemes in Norton Radstock had closed their waiting lists with more than one person in reserve for each unit.

Despite the obvious need for low-cost housing and the dearth of local authority development, little advantage was taken of the opportunity to control the type of development on land released to the private sector under Regulation 5. This manifests both the lack of coordination between the District Planning and Housing Committees and the lack of commitment to such control for the reasons previously discussed. The political complexion and ensuant attitude of the District Council were reflected in its failure to make its own land available to housing associations, poor competitors in land markets. Further, the DPA's adherence to normal physical planning standards for a housing association scheme in Timsbury resulted in its refusal on grounds of density and concomitant piecemeal development of a larger area, but for which the housing association could not secure funds. The Council's favoured scheme on this land, representing its one gesture to assist development for local needs, entailed making available individual plots for sale to, and development by, individuals resident within the district. This reflected the Council's empathy with private ownership. In the event, it seemed an exercise in political symbolism, the pricing of plots being considered by the Land Subcommittee to be prohibitive to first-time buyers.

With increasing competition for fewer sites by highly competitive transient developers building for commuting populations, development for local needs by the local authority and housing associations was becoming increasingly important. However, at the same time it was becoming less available because of lack of funds, poor ability to compete for land and lack of commitment by the District Council to provide positive assistance. Thus, under the SCDP coincidence of planning control and development activity resulted in housing appropriate to the policy intentions in the south of the District. The primary conflict was the invasion of the housing stock by those seeking cheaper housing than in the urban centres. However, no such coincidence appeared to exist later in the study period, commuter demand appropriating the supply of housing throughout the study area. This effectively contravened the intended local functions of settlements. Further, it prejudiced fundamental intentions of the Structure Plan expounded in paragraphs qualifying the strategic policy statements. The plan was concerned (pp 31–32, para. 8.6) to minimize journeys to work by reducing past trends of rapid expansion of settlements beyond the green belt but unaccompanied by increases in employment opportunities in the immediate vicinity. Hence, it was proposed that additional new housing developments should be associated with the creation of additional employment opportunities. In practice, however, the 'quasi-legal' operation of development control (Simmonds, 1978) confined to technical, physical planning considerations, was not attuned to endorsing such qualificatory criteria. This shortfall holds profound implications for the ability of planners to implement broad settlement policy objectives, and in particular to provide housing for local needs, within the context of policies of rural restraint.

CENTRAL GOVERNMENT INTERVENTION IN LOCAL PLANNING CONTROL

The DPA was concerned to 'make provision' for residential development to accommodate needs which were evaluated quantitatively by housing target figures in the Structure Plan. The DPA allocated land according to good physical planning criteria of minimizing the take-up of agricultural land and encouraging the development of derelict and other land where a significant environmental gain could be achieved (Wansdyke District Council, 1980, para. 2.12). This aligned closely with local political planning prerogatives. Thereafter, development control adhered indiscriminately to preventing development other than in accordance with those provisions which formed a more objective basis for physical planning control than the traditional development plan, but also enhanced the visibility and, inherently, danger of precedents. However, such precise land allocation and development control in line with needs evaluated quantitatively further enhanced separation of the material from the human. Structure Plan provisions for development 'immediately adjoining' the larger villages (policy H.5) were negated in the allocation of land and drawing of HDBs. Constraints of the form condemned by Circular 9/80 did abound. However, at least during the period studied, the DPA demonstrated little concern to ensure 'realization' of the development potential.

Central government, however, functioning increasingly as a 'corporate' sector of politics (Jessop, 1978; Saunders, 1981), is characteristically more concerned to ensure that the development potential scheduled is realized. During the period studied, political pressure to regenerate the economy through bolstering economic activity resulted in enhanced central government concern to facilitate development because of its fiscal benefits rather than to ensure housing provision for specific needs. This, combined with belligerent enforcement by the then Secretary of State, was overtly contrary to the inclination of the DPA under the new development plan system adopted at the same time. Circular 22/80 on development control (Department of the Environment, 1980b reiterated more forcefully the provisions of Development Control Policy Note 2 (Ministry of Housing and Local Government, 1969, para. 6), discarding as a sufficient reason for refusing planning permission elsewhere the fact that the housebuilding needs of the area could be met from identified sites (Department of the Environment, 1980b, Annex A, para. 8). Further, it purported to attach less weight to planning objections where suitable land was not available for immediate development but its existence was used in justification for refusing planning applications on less appropriate but readily available land (op. cit., Annex A, para. 7).

The prevailing and conflicting attitudes of central government and the DPA were evident in a number of appeal decisions. Two appeals in Norton Radstock and one in Paulton reversed the principle of development on land excluded from allocation and outside the HDB in the NREDP. A primary determining factor in all three cases seemed to be the doubt that sites allocated in the District Plan would be fully developed during the plan period because of (non-planning) constraints on development land. Another appeal decision on land in the central area of Paulton effectively negated the DPA's attempts to secure comprehensive development of the area accompanied by private funding of the much needed village centre relief road. The DPA's tendency to allocate land for development where a planning gain could be secured was effectively contrary to the prevailing policy of central government to minimize constraints on developers in order to maximize rates of development. The Structure Plan was interpreted in accordance with central government priorities; for example, its allowance of development on the fringe of Paulton (see Table 10.3, policy H5) was exploited and used to justify overriding the specific provisions of the NREDP. Longstanding national aims of agricultural land protection, resistance of development in prominent locations and subjective notions of intensification of existing infrastructure deficiencies seemed to be less stringently interpreted.

In the smaller villages where strategic and local policies of restraint were more in line, appeal decisions relieved the effects of a strict political and technocratic control of development by the DPA. DoE inspectors seemed to assume a more meritorious interpretation of, for example, acceptable 'infill' and 'agricultural need'. This is compared with the DPA's indiscriminate refusal of proposals for such, respectively, outside HDBs defined in the NREDP and failing to qualify within the Ministry of Agriculture's criteria of 'prevailing viability'.

Similarly to officers and politicians of the DPA, DoE inspectors were vulnerable to seduction by the prevailing pressures to which they were most exposed. Not only were the merits of certain proposals evaluated in a different way to the DPA, but also similar objections to similar proposals in similar areas were regarded differently by different inspectors and at different times. The indefinite relationship between the Structure and Local Plans, emanating from physically and politically separate authorities, and the lack of a firm national policy for rural areas, enabled central government agents to legitimate actions which effectively utilized the planning system to further central economic policy. Although the DoE effectively increased the 'availability' of land for housebuilding in all respects, it did little to influence directly the development process in the interests of any specific group apart from developers.

CONCLUSION

The current structure of the planning system seems to generate a polarization of interests in planning control and to do little to influence the development process in the interests of needy groups in rural areas. Structure planning has attempted to integrate social and economic objectives with physical planning ones. However, its embrace would seem to be an activity of planning as defined politically while the statutory, quasi-legal base of development control has failed to adapt to the prevailing political definition of planning. This reflects the enduring assumption that planning policy is omnipotent and social and economic objectives can be realized through mere control of physical order. With increasing development pressure and decreasing public-sector initiatives, the urgency for a review of development control is intensifying.

Enhanced by the prevailing (political) pressures, the DPA, resource and investment agencies, and central government seemed to be driven towards different poles with insufficient regard for each other's objectives. As Stewart (1980) recognizes, the organization of local government effectively sharpens differences in organizational assumptions by drawing organizational boundaries at the same point as professional ones. This can account for the lack of coordination between the DPA and other agencies (water, highway, housing, developers) and the failure of the DPA to address directly the social provision of development. Insofar as the DPA was concerned, the latter was the responsibility of the Housing Authority and, to some extent, the strategic planning authority. The structure of the planning system, however, seems to exacerbate these difficulties by drawing internal boundaries between functions, of uneasy and poorly defined relationship, at the same point as political ones. This would seem to be especially profound since local government reorganization in 1974 and for planning in rural areas where investment priority is low and the voice of restraint loud. Hence, local planning and development control have become increasingly bound to the interests of 'established' residents and the restraint lobby in rural environments at the same time as the need has arisen for greater flexibility and discrimination between the interests of many competing social groups. While local political influences, compounded by reactions to central economic policy, effectively have operated to place greater planning constraints on developers, central political inputs to the planning process have attempted to reduce such constraints. This seems to have further deflected attention from the important issues in planning for rural housing.

A fundamental appreciation of contemporary pressures and requirements in rural areas is urgently required, together with provision for planning control in accordance. Development control must wrest free from the paranoia of precedents and concerns for absolute consistency evaluated in technical, physical planning terms. The intrinsic socioeconomic values of physical planning control must become material considerations in development control, as in strategic planning, and at both central and local levels of the planning system. Social planning must penetrate development control. At both levels, sectional, political planning interests must be taken in context with the range of public interests affected by planning and development processes in rural areas. Local planning authorities must be committed to facilitating realization of the development potential, rather than blindly making provision for it, requiring specific accompaniments in the interests of the local environment, and exerting physical planning control indiscriminately thereafter. Development pressure in Wansdyke enhanced the DPA's ability to implement its physical planning objectives through private means. However, while the development potential may have been largely realized in physical terms, such pressure enhanced prejudice to the intrinsic social objectives. Strategic concerns for housing provision seemed to be regarded by the DPA as prejudicial to the interests of the local environment which must be protected against them and duly compensated. There seemed to be no regard for the local interests of housing provision.

It is thus important that particular sectional (political) interests should not be assumed to be the public interest. Implementation success must be judged in terms of physical *and* social planning concerns. Contemporary rural planning should plan 'with' rather than 'against' or 'irrespective of' commercial forces and infrastructure capacity, and, inherently, on an interagency basis. Equally, development should not necessarily be permitted for its own sake, as prevailing pressures on central government seemed to decree. Central government must consider rural policy for housing development and infrastructure provision on wider than mere economic merits, and must not use the planning system merely to support economic policy. Rural settlements, especially those close to urban centres, are no longer closed entities. Available development land is increasingly part of the land bank for a very broad housing market from a wide area, and it is vital to discriminate between elements of this. If development proposals for a particular housing sector are not appropriate, then the planning system must be geared to control in accordance. Development potential deemed necessary must be genuinely available, but must also be so for the development intended. The material and the human must be interrelated. Failure to fulfil these requirements was undermining fundamental strategic and intrinsic local planning objectives for Wansdyke. The interrelationship between quantity, type and location of residential development is especially profound but difficult to reconcile appropriately in rural areas. It contemporaneously requires much more discriminating and perhaps broader-based planning intervention.

REFERENCES

Avon County Council (1976) *Structure Plan Situation Report — Housing*, Avon County Council, Bristol.

Avon County Council (1980) *County of Avon Structure Plan: Draft Written Statement*, Avon County Council, Bristol.

Blacksell, M. and Gilg, A.W. (1981) *The Countryside: Planning and Change*, Allen and Unwin, London.

Cloke, P.J. (1979) *Key Settlements in Rural Areas*, Methuen, London.

Connell, J. (1974) The metropolitan village — spatial and social processes in discontinuous suburbs. In Johnson, J.H. (ed.) *Suburban Growth*, Wiley, London.

Department of the Environment (1980a) *Land for Private Housebuilding*, Circular 9/80, HMSO, London.

Department of the Environment (1980b) *Development Control — Policy and Practice*, Circular 22/80, HMSO, London.

Harrison, M.L. (1972) Development control: the influence of political, legal and ideological factors. *Town Planning Review*, Vol. 43, 255–274.

Jessop, B. (1978) Capitalism and democracy: the best possible political shell? In Littlejohn, G., Smart, B., Wakeford, J. and Yuval-Davis, N. (eds) *Power and the State*, Croom Helm, London.

Martin and Voorhees Associates (1981) *Review of Rural Settlement Policies 1945–1980*, Martin and Voorhees Associates, London.

McNamara, P. (1982) *Land Release and Development in Areas of Restraint*, Oxford Working Paper 76, Department of Town Planning, Oxford Polytechnic.

Ministry of Housing and Local Government (1969) *Development Control Policy Note 2 — Development in Residential Areas*, HMSO, London.

Pahl, R.E. (1975) *Whose City?* Penguin, Harmondsworth.

Rogers, A.W. (1976) Rural housing. In Cherry, G.E. (ed.) *Rural Planning Problems*, Leonard Hill, London.

Saunders, P. (1981) *Social Theory and the Urban Question*, Hutchinson, London.

Shucksmith, D.M. (1981) *No Homes for Locals?* Gower Press, Farnborough.

Simmonds, D. (1978) Development control 6: planning versus development control, *Planner*, Vol. 64, November, 186–187.

Somerset County Council (1972) *County Development Plan, First Review*, Taunton.

Stewart, J. (1980) Inter-organisational relationships: an introduction, *Town Planning Review*, Vol. 51, 257–260.

Wansdyke District Council (1979) *Norton-Radstock and Environs District Plan: Report of Survey*, Department of Planning, Wansdyke District Council, Radstock.

Wansdyke District Council (1980) *Norton-Radstock and Environs District Plan: Draft Written Statement*, Department of Planning, Wansdyke District Council, Radstock.

11

RURAL GENTRIFICATION AND THE INFLUENCE OF LOCAL-LEVEL PLANNING

Jo Little

INTRODUCTION: THE SOCIAL IMPLICATIONS OF IMPLEMENTATION

The relationship between planning and social structure in rural communities is of fundamental importance in the current debate concerning the allocation of resources in the countryside. Deprivation studies have provided a convincing demonstration of the marked inequalities existing between different sections of the rural population while, recently, the desire to account for such inequalities in the context of planning and decision making in general has gained particular attention. Little progress has, however, been made in evaluating the extent to which planning, as an agent of rural decision-making, has been important in influencing the configuration of social groups and the spatial distribution of poverty and inequality, especially at the community level.

Researchers remain understandably cautious of bridging this gap between the composition of society and rural planning. The issue is far from simplistic and begs a wide range of questions concerning not only the interpretation of contemporary social change but also the role and 'power' of the planning process itself. There are a number of dangers attached to the formulation of direct or causal links between planning and social structures, not least being the problems of simply attributing to 'planning' certain issues which may be a function of much wider social and economic processes. It is argued here, however, that, as an element of state decision-making which cannot be divorced from the society in which it operates, the planning system represents a very powerful influence over the distribution of different social groups within the country-side, particularly through the operation of housing policy and development control in local areas.

The familiar assertion that planning is a technical, politically neutral activity which acts in support of the 'public interest' has recently been shown to lack credibility (Broadbent, 1979; Blowers, 1980, 1982). It is now widely accepted that within the framework of central and local government structures, the planning system can act as a very forceful mechanism of social and economic control (see Chapters 1 and 2).

Despite the fact that many of the powers available to the planning process are primarily negative (for example, development control), it nevertheless has an important role in maintaining the status quo, giving political credence to certain established groups and causes and above all facilitating 'the continuation of the dominant material relationships (the reproduction of the means of production)' (Camhis, 1979, p. 7) and preserving the system in which it operates.

CONTEMPORARY RURAL SOCIAL CHANGE

Recent changes in the social structure of rural communities have been highly significant, far reaching, varied and complex. The prevailing trend — well documented at least on a theoretical level (see, for example, Connell, 1978; Newby, 1980; Phillips and Williams, 1984) while less so on an empirical one (Cloke and Little, 1984b) — has been the movement of middle-class migrants (particularly commuters and the retired) into villages, attracted initially by cheaper house prices but, more recently, by an idyllic rural vision of a healthy, peaceful and 'natural' way of life. Such processes, which are by no means uniform, have led in extreme cases to the gentrification of villages and the almost wholesale replacement of one population by another. These changes in the class structure of rural society have had serious implications for the allocation of resources and the configuration of inequality within the countryside. Conflicts arising over distributional issues, such as the availability of housing, have highlighted the divisions between the local residents and the immigrants. In this chapter it is argued that because of their associations with access to resources and material wealth these divisions are best conceptualized not in terms of locals versus newcomers but within the framework of the rural class structure, and their importance is most effectively evaluated through the use of a political economy perspective.

While commonly adopted in the analysis of urban society, political economy perspectives have yet to be widely explored in relation to changes within the rural community (Hanrahan and Cloke, 1983). And yet, in view of the processes of class change identified above, such approaches would appear to have much to offer by way of explanation of existing social and economic patterns. The political economy approach is also to be valued in relation to its ability to shed light on the wider association of social structure and decision-making by placing both within the context of the role of private capital. Further elaboration of this idea is best undertaken by an examination of actual examples from original research. The following sections of this chapter are consequently devoted to a discussion of social structure and planning in two case study villages in rural Wiltshire.

THE CASE STUDY: SOCIAL STRUCTURE

This study begins with a brief examination of the social structure of two villages in the Kennet district of northeast Wiltshire, moving on to a discussion of planning, with particular reference to the social impact of decision-making in respect of local plans and development applications. (For a more detailed account of particular aspects of social change in these villages see Little [1986].)

The communities in which the case study was undertaken, Milton Lilbourne and

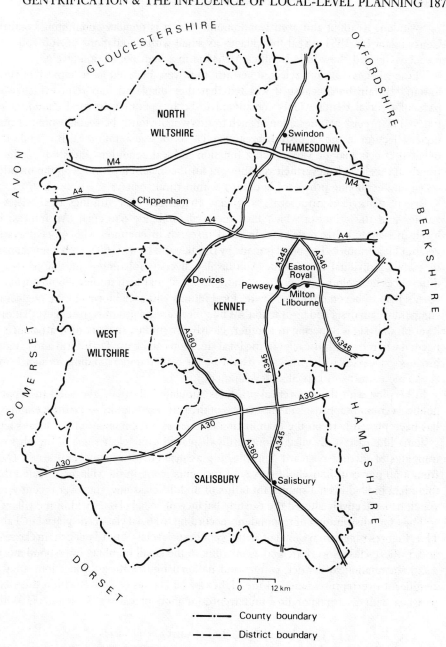

Figure 11.1   The county of Wiltshire

Easton Royal, are situated in an area of rural Wiltshire which, while not physically far removed from quite sizeable centres of population (Marlborough, for example, is only 8 miles away and Devizes less than 20 miles), gives the impression of relative remoteness due to the lack of development in the area (Figure 11.1). Good rail and road communications, however, make this area accessible to large employment centres such as Swindon, Reading and even London and thus it is popular commuting country. Census data for 1981 reveal the villages as small with populations of 466 and 222 respectively, and show little significant change in recent population levels.

These villages were not selected because they were believed to be 'typical' of rural lowland Britain but because it was felt that they displayed important evidence of particular social trends widely considered to be in operation in rural communities today. The precise manifestation of such trends will obviously be spatially unique, and their reflection in the case study area peculiar to these communities. But while the detailed effects may be very much a function of local conditions the study of these trends at this level is nevertheless important for the insight it provides on the broader social and economic processes operating within rural society.

Recent work (e.g. Strathern, 1984) has challenged past attitudes to local-level studies and the criticism which they received for being parochial. An interest in localism is now being developed in rural research in common with other areas of geographical inquiry. The point is made by Bradley and Lowe (1984, p. 9), for instance, that while individual communities will display diversity it is important that just such differences be explored. They go on to add, however, that such studies should not allow researchers to become obsessed with 'local idioms and social forms to the neglect of comparative analysis and abstraction'. While there are no grounds to suggest that one level of analysis is superior to another, clearly, in studies such as this, a balance is needed whereby the intricacies of the local situation can be used to inform and explore broader processes which may be useful in the wider understanding of social and economic patterns of capitalist development.

In keeping with the theoretical priorities stipulated above — the need to adopt a political economy approach in the analysis of the rural community — greatest emphasis has been placed here on the examination of class as a component of the local social system. The case study villages outwardly displayed quite clear signs of the physical trappings of picture-postcard gentrification associated with many rural areas. Data from a 50 per cent household survey of residents living in the villages revealed that there had indeed been a significant influx of middle-class migrants over recent years which had effectively altered the existing balance of social classes within the villages.

The exact distribution of respondents according to social class is displayed in Table 11.1. Figures range from a total of 33 per cent in social class 1 to 13 per cent in classes 4 and 5 (these classes were treated as one due to the small numbers of respondents in each). In relation to district, county and national figures these proportions show a significant overrepresentation of the higher social classes (1 and 2) within the study parishes with a corresponding underrepresentation of classes 3, 4 and 5. When

Table 11.1   Social class of survey respondents

Social class	No.	%
1	39	33
2	34	29
3	29	24
4/5	15	13
Total	117	100

Table 11.2   Social class by length of residence (%) for the study parishes

Social class	0–5	6–15	Length of residence (years) 16–30	>30	All life
1	45	41	21	9	0
2	29	27	31	36	18
3	18	22	21	36	45
4/5	8	7	27	19	37
	100	100	100	100	100

considered in relation to length of residence an impression of the growing importance of the middle classes in respect to the changing social structure of rural areas is immediately apparent (Table 11.2), the percentage of residents of less than 16 years' standing being clearly biased in favour of the middle classes.

The implications of such changes in class composition on the dominant attitudes, behaviour patterns and even physical appearance of the villages were very difficult to isolate, much less to quantify. Certain trends, however, were very noticeable. The general affluence of residents was reflected in, for example, elements of conspicuous consumption such as the levels of car ownership within the villages, with only 7 per cent of households not having access to a car and as many as 38 per cent owning two (this compares with a national figure of 15.9 per cent as recorded in the 1981 Census). Similarly, the percentage of village families who sent their children to private schools (another indicator of wealth) was very high: 34 per cent of children went to either local preparatory or to boarding schools.

The changing social structure of the villages is also reflected in aspects of lifestyle such as residents' workplace, leisure patterns and social contacts. For many of the recent migrants both work and social life took place mainly outside the village. The image of the very self-contained community life traditionally associated with rural areas is becoming increasingly anachronistic. This aside, however, a dominant rural ideology extolling the old-fashioned virtues of a close-knit, caring community, coupled with a glorification of the English landscape and of the health and peacefulness of the countryside, remains very strong in rural areas. In the case study villages a 'sense of community' was considered to be the 'most important aspect of village life' by a high proportion (46 per cent) of respondents, while a total of 29 per cent cited the quality of the environment as an important influence on their decision to move to the village — a higher proportion than any other single reason.

These trends were most apparent among the middle classes. Seventy-five per cent of respondents who mentioned 'the environment' as a factor contributing to their decision to move to the villages, for example, belonged to social classes 1 and 2. There is some conflict here between this finding and the generally accepted belief that it is just such people who have attributed most to change in village society, to a break-up of 'the community' and the spread of development into the countryside. The wish to protect the attributes, real or imagined, which have attracted them to rural life is clearly displayed among these people, however, who frequently become fervent supporters of conservation and dedicated champions of village societies, functions and issues. In this context the household survey attempted to identify residents' attitudes towards potential housing and industrial development in the villages. Again, results showed a strong association with social class; a greater proportion of the higher classes than the lower classes being opposed to development.

The picture emerging from the case study was of the steady inmigration into the villages of middle-class newcomers, many of whom were retired or close to retiring. As noted earlier, neither village had grown significantly either in terms of population levels or physical size and the increase in middle-class newcomers had occurred largely at the expense of lower-class locals. With this growth in the middle classes had come a widespread renovation of old village property and a concern to protect both physical and social images of rural life. The contention of this chapter is that these processes are perpetuated through the protection of private capital and wealth accumulation and that in the reinforcement of individual interests by the planning system, the progressive gentrification of rural areas by the middle classes is not only facilitated but actively encouraged.

In this chapter the ways in which planning is influential in the process of gentrification are illustrated, together with examples from original research. Unfortunately, space restricts this analysis to a study of policy and implementation. Also important, however, is the actual operation of the planning process itself and the way in which this is influenced not only by the political relationship between central and local government, but also by the interests and allegiances of key decision-makers at the local level. The role of individual actors in the operation of the local planning process is a relatively neglected area of research. Newby et al. (1978) and Buchanan (1982), in two of the few studies which have looked at this area, consider the position of landowners in local decision-making and the extent to which conservationist policies, frequently endorsed in rural areas, constitute a deliberate attempt to protect the property interests of particular individuals. Recognizing that this is clearly a very complex issue both authors suggest that it may be misguided to assume that landowners will necessarily use positions of power to reinforce personal interests. Newby et al. (1978), for example, believe that a degree of paternalism can be identified in the policy preferences of both landowners and powerful farmers and that the desire to 'preserve the national heritage' may be a reflection of genuine altruism.

Clearly, the identification of motive is extremely difficult in such circumstances. The position is perhaps best summed up by Newby et al. (1978), however, who suggest that 'irrespective of all claims to altruism' the support of landowners and large farmers for conservation 'functions to perpetuate a situation in which they continue to reap a number of political and economic advantages while less privileged groups continue to bear disproportionate costs in terms of alternatives foregone' (pp 244–245). In Wiltshire both District and County Councils were strongly Conservative and while little information was collected concerning the specific interests of individual councillors it was apparent that at all three levels (county, district and parish) the landowning interest was well represented. There was little evidence of conflict either within or between different levels of the local state, although it is not clear to what extent such apparent harmony represented a true convergence of interests or the skilful management of consensus. Clearly, this area would benefit from further research in order to uncover the true motives of key actors in the allocative process. What was apparent from the little information gathered here was that the political make-up of local government was more likely to lead to support for the interests of private property owners, thus protecting the position of the middle classes within the rural communities at the expense of the poorer sectors of the population. The motives of individuals are possibly easier to identify at the parish level. Thus in the treatment of planning applications (see p. 194) comment is made on the interests and allegiances of specific groups and individuals.

THE CASE STUDY: PLANNING

Before embarking on this analysis it is important to stress that the concern here is as much with the implementation of planning decisions as with the policy statements themselves. Owen (1980) suggests that existing research has concentrated largely on planning objectives rather than the effects of planned action, and believes, like others (see, for example, Knox and Cullen, 1981; Cloke and Little, 1984a) that the implementation process within planning is of crucial importance to the impact of decisions made on the community. Far too much attention has been devoted to looking at written policy, particularly, it is alleged, in the context of statutory plans (Cloke, 1983), rather than at the actual implementation of those statements or of their outworking on the ground.

This does not mean that the failure of statutory plans to deal with rural problems is due entirely to difficulties of implementation. As Gilder (1984) argues, such plans themselves are frequently 'fundamentally unsound vehicles for rural policy', a fact which is particularly accurate in the context of policies directed at local housing needs. It does, however, imply that in any evaluation of the true power and implications of both the planning process in general and individual policy decisions, more is to be gained from a study of policy enactment than from the often rather vague and woolly statements contained in published planning documents. There are numerous constraints, administrative, financial and ideological, operating at the local level to ensure that the intentions of broad strategic policies cannot be (or are not) directly transferred to initiatives within the local situation. To suggest why this is so is beyond the scope of this chapter since it brings into contention a number of issues concerning, for example, the workings of the decision-making process, the relationship between different levels of government, not to mention aspects of the political loyalties of those involved in both formulating and implementing policy.

Finally, as has been mentioned above, planning is as important for its negative aspects and 'non-decisions' in certain instances as it is for its powers of reform. Such importance is likely to be undervalued if analysts confine attention to broad policy intentions. Again, local-level investigation is required in order to assess the full impact of planning as a vehicle for social change.

WRITTEN POLICY — THE WILTSHIRE STRUCTURE PLANS

While the major concern here is with the local implementation of planning rather than with the broad objectives of policy, it is helpful to look briefly at the priorities laid down in the Structure Plan for Wiltshire. Such policies give at least some indication of the dominant trends favoured by decision-makers although, as has been observed elsewhere (Cloke and Little, 1984a), the final published statements are often the result of compromise to the extent that they portray little of the deliberations or conflicts which may have surrounded their inception, nor, indeed, the 'true' intentions of the policy-makers themselves. The general policies for rural settlements as contained within the Wiltshire Structure Plans* (Wiltshire County Council, 1980) can hardly be described as innovative. They reflect, for the most part, the traditional aims of rural resource concentration commonly witnessed in the majority of structure plans (a study by Cloke and Shaw [1983] revealed that only three counties — Gloucestershire, Cumbria and North Yorkshire — demonstrated any form of radical movement away from conventional 'key settlement' type approaches). The North East Wiltshire Plan went as far as to name those individual villages into which growth should be channelled, stating that: 'the development of small groups of dwellings within the framework of each settlement will normally be permitted if that settlement has the following facilities; a primary school, a post office, a food shop and a journey to work service to one or more towns'. Such villages, it was suggested, are likely to be: 'better suited to absorb small groups of housing than the remaining villages' (Wiltshire County Council, 1981a, p. 42). In this way the intention was to establish rural centres towards which the various public and private agencies responsible for providing basic services could be encouraged to direct resources.

The aims of conservation and landscape protection also receive considerable attention within the broad policy objectives of the Wiltshire Structure Plan. While all three plans recognize the competing needs of housing and employment, agriculture, landscape and wildlife conservation and recreation, it appears that the needs of agriculture and environmental protection are given priority with many of the policies directed towards growth in rural areas conditional on development having no adverse effects on the existing character of the environment. For example, the North East Wiltshire Structure Plan (Wiltshire County Council, 1981a), referring to those villages selected for growth, stresses that residential development will be permitted only if it is in character with the existing architecture and if 'there is no overriding objection because of the impact of the scale or design of the development on the local environment'. Again, in non-selected villages development, it was proposed, 'will be acceptable only if it is in scale and harmony with the character of the settlement and provided there is no adverse effect on the local environment' (Wiltshire County Council, 1981, p. 4). It appears throughout the plans, moreover, that the objectives of development and those of conservation are, by definition, considered to be conflicting and mutually exclusive. In essence the real needs of the rural population receive little attention within the stated scope of strategic policy over and above a rather cursory declaration of the intention to safeguard services where possible and to 'promote employment growth by assisting the development of small scale industries in rural areas'.

Such broad directives clearly leave considerable scope for variety in interpretation and implementation at the district and community levels. A study of local plans and,

* There are three separate Structure Plans covering Wiltshire. They are not coincidental with district boundaries. The case study area falls under the North East Wiltshire Plan. Many of the policies are, however, consistent throughout the three plans — especially those concerned with broad rural settlement objectives.

more importantly, planning applications was therefore made to give a much more detailed and realistic idea of both the nature and impact of planning as experienced in rural settlements and, specifically here, the case study villages. Generalizations in the study and analysis of local plans must be made with caution. It is clear, however, that despite the stipulation by the Department of the Environment (DoE) that they should be directed towards land use and, in particular, development control (see DoE, 1979, 3–1, p. 29), local plans are recognized by many authorities as potential vehicles for the construction and implementation of social as well as physical policies. There does indeed appear to be a trend towards 'a wider and more comprehensive response to localised planning issues' (Cloke, 1983, p. 289) at this level, despite concern by the DoE (see DoE, 1981), in terms of economic constraints, that unnecessary priority is not given to local plans, especially where 'the structure plan provides an adequate planning framework or where little or no pressure for development is expected'.

Again, the relationship between district and county levels is all important. Friction between the different levels is likely to be greatest where political control differs (Beardmore, 1976). Conventionally, as Saunders (1982) documents, local state activity shows greater concern for citizenship rights and social needs, while the central state is involved more directly with fiscal policies which are developed through the corporate sector and directed towards private profit and the maintenance of private property rights. To what extent this is reflected in the relationship between district and county is uncertain, the county representing an intermediate level, in some senses, between local and central state activity. It is clear, however, that the detail given to the particular needs of local people is a function of the relationship between district and county. In terms of local planning, policies may be sensitive to detailed social needs, coordinating the activities of different public- and private-sector agencies or they may remain simply mechanisms for the implementation of development control.

LOCAL PLANS

While, at the time of writing, no local plan had been produced to cover the precise study area, two district plans (of a proposed series of nine) had been published by the District Council. One of these was the Pewsey Village Plan (Kennet District Council, 1983) which makes frequent references to the 'rural area' surrounding Pewsey, the area in which the case study villages are located. The major focus of the Pewsey Village Plan as far as the study villages are concerned is the reiteration of general Structure Plan policy in the concentration of resources into Pewsey itself. The Plan states that Pewsey is 'an important service and employment centre for other surrounding villages' (Kennet District Council, 1983, p. 5). The development of Pewsey as a centre was also seen as a way of restricting growth within the neighbouring rural areas, the Plan pointing out that as Pewsey is situated in an Area of Outstanding Natural Beauty (AONB) it is 'important that the village does not spread out into the surrounding countryside unnecessarily'. Many of the respondents in the case study villages suggested, informally, that development was most appropriate in Pewsey where an existing service infrastructure and workforce existed. These comments, however, came mainly from the mobile middle classes, for while the concentration of services and so on in Pewsey was of little inconvenience to such residents, the lack of public transport between the villages and

Pewsey left those without a car, particularly the elderly, relatively deprived.

In terms of local plans it is clearly not possible to come to very detailed conclusions about the relationship between decision-making and social structure in the communities studied. Essentially, in the two plans so far completed (the other being the Devizes District Plan), there appear to be few examples of positive initiatives in terms of social needs policies, simply a commitment to reinforcing the aims of the Structure Plan in both the distribution of resources and the protection of the landscape. In the study of planning applications, moreover, fundamental anomalies were found in the implementation of policy which appeared to contradict the Structure Plan and local plan policies themselves. The extent to which development decisions actually reflect strategic policy is again brought into question, illustrating once more the importance of the implementation process.

PLANNING APPLICATIONS

This section does not undertake a rigorous analysis of all recent planning applications in the case study villages nor make detailed comparisons between refusals and acceptances. Rather it confines itself to a review of those applications which had been rejected or provisionally accepted during a 10-year period immediately prior to the original research for this project (see Little, 1984).

Of those planning applications that have been refused by the District Council over the past 10 years the majority has been rejected on environmental grounds. (Most applications for residential development had been submitted by existing villagers, although proposals to open a trout farm [see below] did come from an outside interest.) Particular concern is expressed by the Planning Department for the prevention of growth beyond the existing boundaries of the villages. For example, plans to build a bungalow on the edge of Milton in Havering Lane were denied because:

> The development would represent an undesirable consolidation of existing building outside the village limits to the detriment of the character of this rural area which is included within the North Wessex Downs AONB. (Kennet Planning Department)

The statement continues:

> The grant of planning permission in the present case would set a precedent for proposals of a similar nature in respect of other small pieces of land in the vicinity which would be equally undesirable and which would then be difficult to resist.

Similarly, a proposal to build a single house in place of a derelict garage on the road between Burbage and Easton Royal (B3087) was refused on the grounds that:

> [. . .] the building of residential development on the land would represent an undesirable extension of building in ribbon form beyond the reasonable limits of Easton Royal to the detriment of the appearance of the area.

This fear of ribbon development appears to be particularly influential over planning decisions made in the area. It is frequently suggested that should one property be allowed along the B3087 then this would soon lead to further applications and more extensive development. One such application for the construction of a small but much needed village shop, and another to build a bungalow for an elderly person presently living with relatives in the village, were also rejected under the 'ribbon development policy'. Both examples clearly illustrate the precedence of environmental and aesthetic concerns over social needs, and the operation of policy to the disadvantage of 'local' people.

The reaction of the Planning Department to infilling is generally found to be more positive, as would be expected from local and Structure Plan policy. Many of the proposals do, however, carry conditions which must be guaranteed before full acceptance is granted. For example, rigid controls on roofing (Welsh slate or thatch), brick type and window size are specified on many of the applications for new development. And in the same way extensions to existing property are carefully regulated under such criteria.

The justification for these strict controls rests overwhelmingly on a desire to maintain the existing character of the villages. Conditions are laid down variously 'in the interests of visual amenity' and 'in order to ensure harmonious architectural treatment' (Kennet Planning Department). A number of applications had gone to appeal and it was interesting to note that where planning permission had been denied on environmental grounds decisions were generally upheld and it was only in the case of highway objections that initial decisions appeared more flexible and open to revision.

While the decisions involved in the implementation of planning policy at this level are not, it can be argued, formulated overtly in the interests of any specific social group within the community, their effects clearly operate to the advantage of the more affluent in the protection of private property. The wholesale preservation of the quality of the environment, not only in the blanket refusal of certain types of development (for example, the ribbon development described above) but in the strict specifications enforced on the design and appearance of any building allowed, acts to enhance the value of property in a society which attaches increasing value and status to rural life and a house in the country. In a survey of house prices undertaken by Wiltshire County Council (1981b), property in the Marlborough area (which includes case study villages) was found to be more expensive than in other parts of the county. More specifically, the value of property within the case study villages themselves was found to be very high and rising sharply. In estimates provided by house owners (which were generally felt to be reliable — many, for example, had recently moved in or had had the house valued for potential sale or for insurance purposes) 34 per cent of respondents believed their property to be worth over £55 000 (at 1984 prices) while, at the other end of the scale, only 11 per cent thought theirs to be worth less than £40 000.

Perhaps more important here is the proportion of houses which are bought relatively cheaply but then 'improved' by their owners such that they become inflated in value. In this way houses are taken beyond the purchasing power of the lower classes and effectively removed from one part of the market and placed in another. While figures must clearly be treated with some caution, the survey did reveal that despite current prices, 47 per cent of respondents had paid less than £25 000 for their house. Moreover, not all such respondents were longstanding residents, nearly one-quarter having moved to the village in the past five years. Almost half those houses bought for less than £10 000 were now worth more than £55 000 — a reflection of both the increase in house prices and the importance of renovating old property in the villages. Indeed, 48 per cent of respondents said that they had undertaken major work consisting of building extra rooms, knocking down internal walls or constructing a garage, one-third of these having totally rebuilt their property.

In many villages of high aesthetic/environmental quality (Milton and Easton included) there is a severe shortage of low-cost housing. Furthermore, a reduction, or more frequently a total absence, of coucil house-building, together with the widespread selling-off of local authority stocks in rural areas, has effectively reduced the option of renting for the poorer sections of society.

It was suggested earlier in this chapter that although many of the powers available to planning authorities are in fact negative or preventative, this in itself does not mean that planning is ineffectual in terms of influencing social structure and wellbeing in rural communities. On the contrary, it is the negative effects of the implementation of planning decisions to restrict development which help ensure that free market forces and the interests of private capital in the ownership of property prevail. The competition for resources which thus occurs quite freely reinforces the position of the more affluent in contemporary rural society.

At times private interests are not merely supported by planning policy but are dominant over it. Political pressure exerted by local councillors frequently, although not always, ensures that the anti-development stance favoured by many middle-class migrants is advanced, although, as certain authors have pointed out (notably Newby *et al.*, 1978; Buchanan, 1982), it may be too simplistic to equate the pursuit of such aims entirely with private interest. Moreover, Lowe and Goyder (1983) believe that the professional and business interests of many local councillors may lead them to favour development (although their evidence was drawn from more accessible rural areas and may not be as applicable in the remoter rural context). The inconsistencies which occur between the implementation of decisions and the actual policies do invite speculation and comment, however. In Milton and Easton residents cited a number of examples where decisions had been taken apparently running contrary to established policy. These included the building of three large detached houses in the centre of Easton, the refusal to allow plans to develop an infill site in Milton opposite the house of the then chairperson of the parish council and the granting of permission, which had apparently been denied to a local resident on two previous occasions, to an 'outsider' to build a garage on the edge of Milton. Similarly, when a planning officer was questioned concerning a particular plot of land on which planning permission had recently been granted after numerous past refusals, he replied that if applicants persevered with a case 'eventually the planning officer may give in and grant permission' even if circumstances had not changed. This hardly implies close links between policy and implementation.

The tendency for planning to operate in support of private interests in rural settlements is perpetuated to some extent by the middle-class residents themselves. On a formal level parish councils have the right to be involved in the processing of applications if they so choose, and although the planning office is under no obligation to comply with the views given, such views are clearly not totally without influence. In the applications studied there were no examples of major development (the building of new housing or large extensions) where planning permission had been granted against the officially recorded wishes of the parish council. While the parish council is supposedly a representative body, it is well known that in the rural areas members tend to be drawn largely from the ranks of the middle classes (Buller and Lowe, 1982; Leverton, 1982). Certainly this was the case in the communities studied here where the majority of those involved with the parish council, either as members (78 per cent) or simply through attendance at meetings (75 per cent), were from social classes 1 and 2. The extent to which this distortion in class representation may affect views expressed by parish councils is unclear and to some degree dependent on the individuals involved. As noted above, the applications revealed a number of rather 'dubious' decisions relating to the rejection of applications on 'environmental' grounds. Perhaps the most noteworthy was the repeated refusal (supported by both the planning officers and the parish council) for the development of what appeared to be a prime 'infill' site located right opposite the house of the then parish council chair. In the case study villages, at least, concern for the maintenance of the rural character of the area appeared to assume considerable importance in terms of the reaction of the 'planning sub-committee' of the parish council to planning applications. In the case of applications where permission had been refused on environmental grounds the parish council generally concurred with the decision of the district. Again, this is another complex and very important element of the debate to which more time cannot be given here but to which further research could profitably be directed.

CONCLUSIONS

In this analysis of local social structure and planning implementation, an attempt has been made to illustrate the relationship between social change and planning in rural settlements, particularly the perpetuation of gentrification through aspects of policy and its implementation. The explanation has been necessarily brief, the topic itself deserving far greater attention than could be attributed in many of the areas touched on in this chapter. The main thrust of the argument presented is that, as an element of state activity, the powers and influence available to planning are severely constrained by the demands of the state. However, this does not make planning or the planning system powerless *per se*; it simply means that the scope available to planning for any form of radical, autonomous initiative is limited. In its protection of private interests, however, planning does exercise a very real power.

At the local level such powers may ultimately be effective in influencing not only the wellbeing but also the distribution of different social groups. In rural areas, for example, the increase in middle-class residents, leading to the gentrification of many villages, has been encouraged by planning policies which show more concern for the aims of environmental conservation and the economic principles of resource concentration than for the alleviation of social need. It can be argued effectively that the dominant rural ideology mediates against the poorer members of society by advocating anti-development and self-help as planning solutions to present-day rural problems. As those living, or wishing to live in, rural areas are left increasingly to the mercy of free market forces the competition for limited resources promotes a change in the structure of rural society and a widening of the gap between rich and poor.

While broad strategic planning may acknowledge (to some extent) the urgency of dealing with rural problems, providing services, employment and housing for the less affluent to ensure that some degree of social (implicitly, class) balance is maintained, at the local level the implementation of resulting policies often falls victim of economic constraints, political pressure or simply the problems of coordinating a wide range of diverse interests. Insofar as decision-making at the community level is in the hands of many different agencies, departments and individuals, it is perhaps inappropriate that planning, as only one element in the whole process (see Wright, 1982), is held responsible for the problems of resource distribution and inequality currently occurring in many rural areas. It is clear, however, that planning cannot be disregarded as a definite force behind social change and that conservative anti-development and *laissez-faire* policies not only protect the interests of the middle classes but actively disadvantage the least affluent. This will result in the continuing (possibly accelerating) social polarization of rural areas in the future and a reinforcement of middle-class exclusivity in the countryside.

REFERENCES

Beardmore, D. (1976) An uneasy partnership in development control, *The Planner*, Vol. 62, 73–74.

Blowers, A. (1980) *The Limits of Power: The Politics of Local Planning Policy*, Pergamon, Oxford.

Blowers, A. (1982) Much ado about nothing — a case study of planning and power. In Healey, P., McDougall, G. and Thomas, M.J. (eds) *Planning Theory: Prospects for the 1980s*, Pergamon, Oxford.

Bradley, T. and Lowe, P. (1984) Introduction: locality, rurality and social theory. In Bradley, T. and Lowe, P. (eds) *Locality and Rurality: Economy and Society in Rural Regions*, Geo Books, Norwich.

Broadbent, T.A. (1979) *Options for Planning: A Discussion Document*, Centre for Environmental Studies, London.

Buchanan, S. (1982) Power and planning in rural areas: preparation of the Suffolk County Structure Plan. In Moseley, M.J. (ed.) *Power, Planning and People in Rural East Anglia*, University of East Anglia, Centre for East Anglian Studies.

Buller, H. and Lowe, P. (1982) Politics and class in rural preservation: a study of the Suffolk Preservation Society. In Moseley, M.J. (ed.) *Power, Planning and People in Rural East Anglia*, University of East Anglia, Centre for East Anglian Studies.

Camhis, M. (1979) *Planning Theory and Philosophy*, Tavistock, London.

Cloke, P.J. (1983) *An Introduction to Rural Settlement Planning*, Methuen, London.

Cloke, P.J. and Little, J.K. (1984a) *Implementation and County Level Planning*, Rural Policy Implementation Project working paper 1, St David's University College, Lampeter.

Cloke, P.J. and Little, J.K. (1984b) *Social Profiles of Ten Case Study Parishes*, Rural Policy Implementation Project working paper 2, St David's University College, Lampeter.

Cloke, P.J. and Shaw, D.P. (1983) Rural settlement policies in structure plans, *Town Planning Review*, Vol. 54, 338–354.

Connell, J. (1978) *The End of Tradition: Country Life in Central Surrey*, Routledge and Kegan Paul, London.

Department of the Environment (1979) *Circular 4/79*, HMSO, London.

Department of the Environment (1981) *Circular 23/81*, HMSO, London.

Gilder, I. (1984) State planning and local needs. In Bradley, T. and Lowe, P. (eds) *Locality and Rurality: Economy and Society in Rural Regions*, Geo Books, Norwich.

Hanrahan, P.J. and Cloke, P.J. (1983) Towards a critical appraisal of rural settlement planning in England and Wales, *Sociologia Ruralis*, Vol. XXIII, No. 2, 109–129.

Kennet District Council (1983) *Pewsey Village Plan, Survey and Options Report*, Kennet District Council, Devizes.

Knox, P. and Cullen, J. (1981) Town planning and the internal survival mechanisms of urbanised capitalism, *Area*, Vol. 13, 183–188.

Leverton, P.J. (1982) Working relationships in local government: the view point of the parish councils in Norfolk. In Moseley, M.J. (ed.) *Power, Planning and People in Rural East Anglia*, University of East Anglia, Centre for East Anglian Studies.

Little, J.K. (1984) Social change in rural areas: a planning perspective. Unpublished Ph.D. thesis, Department of Geography, University of Reading.

Little, J.K. (1986) Social change and planning policy: a study of two Wiltshire villages. In Lowe, P. and Wright, S. (eds) *Rural Deprivation and Welfare*, Geo Books, Norwich (in press).

Lowe, P. and Goyder, J. (1983) *Environmental Groups in Politics*, Allen and Unwin, London.

Newby, H., Bell, C., Rose, D. and Saunders, P. (1978) *Property Paternalism and Power*, Hutchinson, London.

Newby, J. (1980) *Green and Pleasant Land? Social Change in Rural England*, Penguin, Harmondsworth.

Owen, S. (1980) Assessing the effects of local planning. In Owen, S. and Curry, N. (eds) *Gloucestershire Papers in Local and Rural Planning*, Department of Town and Country Planning, Gloucestershire College of Arts and Technology, Gloucester.

Phillips, D.R. and Williams, A.M. (1984) *Rural Britain: A Social Geography*, Blackwell, Oxford.

Saunders, P. (1982) Why study central–local relations? *Local Government Studies*, March/April, 55–66.

Strathern, M. (1984) The social meaning of localism. In Bradley, T. and Lowe, P. (eds) *Locality and Rurality: Economy and Society in Rural Regions*, Geo Books, Norwich.

Wiltshire County Council (1980) *South Wiltshire Structure Plan, Approved Written Statement*, Wiltshire County Council, Trowbridge.

Wiltshire County Council (1981a) *North East Wiltshire Structure Plan, Operative Plan*, Wiltshire County Council, Trowbridge.

Wiltshire County Council (1981b) *Wiltshire Structure Plans, Monitoring Report, Appendix 2, Housing in Wiltshire*, Wiltshire County Council, Trowbridge.

Wright, S. (1982) Parish to Whitehall: administrative structure and perceptions of community in rural areas. In Owen, S. and Curry, N. (eds) *Gloucestershire Papers in Local and Rural Planning*, Gloucestershire College of Arts and Technology, Gloucester.

12

COORDINATION OF RURAL POLICY-MAKING AND IMPLEMENTATION

Gerald Smart

In previous chapters of this book individual aspects of policy-making for rural areas have been examined, such as are the primary concern of special agencies or of service committees of local authorities. Some of these relate to particular resources, water or landscape for example; some, such as housing and education, to specific needs of local communities. The focus of the book now turns to the interrelationship between these aspects, using as a case study the research on rural decision-making carried out at University College London (UCL) for the Department of the Environment (DoE) in the period 1979–83 (Smart *et al.*, 1980, 1982a, b, 1983) and examining briefly some developments which have taken place since then.

This research was commissioned during a period of growing public and political interest in rural affairs, punctuated by various events such as the Countryside in 1970 Conferences, the abortive reports (in the mid-1970s) of the Countryside Review Committee (1976) (note 1), the parliamentary debate (1980–81) on the Wildlife and Countryside Bill (note 2), and the formation of Rural Voice in the same year. Perhaps the greatest emphasis given at the time was to the issue of natural resource conservation; there were, however, some important socioeconomic studies of rural decline by the Development Commission (1982), the Standing Conference of Rural Community Councils (1978), and local authorities (see, for example, Hereford & Worcester County Council, 1975–78; Association of District Councils, 1978; Association of County Councils, 1979). All these undoubted contributions to knowledge of rural affairs stressed the need for improved coordination of decision-making by public authorities, especially central and local government. The issues tended to be seen primarily in organizational terms. However, anyone with experience of decision-making and implementation at the sharp end will know that the processes by which problems are identified and solutions debated and determined are just as important as the actual structure of administration within which the processes are, or should be, taking place. The processes are often incremental and overlapping, far from clearly structural. Individual studies in the fields of organizational theory, too, have tended for obvious reasons to concentrate on administrative or political aspects, and to focus on specific levels of government. There seemed to be a need to draw from the debate on 'agenda creation' which followed these earlier studies (see Bachrach and Baratz, 1982), and to develop a view of the process of decision-making which gives equal emphasis to all levels from 'rural community' to central government.

A CASE STUDY

Thus the UCL project set out to study the administrative and organizational interrelationships of public and voluntary bodies, and to investigate the impact of their policies, aiming to discover to what extent their policy-making accorded, individually and collectively, with the needs of rural communities. Since most previous case studies had focused on upland areas, the UCL team worked on three contrasting areas of lowland England shown in Figure 12.1.

In each area (West Dorset, with its substantial retired population, remote East Lincolnshire, and partially urbanized South Cleveland) the research took the form of widening horizons of study. It started by looking at local-level issue creation and at attempts made to influence the 'agendas' of local government. In the light of collective views of rural problems at this level it then examined the efforts made by these authorities to solve perceived problems. Where the decision-making processes were seen to trace to central government, the study went on to look at functions there and at any measures taken in order to produce a collective view of, and harmonized policies towards, rural areas. What problems, for example, are expressed at parish level and what dialogue is there with higher levels of local government to help authority-wide coordination? What are the district and county views of rural areas and their futures, and how do these compare with the views of residents? What causes any differences, for example communication or feasibility? Is there a central government 'view' of the present and future shape of rural communities and their varying needs? What are the influences on agenda creation at this level, and how do these affect attempts to harmonize policies?

THE STUDY'S FINDINGS

Residents tended to see the impact of policies as a totality. In West Dorset their main concern was with the problems of an ageing community, and the majority was willing to see further development in the hope that this would help to overcome such trends by easing constraints in the housing and job markets. In East Lincolnshire, the residents' worries about shortcomings in job availability and career prospects in this area of exceptionally high farming productivity were strongly related to two other concerns: a lack of housing for young families, and of transport, especially in view of the cost and time penalties of travel along far-flung lines of communication. Not altogether surprisingly, they regarded the sensitive question of balance between farming and environmental conservation as being of low importance; perhaps they were too involved. In South Cleveland the main problems quoted by residents resulted from their experience that policies and provision were primarily designed for the county's urban areas. In all three areas residents felt that their needs were not adequately reflected in policies; apart from parish councils, their dominant impression of government, central and local, was one of remoteness and insensitivity to their needs and to

Location of Study Areas

Figure 12.1   Location of study areas.

the relationship between these needs. Hence there arose an emphasis on self-help: to try to overcome the inadequacies of policy (for example, for public transport or community care) or to facilitate confrontation on occasions when policies were thought to be inappropriate (such as school closures, which were bitterly contested) or conflicting (although such conflicts seemed most acute in natural resource management, about which the strength of residents' feelings varied from one area to another). Residents perceived the need for organizations to facilitate such self-help and to communicate with higher levels of government.

Contrasting with the residents' views, the perspectives of decision-makers were found to start with the whole geographic area they administer, and to sharpen gradually on a particular location, or on the problems of a particular section of society, namely their 'clients' in the service they administer. They, too, saw present characteristics and future possibilities, but primarily within these perspectives.

How might these two perceptions be better related? The project looked at trends in the organization and politicization of local government since its reorganization in 1974 (see, for example, Stewart, 1983). Against this background, the progress made by the counties and districts in the three study areas towards the integrated setting of priorities for specific issues was patchy, as might be expected. There was also the question of how such policies might be communicated and given effect.

One possible vehicle for broad integration and communication is the Structure Plan — the only statutory means of expressing, at the strategic county level, the local authority's approach to the future of its area. Unfortunately the DoE's insistence (Department of the Environment, 1984), from interpretation of the relevant legislation, that these plans must deal with land use and development has severely limited their wider usefulness. Similarly, in local planning in the study areas, there had been few opportunities for such expression at district level; reasons for this included staff shortage, and also the priority being given to urban areas.

Quite apart from the question of policy vehicles, however, the authorities which are best placed to take a strategic view (the county councils) had not always been able to develop strong links between their own policies, and with those of other authorities and agencies. Even the necessarily *ad hoc* initiatives by local authorities towards joint action between county and district levels and the Council for Small Industries in Rural Areas (CoSIRA) to promote economic development, for example in the Lincolnshire study area, could perform only a limited role. This was due primarily to the counterbalancing impact of agricultural development, with its widespread social and economic effects on local communities, assisted financially and technically by the Ministry of Agriculture, Fisheries and Food (MAFF) through its own separate channels of communication with the farming industry (Wibberley, 1981; Smart *et al.*, 1982a, pp 30–32, 52–61, 1983, pp 29–30). (Similar constraints applied in the case of initiatives by local authorities or organizations such as the Nature Conservancy Council or the Countryside Commission to influence decisions affecting natural resource conservation, other than in specific areas; the situation may now have improved with the enactment of the Wildlife and Countryside Act 1981.) There was evidence, however, that the experience of joint finance between local government and the National Health Service (NHS) might augur well for the principle of joint action, given a suitable financial framework (Smart *et al.*, 1982a, pp 37–38, 1982b, p. 115) (note 3).

Thus there was not much progress in the study areas towards the ideal of rural community development in the sense described in the research report, namely the integration of planning and provision of various services for individual or grouped settlements. Indeed, it seemed that in Dorset, at the time of the case study, and in

Lincolnshire, the authorities were to varying degrees unclear about their aims for rural areas, save for the introduction of industry; and that they had no adequate formal means of translating such aims into integrated policies and decisions, and of communicating these to residents. They experienced particular problems in such integration due to the fragmentation of advice or control from government departments. The situation was not helped by the endemic weakness, with notable exceptions, of parish councils. In Cleveland the case study revealed a somewhat unusual situation, that of an area where urban values and inter-authority rivalry predominated in the approach to rural affairs, within a strongly party-political climate. This aroused the suspicion of rural communities. Here, rural policies seemed consequently to lack objectivity, in general, and adjustment to the particular needs of small settlements. In each area rural community councils (RCC) had the potential to strengthen communication between residents and higher authorities, especially through their support to local communities by assistance to parish councils and voluntary groups. Unfortunately this potential was not fully developed; for success in such a role, an RCC must be seen to be sufficiently free of direct local authority control to act on its own behalf, despite necessary dependence on local government for funding, as well as on substantial Development Commission grant.

The study of the role of key organizations at central government level confirmed the indication from local levels that there is a disconcerting fragmentation of aims and decision-making, despite the wide network of resources available to major departments. In particular, the coordinating agency with the greatest potential, namely the Department of the Environment's Directorate of Rural Affairs (DRA), could play only a limited role in initiating or coordinating decisions in important areas of concern, especially in the influence of central government over rural social and economic development. These limitations can be attributed partly to the plurality of responsibilities for such policies between powerful departments other than the DoE, for example MAFF and the Department of Education and Science (DES), and partly to the absence of a strong external community of interest, despite the efforts of organizations such as Rural Voice. The Development Commission, despite its widely cast role, is small and specialized by comparison with such main departments. Even the local authorities seem to have only limited influence, notwithstanding their wide contacts on the ground and the ability of their associations to mount a well-informed lobby.

THE STUDY'S RECOMMENDATIONS

The study revealed a situation which was not one of universally serious shortcomings in policy, nor usually one of dramatic conflict between decision-making organizations, requiring radical solutions. Rather, it showed that there are particular areas of concern where community development could benefit from further practical application of current concepts of administrative coordination and of public involvement. The need for action probably exists in urban areas, too, though different considerations arise in a rural context. Here, the population is sparsely distributed, and practically all services operate on the margin. Thus the failure of policy for any one service can have widespread repercussions on communities and their structure, and on other services. Integration and fine tuning are therefore of the utmost importance.

Being made at a time of severe financial constraint, the study's basic recommendations had to be cautious and capable of gradual introduction. In accordance with the study's main thrust, starting from the level of the local community, they relate as much to community-based organizations, parish councils, voluntary agencies, and the main levels of local government, as to central government itself.

First, in this sequence, it is necessary to remove impediments to discovering, from a diversity of local opinion, the issues which need to be debated before policy decisions are reached. Among the various points of contact between local community and government, such as the constituency MP, county, district and parish councillors, paid officials and voluntary bodies, the experience of the study suggests that the parish council is often the most accessible and suitable agency to reflect, democratically, the 'rounded' view taken by residents. Parish councils can be an invaluable source of advice to higher levels of local government, and can, to a degree, run their own services. The role of the parish council was on the whole inadequately developed in the study areas. This seems to be the case elsewhere, and the study recommended strongly that *the parish council role should be enhanced as a means of articulating local needs and, where possible, initiating action.* In detail, this would involve measures such as: the continued strengthening of parish councils by grouping them into units which are more financially and administratively viable; the better training of councillors and clerks; the more willing acceptance by district and county councils of the ability of parishes to use their own statutory powers to provide local facilities, and of their need for help with finance and advice for this purpose; and the inclusion of parish councils in consultations on all major decisions affecting rural affairs, and more readiness to take heed of what they say.

Second, it was very clear that voluntary agencies in the study areas and elsewhere could supplement local rural services over a wide front, from public transport to community care, often with catalytic effect. Collectively, also, they have much to contribute as pressure groups in rural policy formulation at district and county level. The RCCs are potentially an effective support and a forum for such groups. They can also be a useful source of advice and 'friend at court' to parish councils, with whose local associations they usually have close links. Unfortunately they are not always good at either role, for reasons already mentioned. The study recommended that *there should be greater policy independence and wider sources of finance for RCCs.* This suggests a consideration of the aims of RCCs, and of the balance of their funding as between the Development Commission, local authorities and other sources, to enable them to act as a local 'rural voice'.

Moving, third, to county and district levels, two matters were thought to require urgent attention. The first is that *rural community development should be seen as a major local government responsibility*, not merely in the uplands where present efforts seemed to be concentrated, but also in lowland areas, including those where agriculture is very prosperous. This renewed emphasis would require very considerable efforts by local authorities to coordinate services, and the closest involvement of government departments, especially MAFF, the statutory agencies and voluntary bodies, in a process which local government is in the best position to guide in each area, on the ground. The second matter for attention concerns the means whereby such coordination of decisions can be achieved in strategic and local terms, organizationally and procedurally. The structure and local plan processes appear at first sight to have much to offer to both, but, as suggested above, they do not have the necessary comprehensiveness. Something less formal is required, adapted to the particular relationship between county and district in any one area. Either level may be in the best position to take on a lead role at any given stage, depending on the nature of the problem. Ideas were developed during the study towards the preparation by local authorities of 'rural community development reports' as a framework for harmonizing policies and inviting public participation. There is indeed some similarity in concept to the Development Commission's 'action plans' (for their 'priority areas') and to the European Community's integrated development projects, although the scope is likely to be wider.

A rural community development report might best form a special supplement to each council's annual report, and should set out: the authority's aims for its rural areas; what has been achieved since the last report; what it is hoped to achieve in the next two or three years; and how this affects or is affected by the plans of other public agencies. An incremental approach like this would enable ideas towards a rural development strategy, including conservation, to evolve over time by dialogue between local and central government departments and other agencies, and the general public, in which attitudes of mind are clarified, acceptable departures from policy or new policies initiated, and the context set for longer-term studies of conflicting requirements and their possible resolution. Responsibility for implementation would remain with the individual agencies, with or without any special financial arrangements such as apply in the case of joint finance between local government and the NHS. The study suggested a 'trial run' in one or two local authority areas, to investigate in practice the 'mechanics' of producing and implementing rural community development reports.

Fourth, moving the focus to central government, the study pointed to the absence of a clear lead in the formulation of integrated policies for rural community development. This lead should be given both through the direct actions of the departments concerned, and through their relationships with local authorities and statutory agencies. The need is paramount in the area of economic development, where the interrelationship between agricultural support and other aspects of economic development was thought to be inadequately recognized. But there was continuing concern, locally, over the effects of school closures and of housing policies on rural communities. It is understandable that the DoE, without a strong mandate for coordination in these fields, is unable to influence major policy themes of other departments. Furthermore, there is broad acceptance in some quarters that all that can be done realistically is to mitigate some of the worst effects, such as on rural employment and population age structure.

There has until recently been little recognition among MPs of the need for central government to take a promotional role in rural community development. In contrast to landscape conservation and recreation, the social and economic affairs of rural areas appear to be a minor concern. Symptomatic of this is the absence until recently of a quantifiable public interest. Conservation groups have long had an established membership whose size is quoted to show the importance of their views. Rural Voice's nine member organizations have an impressive membership, but it is not often quoted in this way (note 4).

Most studies of rural socioeconomic affairs have concluded that there is need for an administrative mechanism to coordinate policies, responsible to a Minister for Rural

Affairs. It is often assumed that this requires a major revision of the structure of government. In fact, both governments in the course of the project did make statements of commitment to rural socioeconomic development. A few statements have recognized the relationship between the decline of public services, the purpose of new investment (e.g. in agriculture) and the decline of communities; and, with greater backbench support, there have been statements committing the government to look carefully at the effects of individual policies on rural areas, for example on petrol prices. The study endorsed the need for policy coordination, but suggested that the framework is already present in the administrative and political organization of government. It would seem it is not major change that is required, but rather a renewed emphasis, commitment and determination to strengthen the framework.

The study therefore recommended that the remit of the DoE should be strengthened to enable it to initiate and coordinate more effectively interdepartmental policies for rural areas; and that there should be a corresponding requirement for other government departments and agencies to have regard to the effect of their activities on rural community development. This would imply a more positive interpretation of the then existing role of the DRA in the DoE, notably in areas where ability to take a lead role has had limitations, especially in the coordination of policies affecting rural social and economic development. The study suggested that a more positive stance might require the DoE to produce, in consultation with other government departments, policy context notes as a background for rural aspects of the work of other departments; to exercise a 'watchdog' role; and to establish a system of conflict resolution, parallel to that which already operates for major rural conservation issues, to mediate interdepartmental disputes over principles of rural policy.

The recommendation would also imply a greater concern by departments such as the DES and MAFF to modify policies which may have side-effects on rural communities or on the rural policies of other agencies. In the case of the DES this might require a review of advice given to local education authorities.

For MAFF, the new emphasis might demand a closer involvement with local economic policy-making. It was thought that MAFF's developing interest in the wider implications of agricultural policies in the uplands might lead to a review of its approach to lowland areas, especially those where the effects of prosperous agriculture are extreme. This closer involvement would require, for lowland areas, a gradual increase in the socioeconomic discipline of the Agricultural Development Advisory Service (note 5); a revised commitment to advise people in farming as to new enterprises, including farm-based ones, which might be beneficial to the wider community; a willingness to promote opportunities for job creation through agricultural development itself; and, in particular, greater flexibility within this large and powerful department for officials to reach a common view with local authorities on how agricultural policy can best be interpreted in the interest of local social and economic objectives.

THE PRESENT SITUATION

Thus the recommendations from the final report of the study, developed as they were from those of the earlier case study reports, had three distinct themes, each of which was intended to contribute towards the improvement of rural community development:

To establish a stronger, essentially community-based means of organizing self-help and communicating residents' needs to higher authority.

2. To promote a new impetus for integrating rural policies within central government.

3. To create a means whereby central and local initiatives in rural community development could be coordinated through the local government system.

It is unrealistic to expect a research report, commissioned within a single government department but affecting many other interests, to have an immediate effect on attitudes and policies. The detailed case studies had resulted in the project being spread over three to four years, during which time many individuals and organizations had been developing their own ideas about the needs of rural community development and possible improvements to means of provision. Major events which had direct or indirect connections with such ideas include the Wildlife and Countryside Act 1981; the government's review of the Development Commission, completed in 1982 and given effect from 1 April 1984 (note 6); the Countryside Commission's Report *A Better Future for the Uplands* (1984); and the progressive reduction of European Community and MAFF financial support for farming. All these, and the National Farmers' Union policy statement *The Way Forward*, in December 1984, have resulted, or may result, in new thinking about the areas covered by the study's recommendations. The most important thrust, however, has been the increasingly active role of the Development Commission itself, as the arm of central government most comprehensively involved in rural socioeconomic development. The Commission is now an executive body in its own right, with a 1983–84 budget of £23.7 million (Development Commission, 1984a).

So far as the first of the three themes is concerned, the Commission has for many years regarded RCCs as the main channel for its support of community development, and had been reaching the same conclusions as the research study about the need for reappraisal of the roles of these organizations. A review was set up after discussion with the Standing Conference of RCCs, to report in April 1985. The terms of reference for this were very wide: to clarify the role and relationships of RCCs (for example with local authorities, the Commission and the voluntary sector); to consider how these roles and relationships might be reinforced; and how the assistance of the Commission itself might be strengthened (Development Commission, 1984a). Although the review's conclusions are still being considered by the Commission, it is clear that greater independence for RCCs has become an important objective. The research study had also concluded that RCCs would service the purposes for which they were set up more effectively if they were less closely identified with local government, and had recommended a very similar review.

To strengthen voluntary bodies such as RCCs is one thing; to do the same to the lowest tier of statutory local government, the parish council, as also recommended by the study, is quite another. Review of parish boundaries is a district council responsibility, in conjunction with the work of the Local Government Boundary Commission, and about one-third of districts in England (and all in Wales) have now completed their reviews. Many more are under way, but the very nature of the work makes progress piecemeal and slow. The results amount to tidying up, rather than radical change (J. Clark, personal communication, National Association of Local Councils). The Dorset case study underlined the importance of grouping parish councils (as distinct from parishes) into useful joint councils, as had been done in that area. It was thought that this process might be more widely applied, but it now appears to be fairly unique; grouping seems to have been superseded by review, at least for the time being.

Much, therefore, remains to be done before the first of the three themes incorporated in the research study's recommendations is properly tackled. Unfortunately this is also the case with the second theme. The new impetus which the study advocated at the level of central government might well have been focused through the DRA. It is interesting to note that the House of Commons Environment Committee (1985), reporting on the operation of Part II of the Wildlife and Countryside Act 1981, recommended that the government should urgently undertake a review 'of the whole rural estate', and produce a White Paper. The subsequent White Paper (HMSO, 1985), explicit as it was about achievements in problem areas such as the uplands and the Norfolk Broads, did not quite match up to these comprehensive expectations. Furthermore, the recommendation itself, influenced no doubt by evidence from the Nature Conservancy Council and the Countryside Commission urging a review of all priorities in government spending on the countryside, probably does not go far enough. Meanwhile, for entirely understandable reasons which have their political and administrative overtones, the DRA, somewhat scaled down in staff, has become regarded as the 'green arm' of the DoE, handling mainly questions of landscape and wildlife conservation and countryside recreation. The DRA's former remit on socioeconomic development has been transferred to another division which is primarily concerned with the DoE's input to regional development and job creation. There is a certain institutional logic in this, but has an opportunity been missed? Will the all-embracing question of future agricultural policy, referred to below, compel rural affairs to be seen once more as a whole?

It is in the realm of the third theme that most progress seems to have been made, through the Development Commission's new sponsorship of rural development programmes (RDP) (Development Commission, 1984b), a concept similar in scope, though not in its application, to the reseach study's rural community development reports. To be introduced albeit gradually, the latter were visualized as a feature of rural local government generally. The RDPs, however, are intended for certain areas only, but introduced in one fell swoop. Indeed, it is not surprising that the Commission, with its tradition of giving priority, through CoSIRA, to areas of greatest need, should to some extent be concentrating its efforts. The criteria used in selecting its rural development areas include lack of employment, population decline or sparsity, and poor access to services (see National Farmers' Union, 1984, p. 21 and Figure 12.1). The resulting areas cover between one-half and one-third of rural England, including some lowland as well as upland areas. It is in these areas that, in addition to offering a wider range of grants for industrial development, village halls, etc., the Commission is promoting RDPs.

The RDPs are concerned with socioeconomic priorities, as befits the Commission's remit from government, and they have to be submitted to the Commission. In fact, the Commission has few special funds for them and is anxious to avoid giving any impression that it 'owns' them, though they will clearly be of use as a context for grants and advisory services. Nevertheless, while the RDPs are prepared and serviced mainly by local government (sometimes by existing joint committees which include RCCs, occasionally even parish councils), they are not entirely the locally accountable rural strategies, including conservation, which the study envisaged. They are, however, in their second year of operation and, in addition to achieving fairly wide coverage of rural areas, they have got beyond the stage of being *ad hoc* assemblies of 'pet projects' (see Development Commission, 1985). With guidance as necessary from the Commission, they now contain creditable assessments of needs, statements of objectives and self-generating programmes which are monitored and rolled forward each year. Indeed, focusing on economic development, housing, transport, services and social facilities (sometimes even education), and with regular involvement of bodies such as MAFF and the Tourist Boards, the RDPs could in time begin to 'read across' at central government level. Thus they could enable government departments to identify policy and organizational decision issues that might not otherwise be seen.

THE FUTURE

Nothing but good can come of the RDPs as a means of coordinating rural decision-making to useful effect, provided that the process actively involves the grass roots of rural communities. It would be even better if the concept, in whatever form, were also taken up in counties which are not rural development areas as such, including those with urban fringe problems. Here the need to take up initiatives lies firmly in the lap of local government, and the process would be more directly identified with local democracy, as was visualized in the study report. Integration with other local programmes and with conservation might thereby be easier. But ignorance and suspicion of authority, as revealed in the case study areas, may persist: they could frustrate the success of project formulation and implementation at the sharp end if more is not done to strengthen parish councils and to enable RCCs to assume an independent role as 'friends at court'.

Looking to a wider scenario, the cuts in agricultural support and changes in output may cause further loss of jobs in some areas, and it is all the more necessary for the farming industry to be involved in the promotion of farm-based enterprises in order to assist economic development. MAFF's view of its role, influenced no doubt by the duties laid on it by the Wildlife and Countryside Act, appears to have changed dramatically in the past two years or so, and could diversify further in future (see Smith, 1984). How will this, and the comprehensive view of rural policy requirements expressed by residents during the course of the research study, affect approaches to decision-making? Will there be demands for central government to unify and intensify further its ability to take an 'overview' of natural resource conservation and rural socioeconomic development? If this were to come about, and the grass roots were strengthened, then the motive power of local government, supported by agencies such as the Development Commission, Countryside Commission and Nature Conservancy Council, might become a great unifying force for rural policy. Its role would bring together, far closer than before, central, local strategic and local community potential. Thus the 'lack of fit' in rural decision-making of the past two or three decades could become a thing of the past.

NOTES

1. This was followed by four further Topic Reports, 1977–79.
2. See, in particular, *Hansard* (Lords) 12 March 1981, cols. 481 & 483, and *Hansard*, 27 April 1981, col. 533, and *Standing Committee* 'D', 9 June 1981, cols. 509–511.
3. It now appears, however, that joint finance is regarded with suspicion by both sides in local government and the health service, due to the lack of long-term funding for projects started by such means, and to the consequent distortion of spending priorities (R. Stockford, 1985, personal communication, Cambridgeshire County Council).
4. The nine member organizations of Rural Voice have, between them, some 20 000 local branches, and well over 750 000 members (National Council of Voluntary Organizations, personal communication).
5. At the time of the East Lindsey Study, there was only one specialist ADAS socioeconomic adviser for the whole East Midland region.
6. Given effect through the Miscellaneous Financial Provisions Act 1983. The duties laid upon the Commission require it to 'keep under review and advise the Secretary of State (for the Environment) upon all matters relating to the economic and social development of rural areas in England'; and to 'carry out and assist others to carry out measures likely to further such development'.

REFERENCES

Association of County Councils (1979) *Rural Deprivation*, Association of County Councils, London.

Association of District Councils (1978) *Rural Recovery — A Strategy for Survival*, Association of District Councils, London.

Bachrach, P. and Baratz, M.S. (1962) Two faces of power. Reprinted in Castles, F.G. *et al.* (1976) *Decisions, Organisations and Society*, Penguin, Harmondsworth.

Countryside Commission (1984) *A Better Future for the Uplands*, CCP 162, Countryside Commission, London.

Countryside Review Committee (1976) *The Countryside — Problems and Policies*, HMSO, London.

Department of the Environment (1984) *Circular 22/84*, HMSO, London.

Development Commission (1982) *Fortieth Report (1981–82)*, HMSO, London.

Development Commission (1984a) *Forty-second Report (1983–84)*, HMSO, London.

Development Commission (1984b) *Guidelines for Joint Rural Development Programmes*, HMSO, London.

Development Commission (1985) *Rural Development Programmes: Further Guidance from the Commission*, HMSO, London.

Hereford & Worcester County Council (1975–78) *Rural Community Development Project*, Hereford & Worcester County Council, Worcester.

HMSO (1985) *Reply to First Report from the Environment Committee*, Cmnd 9522, London.

House of Commons Environment Committee (1985) *Operation and Effectiveness of Part II of the Wildlife and Countryside Act*, Vols I and II, HMSO, London.

National Farmers' Union (1984) *The Way Forward. New Directions for Agricultural Policy*, National Farmers' Union, London.

Smart, G., Wright, S., Hursey, C. and Roberts, J. (1980) *Decision Making for Rural Areas: Report of Pilot Project — West Dorset*, University College London.

Smart, G., Wright, S., Futers, C. and Hursey, C. (1982a) *Decision Making for Rural Areas: Report of Main Project (Phase 1) — East Lindsey, Lincolnshire*, University College London.

Smart, G., Wright, S. and Futers, C. (1982b) *Decision Making for Rural Areas: Report of Main Project (Phase 2) — West Cleveland*, University College London.

Smart, G and Wright, S. (1983) *Decision Making for Rural Areas: Final Report*, University College, London

Smith, E. (1984) Agriculture and the environment. Paper read to the Royal Society of Arts Conference on Compensation and Incentives in the Countryside, Royal Society of Arts, London.

Standing Conference of Rural Community Councils (1978) *Decline of Rural Services*, National Council of Voluntary Organizations, London.

Stewart, J.D. (1983) *Local Government — The Conditions of Choice*, Allen and Unwin, London.

Wibberley, G.P. (1981) *Strong Agricultures But Weak Rural Economies*, European Centre of Agricultural Economics, Brussels.

CONCLUSIONS

13

RURAL PLANNING: A CASE
OF PRAGMATISM?

Paul Cloke

The introductory chapters of this book painted a bleak picture of the future for planning in rural areas. In the face of widespread restructuring in economic terms, and polarization in social and political terms, planning was characterized as hamstrung by the constraints of its role as part of wider state activity. Attention was drawn to the problems of developing responses to rural problems when planners have few corporate responsibilities and even fewer resources with which to underwrite their objectives. The trend, therefore, was for planning in a negative mode using control mechanisms but unable to promote progressive action against rural problems because of the claustrophobic constraints on positive planning. Such activity that did occur was pragmatic in nature, conforming to an 'art of the possible' within current constraints, and given these circumstances planning *action* in rural areas constituted more of a political gesture than a real attempt to resolve problems.

The case studies of how policies have been implemented in various sectors of rural life have challenged this analysis in some respects, and lent compelling support to it in others. In general, significant deviations from expectations raised in the introductory chapters occur where evaluation of rural planning performance has been measured *within* the limits of a constrained planning process, rather than taking equal account of objectives which might be achieved if some of the constraints on planning were to be released. The first point of issue, therefore, relates to how rural problems and policies are perceived, both by policy-makers and by researchers.

PERCEPTIONS OF THE PROBLEMATIC

If viewed from a particular perspective, planning in rural areas need not be problematic. For example, in Chapter 12 Smart clearly suggests that contemporary analyses of 'problems' in rural planning (as reflected in Chapters 1 and 2) are overstated. His conclusion mirrors that of the research project for the Department of the Environment (DoE) on which his chapter is based, namely that there are no universally serious shortcomings in policy, neither are there dramatic conflicts between decision-making organizations requiring radical solutions. Rather, such improvements as are necessary should reflect the time of severe financial restraint, be cautious in nature and capable of gradual introduction. This view of 'no serious shortcomings' is adopted despite the fact that two of the local authorities studied in detail (Lincolnshire and Dorset) were found to be both unclear about their *aims* for rural areas and unable formally to *translate* aims into integrated policies. With no clear expectation of policy objective or policy enactment, the ability to differentiate between success or failure, problem or no problem, can easily become a clouded issue.

Chapters 6 and 7 also offer a view of rural problems being overcome to some extent. In Chapter 7 Pettigrew's analysis of industrial development policy and practice in Mid Wales is that the results vindicate the planning methods and approach adopted. In some ways the notion of success in overcoming problems in this case is wrapped up with the very survival of the planning agency concerned (the Development Board for Rural Wales). Pettigrew's conclusion that 'real results' have ensured the Board's survival on the political roller-coaster suggests that 'results' which are politically acceptable are at a premium, and indeed the Board has undergone a significant change of image and style over recent years to suit the predilections of contemporary central government thinking. In Chapter 6 Patmore's view of the North York Moors National Park Committee is prefaced by a catalogue of the factors inhibiting landscape management: lack of land ownership, restricted powers, restricted policy options and insufficient resources. Nevertheless his evaluation of problem-solving in the Park focuses on the criteria of quality of landscape and recreational experience, and by these measures he sees grounds for pride in the Committee's achievements.

Most of the case study chapters reflect the immense fund of initiative and expertise found among professional and some political planners working within an environment of constraint. The studies by Smart, Patmore and Pettigrew (Chapters 12, 6 and 7) in particular highlight the success of available planning measures and this perhaps reflects the fact that these three authors have been closely involved with the organizations concerned — through a research contract and agency memberships respectively. These contributions are invaluable as they demonstrate that even within a severely constrained planning process, incremental improvement and 'success' have taken place and may further be prescribed.

Other chapters, however, illustrate that a policy successfully carried out may be irrelevant or even derogatory to rural problems. Little, for example, suggests in Chapter 11 that technically 'successful' planning has in fact exerted a powerful influence over the distribution of different social groups in the countryside. If social polarization is deemed to be a 'problem', then planning policy and action have directly contributed to that problem. In similar vein, Rocke (Chapter 10) demonstrates that a focus on physical aspects of residential development in rural areas is detrimental to consideration of social criteria.

These different perspectives on what constitutes a 'problem' or 'success' in planning merely reflect the various conceptual viewpoints on implementation discussed in Chapter 2. To be involved with decision-making, agencies will often adopt a narrowly defined culture of planning action concerned with getting things done with whatever means are available. In such a situation actors might well be satisfied with the type of pragmatic and incrementalist policies which Cox and his co-authors in Chapter 4 find so 'depressing' in the context of the Wildlife and Countryside Act 1981.

THE QUESTION OF POWER

Involvement with a decision-making agency (and therefore to some extent with its collective views) is certainly not the only characteristic which promotes differences of perspective among the preceding case studies. Several authors have encased the themes of implementation and enactment firmly within the realms of the distribution of power within both public and private sectors. The assertion in Chapter 1 that the evaluation of rural planning and decision-making should entertain an overtly political focus finds widespread support. For example, in Chapter 5 Blowers (himself a leading county councillor) suggests that the implementation of policies for mineral extraction reflects social conflicts over the control of land and is thus a directly political matter. The intensity of these conflicts and their resolution reflect the power exercised by different interests. Cox *et al.*, in their review of landscape protection policies (Chapter 4), also emphasize that the policy process is anchored in the social construction of power. In addition, and showing the reverse side of these findings, Tricker and Mills (Chapter 3) describe the feelings of powerlessness and alienation from decision-makers experienced by rural families affected by school closures.

In some cases power is illustrated within fairly classic elitist situations. We have come to expect that local authorities in rural areas will display an innate conservatism in planning decisions. A very neat example of these conservative attitudes is provided by Rocke's investigation into local housing policies in part of Avon. Here, he discovers, there are often political difficulties in obtaining permission to build garages for those types of houses (usually at the lower end of the market) which do not already have them. By stark contrast, the attitudes towards conversions of barns to residential use are far more favourable, these developments being much more in tune with the conservationist view of how development should be accommodated in the countryside.

Elsewhere power in the hands of managers is rated as important. In Chapter 8, on the decision-making roles of water authorities within rural planning, Bell provides a good example of effective liaison between the managers of water and planning authorities to produce compatible and workable programmes of action. Patmore's account of the workings of a National Park committee equally stresses the 'objective' and 'constructive' nature of policy debate, noting that overt political considerations rarely intrude into this process. In such a climate of decision-making the managerialist role of senior officers and members can be effectively pursued.

In many of the case studies, however, the distinct concepts of elitism and managerialism are blurred by the importance of cross-cutting alliances of power. In Chapter 5 Blowers shows how such alliances can spread and intensify planning conflicts. In his investigation of planning for mineral extraction, he found examples of major developers lining up alongside dependent workforces to oppose a broad conservation lobby. Thus fractions of capital and the working class may jointly oppose conservation-minded middle classes and other environmental interests over this particular issue. Similar cross-cutting of traditional interest groups is uncovered by Patmore in Chapter 6. Concern over the protection of moorland landscape in the North York Moors National Park led the Park Committee to advocate a system of planning control over agricultural land-use change, despite the fact that the Committee's membership contained a strong farming element. This departure from the expected decision-making behaviour of farming interests involved in land management agencies is in direct contrast to Cox *et al.*'s evidence from Exmoor where National Park authority members, many of whom had a background in farming or forestry, were found to be favourably disposed to agricultural developments and permit many landscape changes 'on the nod'.

The evidence of power distribution within the various case studies is therefore variable. There is, however, a clear trend in the outcome of policy and implementation towards consensus options. Cox *et al.* suggest that the politics of landscape protection and nature conservation are dominated by consensus building as represented in the Wildlife and Countryside Act 1981, which serves as a bridge between the polarities of conservation and farming interests. Even within the implementation of the Act they suggest that agencies such as National Park authorities will temper their objections to land-use modification and limit them to those cases to which they expect agriculture departments of central government will concede. Consensus then represents the identification of, and operation within, a commonly recognized 'art of the possible' reflecting prevailing distributions of power. Different minority interests in rural planning may win their battles *within* this arena, but rarely *beyond* it. Equally a majority consensus between powerful interests is quite capable of inducing flexibility into statutory planning procedures providing that the 'art of the possible' is not breached. Blowers describes how a consensus in favour of mineral extraction in an Area of Great Landscape Value can overcome any reluctance to permit intrusive land use there provided that conservation objections can be legitimated by the promise of careful planning with tight conditions on the developer.

This notion of flexibility *within* the art of the possible serves to emphasize the overwhelming importance of structural factors which set the limits of feasible policy prescription. Thus the role of the state–society relationship, of which planning is one small part, and the function of the central state in relation to its local and regional counterparts remain crucial to an understanding of the delimitation of planning action in rural areas.

RURAL PLANNING AND THE STATE

In Chapters 1 and 2 it was asserted that the relationships between the central and local states, and indeed between agencies representing the local state, set crucial constraints on planning activity. The role of the state in the preservation of societal status quo and in the support of capital expansion and accumulation underwrites interaction at central and local levels and between public and private sectors. This overarching role of the state is emphasized by Little (Chapter 11), whose conclusions regarding the influence of local-level planning are that the planning system protects private capital and encourages the progressive gentrification of rural areas by the middle classes. Thus, although the scope which is available for planning to perform radical autonomous initiatives is limited, the power of planning in protecting private interests is very real indeed.

Clear evidence of the increasingly important function of the central state in rural planning emerges from the case studies. In the sphere of education services, Tricker and Mills trace the displacement of philanthropy by efficiency as the dominant motive behind central state policies. As a consequence, rural areas have suffered the impacts of a series of programmes to rationalize the provision of education facilities. As a result of clear central state instructions in the form of DES circulars and advice notes, local education authorities are faced with greatly increased pressure to close small rural schools. In his investigation of water services, Bell indicates the likely effects of central government controls over water authority charges and investment, and speculates on the ideologically inspired moves towards the privatization of these authorities. In similar vein, Edwards (Chapter 9) analyses central government expenditure cuts in spending on highways and public transport and looks ahead to the impact of the deregulation of bus services in rural areas.

In these and other issues involving uncompromising attitudes towards central government expenditure on service provision, clear directives from the centre often minimize the scope for discretionary action at the local level. In other issues, for example landscape conservation strategies, where central government policies themselves represent attempts to reach consensus between different fractions of capital and of the ruling classes, there is perhaps more room for manoeuvre at the local level. Blowers clearly demonstrates a gradation in this discretion in his Bedfordshire case study. Decisions over the extraction of Fuller's earth and Oxford clay met with demands from powerful monopoly interests who were supported by central government in their negotiations with local authorities. Applications concerning sand and gravel extraction, where strategic value is less important and development interests are more dispersed, receive less support from central government, which can afford in this instance to seek consensus with environmental interests. Perhaps even further down this sliding scale of discretion, the legally constituted designation of Sites of Special Scientific Interest (SSSI) is shown by Cox et al. to have been regarded by farming and landowning interests as eminently contestable with the expectation that central government would go along with shifting 'market forces' of power in this issue in which the central policy stance was one originally based on a consensus of these very forces.

Even within the more restricted central government policy areas where financial restrictions tend to be paramount, some localized flexibility is still achieved. Tricker and Mills describe the cost criteria laid down by central government with regard to school viability. Given no local government discretion these cost thresholds would be rigidly applied in a manner undisturbed by local political factors. In selected cases, however, local authorities have been able to massage cost criteria so as to demonstrate to their central paymasters that the savings from school amalgamation would be less than the additional costs of transporting schoolchildren to the more distant centralized school facilities. The various options for local state organizations actively to pursue any available discretion are clearly demonstrated in Edwards' work on highways policy in rural areas. By investigating three localized case studies, each within a different county council policy framework but subject to common central government directives, he illustrates the variations of policy-making impact on implemented maintenance programmes:

1. In Llanfachreth (Gwynedd) activity has predominantly been affected by central government policy decisions.
2. In Llanarth (Dyfed) by a combination of county level and national decisions.

3. In Llandyssil (Powys) by local policy formulation.

As a result, in this little known but interesting area of rural policy, maintenance decisions at ground level are not found to reflect any one overriding policy constraint, but rather represent a compromise between competing interests which happen to exercise varying degrees of influence in the three selected local areas. By contrast, Edwards's conclusion for local rural *transport* policy is that it is doomed to failure unless central government expenditure restrictions are lifted. In this case, then, there is far less room for manoeuvre at the local level.

AGENCIES AND THE PRIVATE SECTOR

The difficulties in coordinating the policy-making and decision-taking activities of different agencies involved in rural planning were highlighted in Chapter 2. Most of the case study chapters reflect this issue. For example, Blowers (Chapter 5) records disagreements between county and district authorities, and indeed between officers and members in single authorities over issues of mineral extraction. Clearly, however, the problems of interagency conflict do not loom as large in these case study examinations of rural planning in action as might have been anticipated. Is there evidence, therefore, for Smart's assertion that the lack of fit in rural decision-making could soon be a thing of the past?

There certainly is some evidence of policy cohesion between relevant agencies within the statutory planning process. Rocke's analysis (Chapter 10) of the implementation of rural housing policy, for example, demonstrates fruitful relations between highways authorities and planning authorities. Similarly, in Chapter 8 Bell records a close liaison between Southern Water Authority and the planning authorities within his chosen case study area. Two reasons may be advanced for this integration of working relations. First, the overall policy direction in both cases — strategies of conservation and general restraint of development — suited the ambitions and resources of the agencies concerned and therefore constituted clear common ground within which conflict was less likely and could be overcome through close liaison. It could be that in areas of more rapid development that greater potential for conflict occurs between strategic or development planners and the servicing agencies who find their resource-allocation decisions pre-empted by the demands of locational planning policy (or vice versa).

A second explanation for the seemingly parallel policy courses of these agencies involves their relationship with private-sector development interests. In an age where contributions from private developers towards the cost of the road and sewerage systems are necessitated by their development, a *culture of negotiation* has arisen within the processing of development applications on a scale not seen before. Instead of a clear decision that highway or water authority objections would pre-empt the development of a particular site, the authorities concerned are now more anxious to secure significant levels of planning gain for the area concerned. Where previously rural planning in some areas was characterized by restriction and embargo, there is now a clear recognition that developer contributions can 'unlock' certain areas for development. This situation places public authorities in a position of bargaining rather than attempting to dictate to each other as has often happened previously. Equally, the

conflicts between the desire of planning agencies to support the expansion of development fractions of capital, and their inability to do so in many cases because of the lack of
public-sector resources available for servicing, may well be diminished through the
increasing achievement of planning gain.

In Chapter 8 Bell comments that the philosophy of water authority policy appears to
be based on a perceived duty to support various production interests and functions.
Such a policy rationale is reinforced by the fact that many senior managers in the
authority have backgrounds in private business and industry, and will presumably only
be further reinforced in the climate of potential privatization. In this way, the
conceptual view of the role of planning in support of capital interest becomes more
visible. So much so that in the case of major planning issues of the day — such as the
proposed new settlements in green belt areas, for example Tillingham Hall in Essex —
infrastructural problems are nullified by securing the provision of services totally at the
developers' expense. This input of private-sector resources into previously public-
sector decision-making realms removes some causes of interagency conflict. The issue
will thus now be resolved by the central state's inclination (or otherwise) to support
these fractions of development capital against the powerful environmental conservation
interest.

Although these examples apply to specific cases, there does appear to be evidence of
a shift in the relationships between the private and public sectors in Britain. This shift
has been centrally inspired and will in turn forge important changes in the balance of
power which determines the consensus over levels and locations of rural development.

THE WAY AHEAD?

Smart's study of rural decision-making, commissioned by the Department of the
Environment, recommended three themes for the improvement of rural community
development:
1. To establish stronger and more community-based means of self-help.
2. To achieve greater integration of rural policies within central government.
3. To coordinate central and local initiatives for community development through the
    local government system.
Such recommendations have deliberately been generated for application in conditions
of economic restraint and are therefore born out of pragmatic necessity. Undoubtedly
voluntary initiatives in rural communities can be beneficial if directed towards suitable
activities which do not attempt to replace functions or services more suited to
public-sector intervention. Such notions of 'suitability' are discussed at length elsewhere (Cloke, 1983). Equally, some of the more glaring contradictions of central state
policy appear ripe for integration. A situation in which the agricultural arm of
government pays a farmer to improve his land while the environmental arm of government pays him not to is clearly ludicrous by any framework of analysis. In the same way
it *is* possible to envisage local authorities in a role of coordinating clearly stated and
apolitical initiatives from above and below, although according to the evidence from the
case studies presented here such rational concepts of rural action tend not to be
prominent in current rural planning. Pettigrew's assertion that a single development
agency dealing with clearly defined policy objectives relating to industrial development

would experience real advantages in implementing its programme is interesting in this respect. Despite the indicated rapport with both central and local government, the Development Board for Rural Wales has suffered because of the withdrawal of central government regional aid from its area, and has also been the subject of criticism from some sections of the local community over its policy directions (Wenger, 1980). The integration of policy initiatives within a single agency, therefore, is not necessarily the panacea it might first appear to be.

Clearly some short-term incremental advances can be made by adopting some of these pragmatic measures for rural planning. But the overwhelming conclusion from the material presented in this book is that current planning advances in rural areas are opportunistic in nature. Far from being a rational process whereby clearly conceived objectives are enacted via calculated channels of implementation, planning action constitutes a search for consensus within prevailing arenas of power — a search which usually precludes any radical or progressive prescriptions. For rural planning, a dramatic change in attitudes towards rural communities and environments is required before this situation can be significantly altered. For rural planning research the task is to gain a greater understanding of the distribution of power and within the political arena to begin to prescribe how the constraints on planning action might be removed.

REFERENCES

Cloke, P.J. (1983) *An Introduction to Rural Settlement Planning*, Methuen, London.
Wenger, C. (1980) *Mid Wales: Development or Deprivation?* University of Wales Press, Cardiff.

AUTHOR INDEX

SUBJECT INDEX

rational models 20–1
recreation 97–101
regional policy 116
roads 145–51
Royal Society for the Protection of
  Birds 62, 65
rural community councils 204–6
rural development programmes 209–10

sand extraction 78–80
section 52 agreements 131
self-help 197, 202–3
Sites of Special Scientific Interest 57,
  61ff
social impact assessment 47
state: central 9–14, 132ff, 146–7, 180–1;
  local 14–16, 147–9; regional 14–16

top-down approaches 20–22
Town and Country Planning Acts 11, 38,
  57
Transport Act 1985 12

Vale of Belvoir 13
Verney Report 81

water authorities 122ff, 171
Welsh Development Agency 117
Welsh Office 109
West Sedgemoor 65
Wildlife and Countryside Act, 1981 13–
  14, 56ff, 94, 203, 208
Wiltshire 186ff
Windscale 13
working class 6, 7, 12, 15, 188–91

DEPT. Economics

O.N. 10,017

PRICE

ACCN. No. 200774204